PHOTOGRAPHING NATIONAL PARKS

A GUIDE FOR SCOUTING AND SHOOTING AMERICA'S MOST CHERISHED LANDS

BY CHRIS NICHOLSON

Sidelight Books - Connecticut

2015

Cover and interior design by Kirsten Navin
www.kirstennavin.com

Copy editor: Alison DeNisco

All photographs by Chris Nicholson, except:
National Park Service, p. 15, 73, 97, 120, 127, 137, 147, 166, 186
NPS Photo/Tim Rains, p. 61
NPS Photo/Brett Seymour, 62
NPS Photo/Jacob W. Frank, 94
NPS Photo/Michael Quinn, 138
NPS Photo/K. Jalone, 160
NPS Photo/Sierra Coon, 193
Back-cover author portrait by Elizabeth Cecere

Printed in the United States of America
First Printing, 2015

ISBN 978-0-9835038-2-8

Sidelight Books
Connecticut, USA

www.PhotographingNationalParks.com

To Maggie, my daughter, who gives me new ways to love.

Thank you…

to my wife, for magically creating extra hours for me to write this.

to Mom and Dad, for cementing my love of wilderness.

to friends who supported this in concrete ways.

to my brother Colin, who seems always willing to talk with me about the parks, and to accompany me into them.

CONTENTS

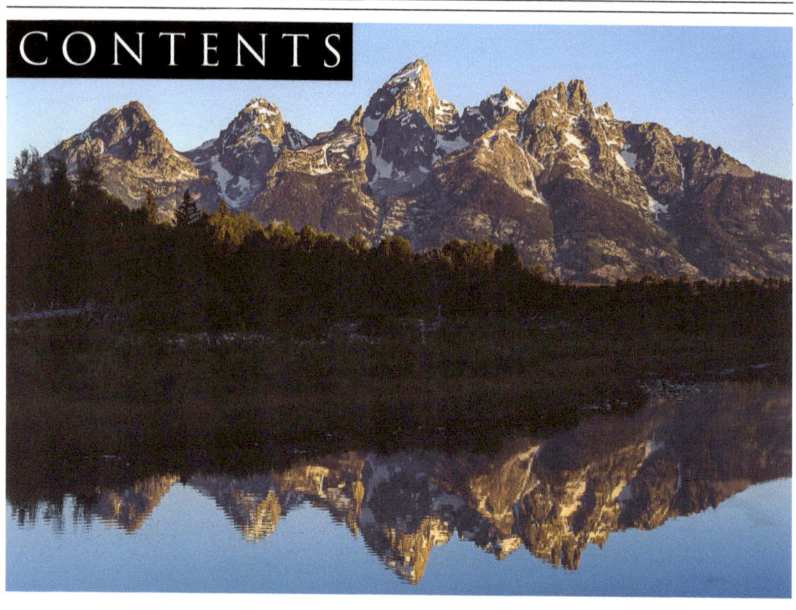

DISCLAIMER

Please be forewarned that although I mention or suggest some activities in this book, that does not mean I advise engaging in them without proper knowledge, experience and/or training. If I state that a park road is navigable with a four-wheel-drive vehicle, that doesn't mean I'm advising you to rent a Jeep and venture off without proper research and planning, especially if you have never previously driven a primitive road. The same applies for snorkeling coral reefs, hiking high-altitude mountain peaks, snowshoeing across winter tundra, fording backcountry rivers, kayaking coastal inlets, photographing lightning, and so on.

These activities are not only useful tools for a nature photographer, but are wonderful outdoor experiences in general. However, they involve risk, particularly when embarked upon by an unprepared novice, and particularly when attempted solo. While people engage in these activities every day without incident, prudence and proper education are advised before undertaking them. This book is not intended to be a tutorial for these activities, nor for the safety precautions necessary while engaging in them.

While spending time in the wilderness of the national parks, visitors may encounter wild animals, toxic plants, challenging terrain and hazardous weather. Dangerous encounters are uncommon, but are otherwise almost always avertible with pertinent knowledge that can be gleaned from park websites, park rangers, visitor facilities and many other easily accessible resources.

Readers assume full responsibility for their safety. The author and publisher assume no liability for the actions of the reader, nor for the consequences of those actions—including injury, suffering or property damage—while traveling to the locations or undertaking the activities referred to in this book.

PHOTOGRAPHING NATIONAL PARKS

I used to envy the father of our race, dwelling as he did in contact with the new-made fields and plants of Eden; but I do so no more, because I have discovered that I also live in "creation's dawn." The morning stars still sing together, and the world, not yet half made, becomes more beautiful every day. —John Muir

INTRODUCTION

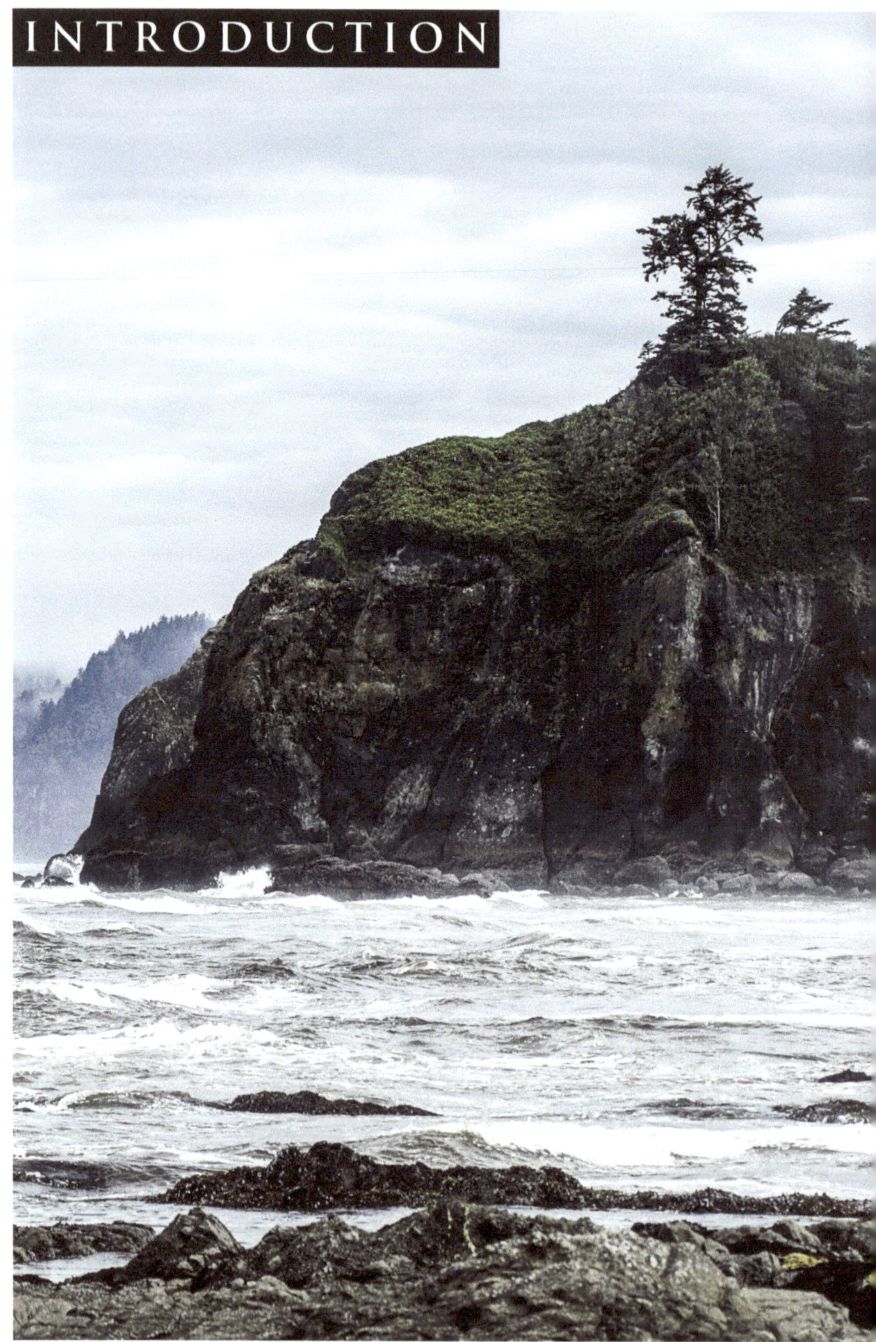

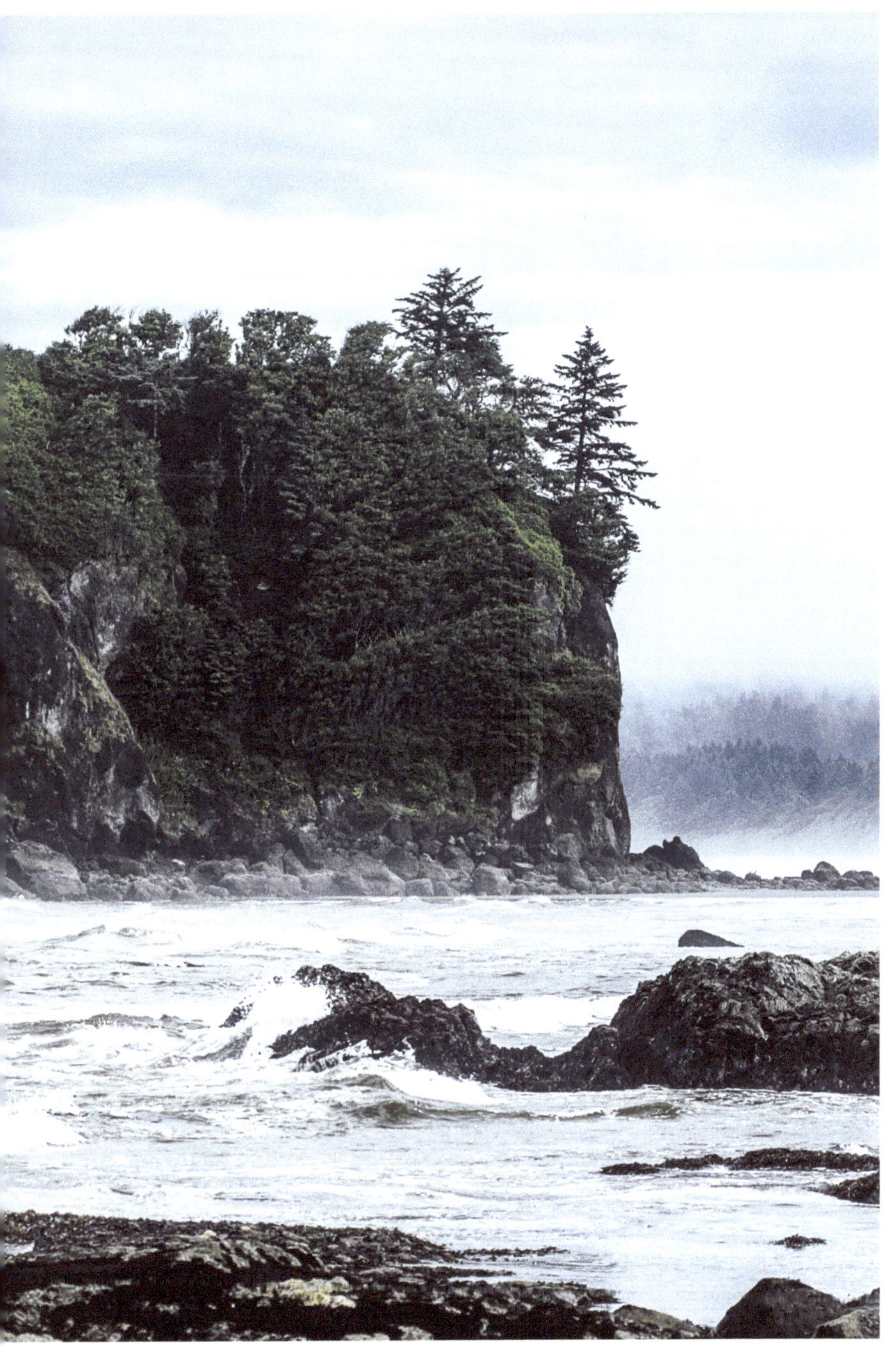

Sea stack, Olympic National Park

THINGS I THINK ABOUT

MY WIFE IS NOT OUTDOORSY. She's a city girl. She doesn't like spiders, she doesn't like dirt, she doesn't care much for forests or meadows, nor the things that live in and around them.

We dated for over three years before I was finally able to convince her to accompany me on a trip to Grand Teton National Park. But her reason for agreeing to go was not the splendor of the Teton Range rising dramatically from the valley floor, nor the bears and bison and moose we would surely see. Rather, she was persuaded by the fact that my brother and his girlfriend were working in the park that summer, and she could spend some girl time drinking wine by a campfire five feet from the front door of a large, homey recreational vehicle.

Still, she accompanied me. I was there for 10 days of photography, and my wife was staying for four to see a few sights, as long as they involved hard floors, or at least paved trails. She loved the shopping in Jackson, and the horses in the pasture in front of the cabin park my brother worked in. She even loved sitting on the patio at the back of Jackson Lake Lodge, with its awe-inducing view of the water and the mountains—until a tiny jumping spider hopped onto her arm.

We decided we'd make a day trip into and around the Yellowstone loop. It was an ambitious adventure, but all of us except my wife knew the park well enough so we could maximize the hours. We drove to Old Faithful and walked around the Upper Geyser Basin, seeing several geysers erupt—including the main attraction, twice. We headed north to Mammoth Hot Springs, where we hiked the boardwalks around the geothermals, and then ate ice cream at the lodge while watching the elk glare at the early-summer tourists. We drove through the Blacktail Deer Plateau to Roosevelt, then meandered through Dunraven Pass, where we saw a black bear sow and her two cubs. We stopped at Artist Point to see Yellowstone Falls spill over the top of the canyon, one of the truly magnificent vistas in all the national park system. We followed the Yellowstone River through the Hayden Valley, then circled back around the western shores of Yellowstone Lake. We left the park the way we came, heading south toward Grand Teton. Immediately before we arrived back at the cabin park, we spotted a bull moose wading through wetlands.

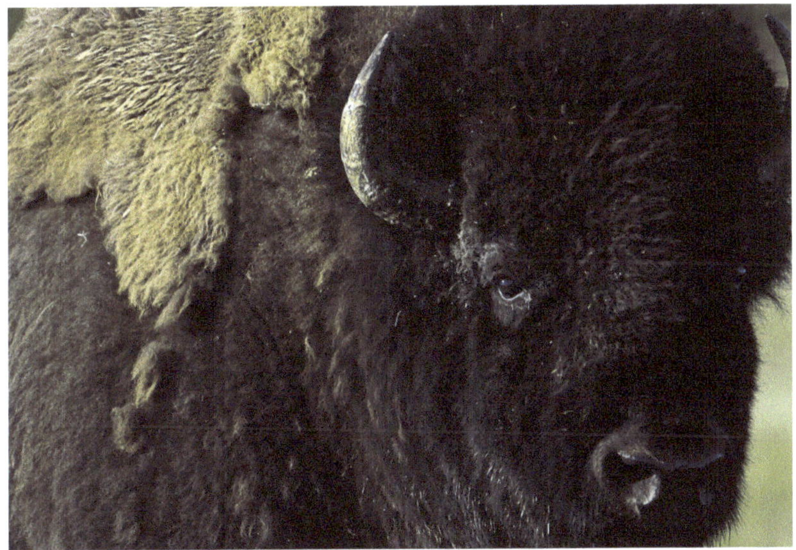

Yellowstone National Park

The next morning I drove my wife to the Jackson Hole airport. The sun had just risen as we snaked through the valley on the John D. Rockefeller Jr. Memorial Parkway, past buck-and-rail fences and old homesteads, past meadows and aspen groves, past view after stunning view of the Snake River and the Teton peaks. We drove around a bend, and a wide prairie came into view on our left, grassland glowing in the warm light of early morning. At the center, spaced apart in the open meadow, stood a herd of a few dozen bison, silently grazing.

My wife watched the bison, and she was quiet for a moment. Finally, she said, "Wow. This really is amazing."

WHAT MY WIFE experienced in Grand Teton was the feeling I yearn for almost every day—being out in nature and seeing the natural things, being as close to our primal home as a modern human can be. Hiking in the woods, wading in mountain rivers, strolling through meadows, watching the sun setting while standing on high ridges—these are the experiences I was raised to love. I long to be in places where clocks and calendars are irrelevant, where time feels different, because nothing there measures it the same as I do.

When I was a kid, my family camped, often. I grew up thinking that spending time in nature, walking and eating and sleeping in the woods, was a commonplace way to spend a weekend or a week. My dad, an avid former Boy Scout and a

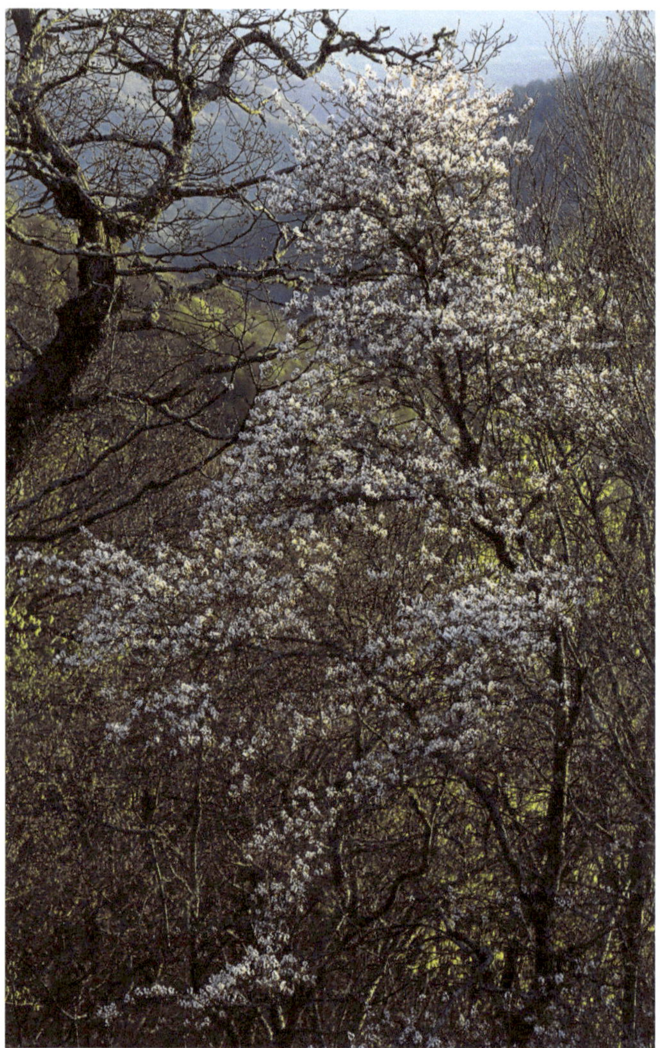

Great Smoky Mountains National Park

passionate Scout master, marine biology major and high-school science teacher, loved ambling among the trees, the fields and the coastlines, seeing the plants and animals, picking them up, identifying them by common and scientific names, and teaching about their place in the ecosystem and in our world. When not camping with my family, Dad would take me into the woods alone—usually with a tent, but sometimes not. We did this often enough that I thought the "Father-Son Camping Trip" was an activity that all kids regularly experienced.

My love of photography was also born from the same source. Dad owned several 35mm cameras, of the Minolta (and even the old Miranda) variety. I saw his passion for photography and I wanted to learn to enjoy that, too. And in this realm, I found even more inspiration: My uncle was a professional photojournalist, and a good family friend was a longtime wedding photographer. I was surrounded by photography. Still, I didn't pick up a camera with any serious intent until college. I was an editor for the university newspaper, and was intrigued by the mystery of the darkroom. So one day I said to the photography editor, "If you ever need an extra person to shoot something, I'd be interested in learning." I really am not sure if I finished that sentence before a camera was in my hand.

From there, I pursued photography mostly through experience. I took only one formal course in the field, and that was "The History of Photography." I knew little about this world, which was apparent in my research. One assignment from the professor was to choose a photographer—any photographer who moved us in any way—and study his or her work, then write a paper about it. The one caveat was that the photographer could not be famous. We had to choose an unknown artist, someone obscure, someone whose catalog was hiding in the shadows of photographic history. I chose Ansel Adams.

These were the blocks that became the foundation of my photography career. A long time would pass before I started producing any work I now consider worthwhile. Henri Cartier-Bresson was right when he said, "Your first 10,000 pictures are your worst." But like many others, I had a lot of fun while learning.

My friend J.P. and I spent a considerable portion of our 20s driving around our home state of Connecticut, around New England, around the United States, finding places to photograph. We would plan long trips to tour the Midwest, or Texas, or the Maine coastline. We drove from the East to West Coast and back three times along three different routes. We drove the highway south down the Pacific Coast, from Seattle to San Diego, in a rented Mustang convertible that we had to keep the top on until Los Angeles. On all of these trips, we stopped at every national park that was on our path, and we diverted our path toward any national park we saw on the map. (Yes, we were using maps. In those days, the letters G, P and S meant nothing to us.) We visited Acadia, Big Bend, Glacier, Yellowstone, Mount Rainier, Redwood, Everglades and more.

Eventually I found ways to make these experiences pay for themselves, and then to pay for some food and bills between the trips. Eventually I began working as a photographer, and even if assignments didn't call directly for nature photos, I would often find a way to work them in. When on assignment in Marco Island, Florida, I mentioned to the art director that Everglades National Park was a short distance inland—surely we wouldn't want to leave out such a conspicuous destination. When on assignment in Palm Springs, California, Joshua Tree National Park was just an hour north—so I ensured it would be part of the trip. Other articles and book projects brought me to national parks as well, mostly because that's where I would choose to steer them. A chapter on shooting star trails? I'll go to the Everglades. An article on winter photography? Let's go to Acadia. And if I just wanted to take a vacation—heck, I'd pack my cameras and my tent and pick a park.

My interest doesn't wane when I'm home. When I see parks in the news, I read about what's going on there. When I notice books on parks in the store, I buy them and read them. When I talk with other photographers, I ask about what parks they've been to and how and why they enjoyed photographing there.

Though I do plan to visit more parks that are new to me, I also experience a lot of joy in returning to places again and again. I have visited and photographed my "top six"—Acadia, Yellowstone, Grand Teton, Olympic, Great Smoky Mountains and Everglades—a cumulative 24 times. Revisiting has given me opportunities to photograph in different seasons, to return to locations in different light and weather conditions, and to learn and know these parks more intimately.

The most important byproduct of all of this is that I am doing something I love, something I would want to do whether or not it was part of my career. Making income along the way is a bonus for me, because it allows me to dedicate even more of my days and weeks to this passion. In this book, I want to share how I go about pursuing all of this, in the hopes that some of what I do may help you expand upon what you do, may help spread some of the joy I have found in photographing these wonderful landscapes that we, as a nation, have set aside for the purpose of preserving our country's natural and aesthetic heritage.

This is not a travel guide, exactly; it is more of a manual about how to approach photographing the parks. I intend to explain what I believe is a diligent way to go about planning

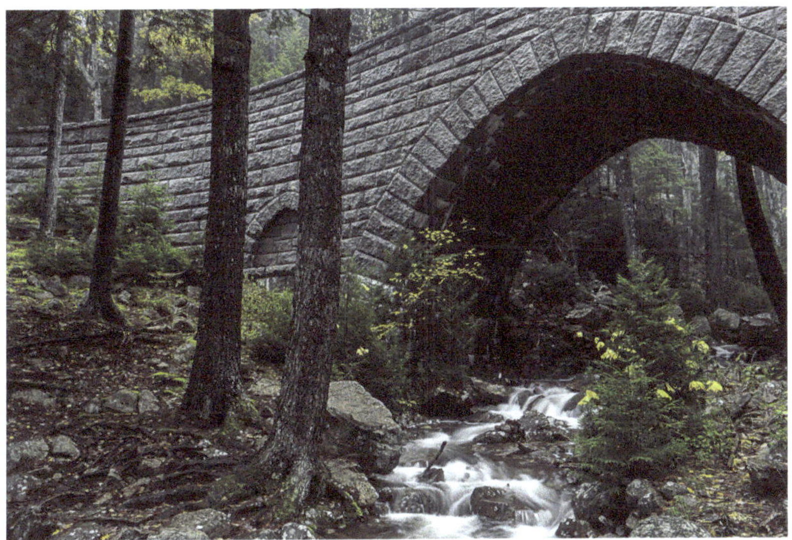

Acadia National Park

and executing a shoot in a national park in order to maximize your experience as a photographer. I will discuss the myriad ways to research a park shoot, the best strategies for logistics such as lodging and food, tips on gear and keeping batteries charged, safety guidelines for spending time in the wilderness, how to avoid needing a photography permit, how to know where you're going and where you've been, and more. And yes, I will offer a breakdown of each park and why you, as a photographer, would want to visit.

Because right now a grizzly in Denali is protecting its cub. A wolf pack in Glacier is devouring its latest kill. A geyser in Yellowstone is about to erupt. A dune in Death Valley is about to shift. All this and thousands of other moments are seconds away from commencing—amid trees, under seas, in canyons, on badlands, over tundra or snow. Let's find them and be there. Let's grab a camera and go shoot some national parks. It'll be some of the best fun we have as photographers.

CHAPTER 1

KNOWLEDGE

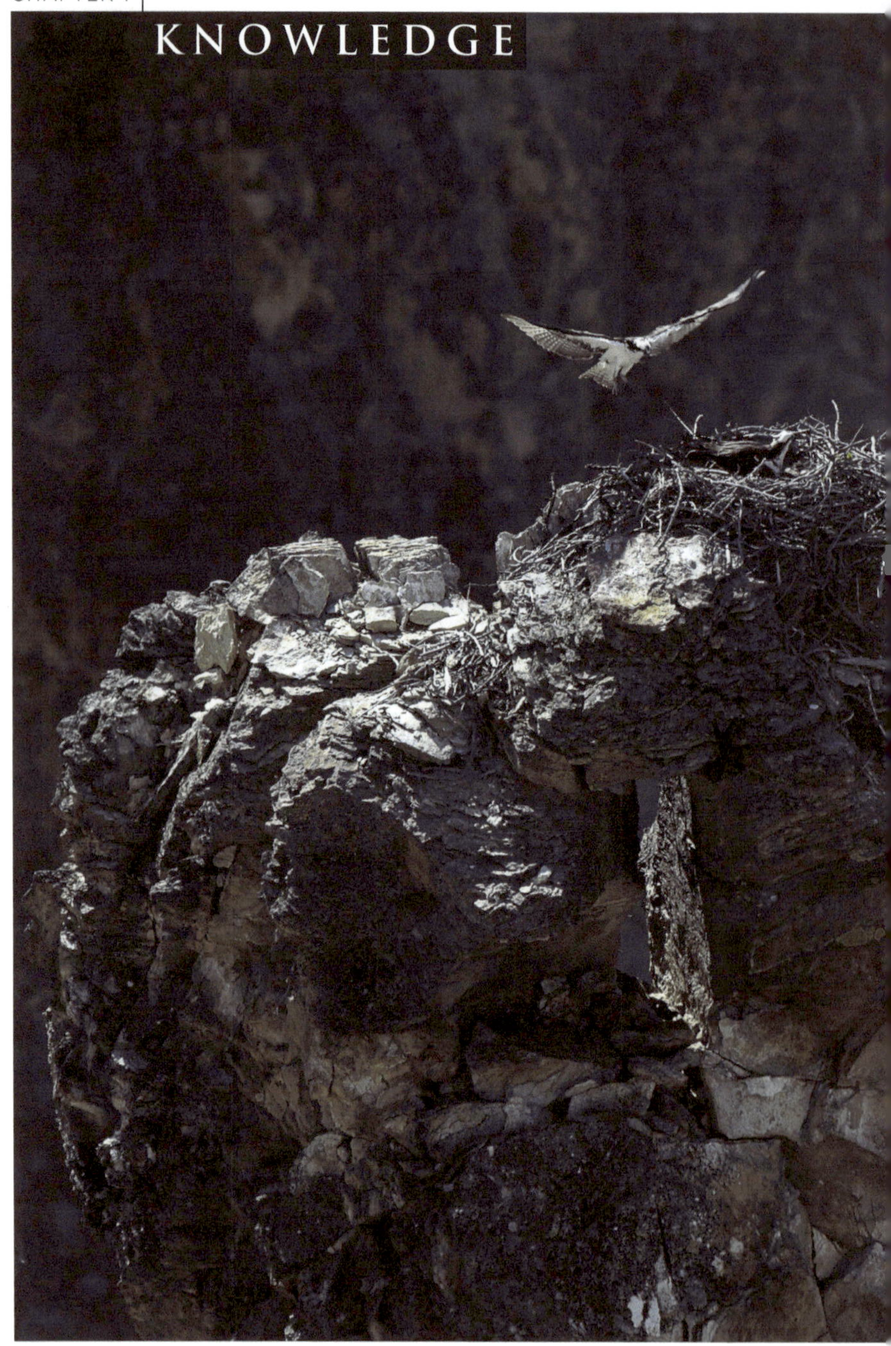

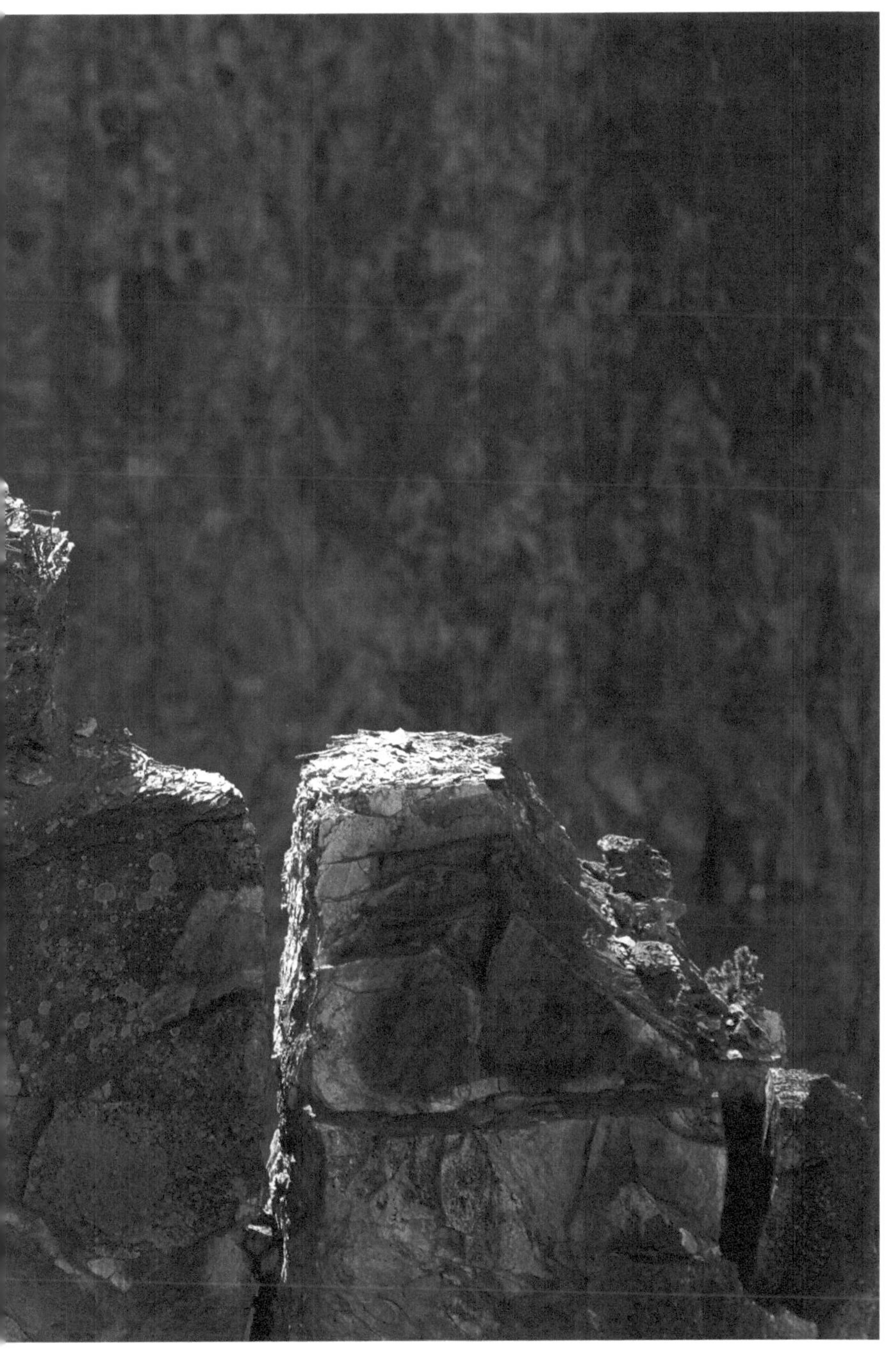

Osprey, Yellowstone
National Park

IMPORTANT THINGS

DURING my early- to mid-20s, I traveled around the United States a lot with a photographer friend. Our impetus was threefold: We were seeking a little cultural education. We were eating some good local food. And we photographed.

We photographed agricultural landscapes, Americana, rainstorms, wildlife, livestock, flowers, architecture, Main Streets, old railroad trestles, and whatever else looked new and interesting—which was just about everything. Clearly our photography efforts were not focused. On these trips we would also often visit the national parks in our path, and we would stay there and photograph for as long as an entire afternoon. Clearly we didn't get to know the parks well. If any quality photos resulted from those brief visits, they were almost certainly accidental.

Here are a few examples from those experiences:

The first time I photographed Everglades National Park, I was there for half a winter day. I shot a beautiful sunset in Ten Thousand Islands, and that's about it. Because I had time to explore only one short road, I missed the owls at Mahogany Hammock, the crocodiles at Flamingo and all the wildlife an imagination could muster along the Anhinga Trail.

The first time I shot Acadia National Park, I stayed one day. I was able to photograph the Duck Brook Bridge and its carriage road, but did not have time to walk even a few hundred yards toward Witch Hole Pond to see the magnificent views over Frenchman Bay. I photographed Bass Harbor Head Light, but only from the east side of the clifftop on a cloudy afternoon, not from the rocky shore in the morning when the pink sunrise light illuminates the lighthouse. I didn't even see Little Long Pond or The Bubbles.

The first time I visited Yellowstone National Park, I was there for one afternoon. I photographed a few hot springs, Lower Yellowstone Falls and a fly fisherman in the Madison River. I bypassed Old Faithful because an eruption was imminent and the parking lot was full. I did not see Mammoth Hot Springs, nor the Hayden Valley, and I didn't even know about Dunraven Pass or the Lamar Valley. I could fill an entire book with what I missed that day.

All the sights I neglected in those parks on the first trip are things I would likely have found had I stayed even a few days. If I had visited for a week or two, I would have learned those parks well enough to know when and where I wanted to be in

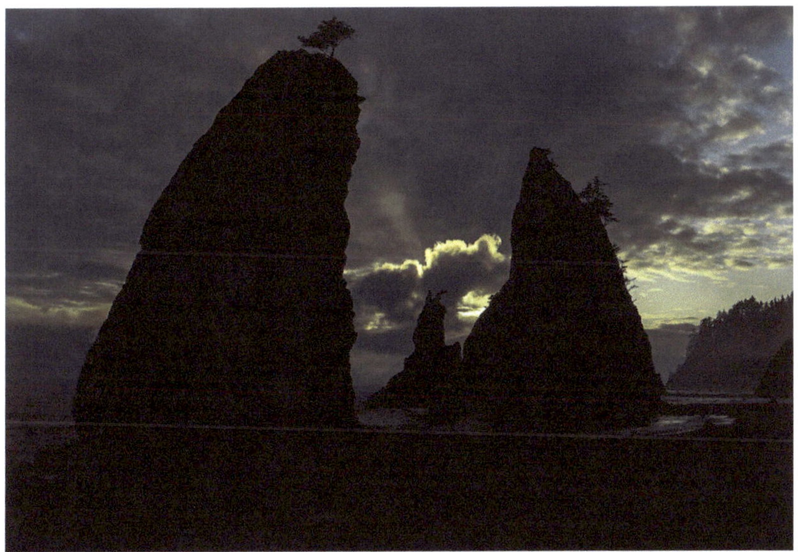

Olympic National Park

just about any light or weather condition. I would have made better photographs, and I would have made myself a better photographer through more knowledge and practice. (Fortunately, I did get to revisit all of those parks for longer periods over the following two decades.)

TIME

Now, if I have less than five days to photograph a national park, I feel like I'm missing opportunities. When I'm in a park, I want time to return to locations in different light, and in different weather. I want time to make mistakes that I can learn from and correct—time for second and third and fourth chances to hone my vision into a photographic reality that I'm happy with. I want time to experiment with unfamiliar techniques, or to create new ones of my own. I want time to methodically move through my list of possible subjects, whether they're ideas I researched beforehand or ideas I happened across once there. I want time to execute my plans, and I want time to meander. I want time to find the wildlife as it wanders into scenic locations. I want time to see a primitive road that wasn't on the map and drive it, and I want time to see a trail I hadn't noticed before and start walking to discover where it goes. I want time to read the displays in the visitor center, to talk with strangers I meet in a valley, to wander alone and be creative in the solitude and the harmony that is the wilderness.

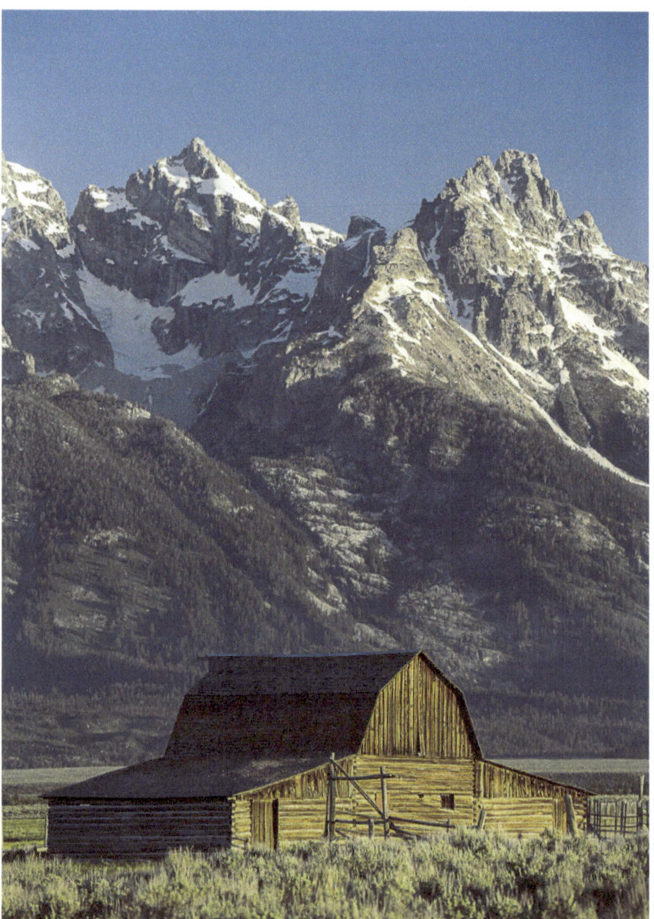

Grand Teton National Park

Spending an extended period in a national park will allow you to truly explore the various layers it offers to the photographer. You can learn how the landscape formed and why its wildlife lives there, which will help you photograph them better. You will have time to determine the best hours of the day and the best weather conditions to photograph different subjects in, and you will have opportunities to revisit places to vary and hone your interpretation of them. Moreover, there's a long-reaching benefit: You might be amazed how much your skills can improve by immersing yourself in a beautiful location.

Five days is my minimum for feeling that I am doing my work well. Seven days or 10 or 14, and I'm feeling that I can explore a little more, I can follow hunches and have them be wrong without feeling anxious that I wasted hours. With a week or more in the park, I have time to experiment with different techniques, and I have time to make notes and study my best options. Furthermore, I'm feeling at home in the park.

For all those reasons, time is important when photographing one of these amazing places. Subsequently, time will be a theme throughout this book. Much of what I discuss will be based on the premise of allowing yourself enough days to accomplish all the aforementioned goals. Only then are you likely to feel that you really experienced, and intimately photographed, a national park.

RESEARCH

Another premise that stems from this is the importance of research. Sure, you can just climb into a car or board a plane and journey to a national park on a whim, with nary a care or worry about what you'll do once there. You can ignore the maps and the experience of those who have gone before, and just explore the turns of trails and the bends of roads as they appear before you. I've done that, too, and it can be fun. But there's another way to photograph a park, and it's better.

If you're going to spend your money (or your client's) and your time to travel to a national park for photography, planning what you'll do once there will make your trip more focused and more productive. And by "productive" I don't mean that you'll make more photos—I mean you'll make better ones.

Planning has one objective: to maximize your time in the park. I promise that if you research your options in advance, and that if you actively refine your strategy while working, your photography and your overall experience will improve dramatically. Whether you are on assignment, on vacation, or something between those two extremes, research will make your national park trip better. It may even save you from wasting good light while hiking to someplace that turns out to have no good view of anything.

That doesn't mean you can't be spontaneous. If you're in Great Smoky Mountains, heading toward Cades Cove to photograph the trees flanking Hyatt Lane backlit by the setting sun, then of course you can change your plans when you see a bear swimming with her cubs in the Little River. If you're in Olympic National Park to photograph the deer at Hurricane Ridge, you can still head out to the coast when you hear that the weather reports call for a moody fog to roll in. Even when you have a plan, you can still change course. You can still adjust. You can still jettison your schedule when you notice a better opportunity developing. But having that plan gives you structure, gives you confidence, gives you an outline and an objective. Moreover, it gives you a means for being constructive and creative in the moments that fail to bring serendipity and surprise. Having a plan, knowing what you want to do and where you want to go, will make you a better photographer.

LAY OF THE LAND

THE world is full of useful sources of information about the national parks. They come in the form of books, magazine articles, pamphlets, films, apps, internet forums, personal knowledge of others, etc. Be a sponge for this information—absorb all that you can. Know about where you go. Then use that awareness of the location to make great photography.

After doing all of this research, you'll have a lot of information about places to be and when to be there. Of course, you don't have to follow any of that guidance. You can use it to follow others' paths while looking for your own way to interpret the things you see, or you can use it to help you avoid treading in others' tracks. Both strategies can be lucrative.

SHOOT THE STANDARDS?

Of course, a lot of the research you do will reveal information about the famous scenes in the national parks. A common topic of conversation among photographers is about the value—or lack of value—in photographing these. Some photographers refer to such locations as having "tripod holes" because of the number of shutterbugs who have recorded nearly the exact same photo there, over and over, for decades.

My feeling is that I want to photograph these places anyway. Why? These spots are famous for a reason. There is some aspect of the place that is responsible for having drawn so many visitors, and I want to see what that is and perhaps try to capture it in a photograph. I know that millions of cameras have been aimed at Yellowstone Falls from Artist Point, but that doesn't make the scene any less beautiful.

Also, I like the challenge of finding a new way to photograph a famous scene. It forces me to be more creative than perhaps I would have been if I had found the spot first. I like

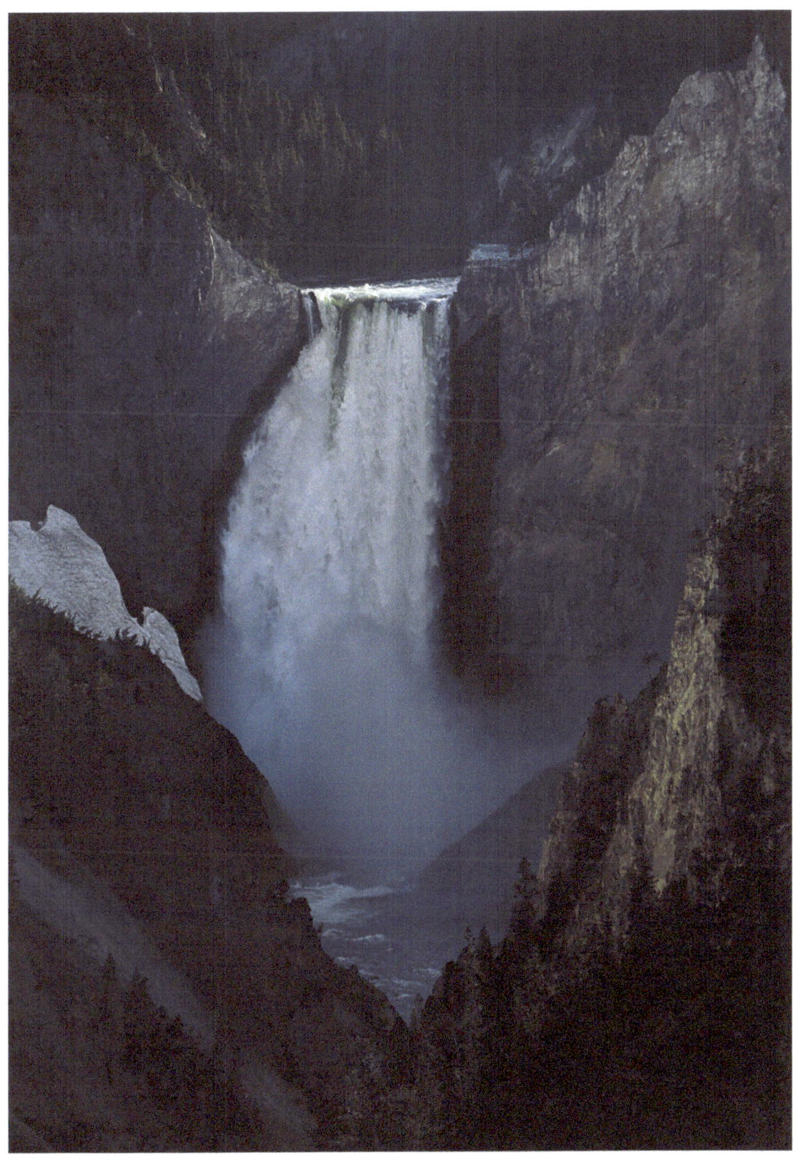

Yellowstone National Park

to disregard the "best practices" of the location and see what happens. In the aforementioned example of Artist Point, the common wisdom is to shoot in morning, when the early-day light is warm and direct, and when rainbows may appear in the mist of the falls. So I tried late afternoon. I was the only person there with a tripod, and I loved the way the backlight

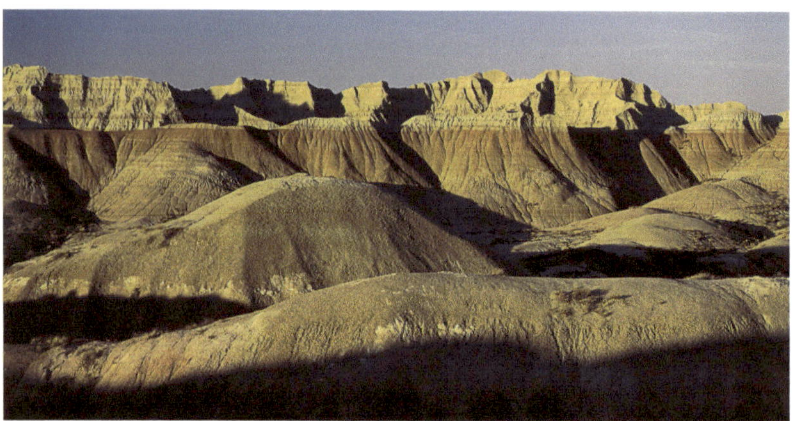

Badlands National Park

highlighted the fringes of rock face in the canyon, and how it brought a new dimension to the scene that is not apparent at other times of day.

Photographing these hot-spots has business implications, as well. If you sell stock images, or if you market fine art prints based on locations, then potential customers will surely ask about famous scenes. If you don't have them in your catalog, you don't make the sales. Even if you're photographing a park as a personal project, you might not feel that your work is complete without some images of its iconic sights. Yosemite's Tunnel View is one of the most photographed vistas in the world, but could you imagine it not being included in a book about the park?

BEYOND PARK BOUNDARIES

While the national parks showcase some amazing scenery, they're not the only pretty places. Many of the parks are situated in areas with lands that have been preserved in other ways—as wildlife refuges, national forests, state parks, etc.

For example, Everglades' neighbor is Big Cypress National Preserve, which while located in the same overall terrain, has an entirely different aesthetic. Grand Teton is flanked by Bridger-Teton National Forest, which contains mountain roads with fantastic views of Jackson Hole valley. Shenandoah and Great Smoky Mountains are connected by 469 miles of the Blue Ridge Parkway, which, among many other traits, is one of the nation's premier fall-color destinations. Badlands borders Buffalo Gap National Grassland and is less than a two-hour drive from Mount Rushmore.

Explore these places and others like them, either as a break from the national park, or in an effort to get a more complete picture of the region. Many are also visited less than their higher-profile neighbors, which means they can be quieter places to work on weekends and holidays.

EXPLORING FROM AFAR

When I'm planning a trip to a park, one of the first things I do in the weeks prior is get a map. If the shoot is at a park I've visited before, then I probably have an official park map in my files, because I usually try to bring home an extra. If I have not been there, then I visit the National Park Service's cartography webpage (see Appendix) and download a map. Because these maps are published by the government, they are in the public domain, so printing one at home or in an office-services store is perfectly legal. I print the map on a large sheet of paper so I have room to write on it. Then, as I'm reading books and articles and such about the park, I can make notes—right on the map—about locations to scout once on site. If you prefer something larger than you can print, or perhaps more detailed than the official map, visit the website of the support organization for the location you're planning to visit (for example, Friends of Virgin Islands National Park). Many such organizations sell maps directly through their online store.

BOOKS, ETC.

Then I start looking at books. Many have been written about the individual national parks. Some are historical or pictorial books, and those can be useful. Some are travel guides geared to general tourists, or to hikers and campers. Trail guides in particular can contain good tips about locations left out of most other travel guides—hikers tend to like nice scenery, so in that regard they're kinfolk to photographers. Some travel guides cover very specific topics about the parks, which may or may not be useful to individual photographers, depending on your visual interests. For example, there's *The Guide to Yellowstone Waterfalls and Their Discovery*, and *Wildlife Watching in America's National Parks*.

The most useful books, though, tend to be the national park travel guides written specifically for photographers. Many are available, though primarily just for the most popular parks. The best are usually those written by photographers who have spent good time working in the park they write about, as opposed to those written by generalist travel writers who might not fully understand the nuances of photography needs. When you're heading to a park, buy any book that another photographer has written about it. If more than one is in print, buy them both—or all. Different photographers' perspectives are valuable, and each is sure to offer some locations and tips that the others don't.

And don't stop with just online or brick-and-mortar book retailers. Also search online for photographers who may offer inexpensive (or even free) e-books or small guides about parks they happen to be an expert about. One of the best resources available is the "Photograph America" newsletter, written and published by California-based photographer Robert Hitchman. Since 1989 he has released quarterly reports about locations he has photographed. They include maps, tips for photo locations, ideal times of day and year to shoot, etc. His entire catalog is available for purchase as a whole, by region, by topic, or piecemeal. Make it part of your pre-trip routine to check if one Robert's newsletters is about where you're going, and if one is, buy it.

Another resource is *Outdoor Photographer* magazine's column "Favorite Places." Each issue contains a one-page piece about a photography location, written by a photographer who is experienced in shooting there. The write-ups include information about the best seasons for photography, gear recommendations for the area, and resources for further information. Many of the locations covered are national parks, or parts of national parks. You can likely view past issues at a local library; alternatively, many of the Favorite Places are archived on the magazine's website. Most other photography magazines focus more on new gear and techniques, but some do offer travel pieces—they're worth looking into when you're researching.

ONLINE SOURCES

Some of the best information you can find will be from other photographers, and fortunately the internet makes reaching them extremely easy. Search for images of the park you're researching. Also, search for photographers who have served as artist-in-residence there—they tend to find obscure and far-flung locations. If you see a photo that you like on someone's website, write an email and ask if he or she would be willing to

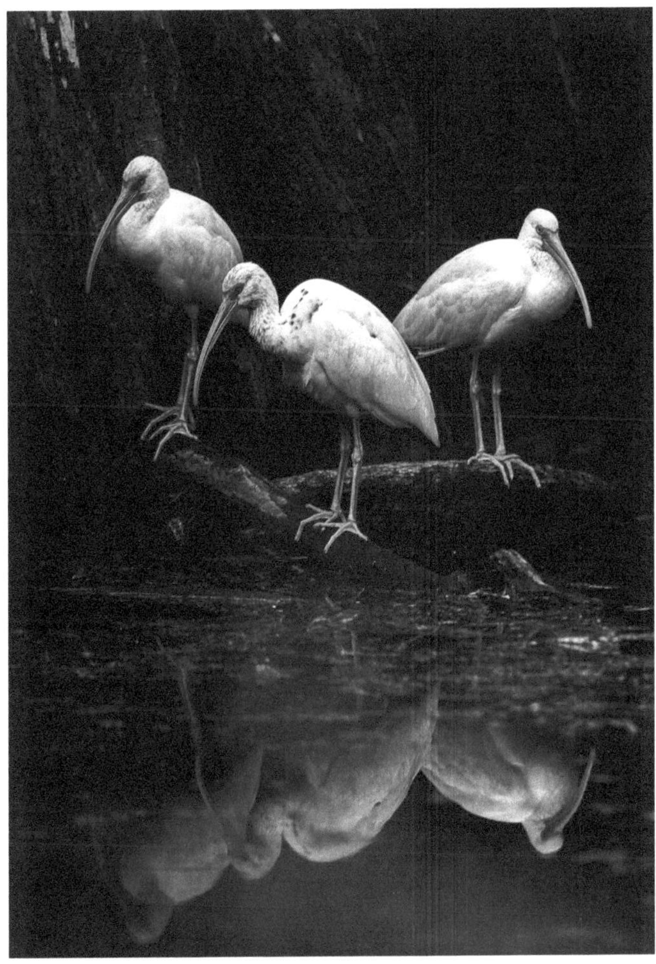

Big Cypress National Preserve

share some tips they learned about working in that park, or in the area of the park where the photo was made. As long as you don't sound like you're trying to copy their photo ideas, you will probably get a friendly response.

I have never failed to find helpful photographers by just reaching out, whether by emailing people through their websites, or by asking for group advice on a forum. Website forums that have especially helpful members include Luminous-Landscape.com and Photo.net. And NaturePhotographers.net has region-specific forums where members tend to be generous with their local knowledge. Also consider posting to hiking forums—the users aren't usually photography experts, but they have seen some great out-of-the-way scenery and are generally happy to share their experiences.

Some apps also can be good tools. National Geographic sells an app that contains their trail maps of 15 national parks, and another that pinpoints places of interest in the parks, along with tips from their photographers about working in those locations. Chimani offers a suite of free apps that details the highlights and logistical information for the parks, along with photos and maps. And the National Parks Conservation Association has a "National Parks Field Guide" app with information about many of the plants and wildlife you may encounter.

Google is another invaluable source of information—and I don't mean just for finding the other items already mentioned. In the months before traveling to a national park, visit Google News and set up an email alert for news about that park. For example, if planning a trip to Biscayne, create a news alert for "Biscayne National Park"—then whenever it's covered by the media for any reason, you'll receive a link in your inbox (or you can stipulate that you want notifications only daily or weekly). This tactic will keep you apprised of road and trail closures, rare wildlife sightings, park events that might interest you, etc.

Another useful tool is Google Earth, a highly detailed searchable atlas that you can download and use for free. It accesses Google's massive stock of maps and satellite imagery, along with street-level views. You can examine the topography from overhead and, using the software's "Sun" feature, you can see how natural light strikes the landscape at any time of day, any time of year. The preview of the sunlight takes terrain contours into account, so you can see what land features will be in sunlight and what will be in shade. This is invaluable visual data for planning how you want to cover a location, possibly even months ahead of time. You can use Google Earth also to find possible photography locations that you would otherwise have to chance upon if just hiking through the park. For example, while looking through satellite images of Shenandoah, I saw a beautiful small meadow in the woods that a trail passes near, but not through. I never would have seen it from ground-level while hiking through the area.

Lastly, check the park's website. Many of them offer tips that are either specific to, or that would help, photographers. For instance, Arches has a chart detailing whether early-morning or late-afternoon light is best at almost two dozen of the park's most popular rock formations. Mesa Verde breaks down the best light at different cliff dwellings by season, and lists photography tips specific to each site.

RESEARCHING IN PERSON

ONCE at the national park, the research doesn't stop. Now is the time not only to start scouting the locations that your figurative legwork has piqued your interest in, but to start finding more locations by doing literal legwork. It's also time to perhaps reject some of the locations that don't look as good as they sounded beforehand.

On my first day in a park, I do hardly any photography. Instead, I drive around, I walk around, I collect new information, I scout locations. I make a lot of notes, and I start planning how to approach my photography for the rest of the trip. I drive as many roads as I can, just to look. I especially explore primitive roads that aren't on the official map (many parks have some), which can give easy access to some nice spots that

WHAT'S THAT?

Getting "lost" in the creative process of photography is easy. So remembering to take notes about what we're photographing in an unfamiliar place can sometimes be hard. A few tricks can help us easily identify the names of our subjects once home:

- When photographing a location, shoot a frame of a park information sign that indicates where you are or what you're looking at. Or photograph the name of the place on the map. When you're reviewing your files at home later, your "ID" frame will appear amongst the photos of that location.
- If your camera has a sound recorder, use it to make audio notes of your locations. The sound file will appear in chronological order with your image files.
- If you have a means of geotagging your photos, use the GPS metadata to load the location into Google Earth. Using a combination of ground-level view and the labeled satellite imagery, you can identify the names of lakes, meadows, mountain peaks, etc.

Collect as much information on-site as possible. It will make captioning and keywording a lot easier later.

no one else is looking for. I drive down any road that doesn't have a "Do Not Enter" sign, especially if I don't know where it goes.

At most parks, you receive a map and perhaps a park newsletter on your way through the entrance. If not, they will be available at a visitor center. Take them both, because the information within can be valuable. Even though I usually print a map before traveling, I still get a fresh one—I might need it for keeping separate on-site notes, or perhaps to have a clean copy to use solely for navigation. The newsletter can provide good information about what is happening in the park at the time of your visit, such as events, or seasonal changes regarding wildlife locations, or where the wildflowers are blooming. It will also alert you to any restrictions, especially if they're unusual—such as a particular trail or campground being closed due to recent bear activity.

Also at the visitor center, stop at the bookstore or gift shop. It will usually have a selection of postcards, calendars and coffee-table books that feature park photos. Look through them for ideas of locations to scout. You're almost certain to find some that you didn't see in the guide books. If you see something that interests you but don't know where it is, just ask around at the store or visitor center—someone will know how to find it.

SIDESTEPPING CROWDS

National parks usually bear their highest visitation levels on weekends, holidays and the occasional fee-free days—such as Presidents Day and Independence Day. So if you want solitude, or you don't want your tripod bumped by a little Johnny or Jane, those are good days to avoid popular park attractions such as Brandywine Falls in Cuyahoga Valley, eruptions of Old Faithful in Yellowstone, or sunrise at the summit in Haleakala.

If your stay in a national park coincides with a time that sees a massive influx of visitors, you may want to adjust your schedule so you're photographing in more secluded spots those days. This is a good time to get on the trails, or to visit area national forests or state parks. And if you really want to visit a popular location on a popular day, try to do so first thing in the morning. Most tourists aren't crazy enough to be out before sunrise—not like photographers.

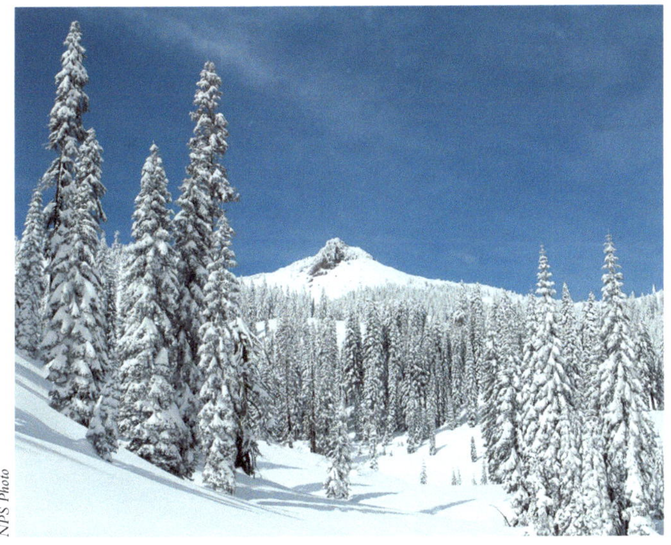

NPS Photo

Lassen Volcanic National Park

OTHER PEOPLE

Just as other photographers can be helpful when planning a national park shoot, they can also assist you on-site. You'll see them everywhere, especially at the more popular parks, especially at the famous spots, particularly in good light. In my experience, most of them are friendly. They are like-minded people, so starting a conversation is usually effortless, and since we all share similar challenges, finding empathetic ears is usually easy. At least some of the photographers you meet will have already been in the park for a few days, so ask them what they've seen, where they've been. (Then, later in your trip, after you've been there for a few days—impart the same favor to others.)

Also, be sure to talk to the people who know the park best: the rangers. They will help you. They know what's happening there—even what's happening today. Many times I have heard a ranger say something like, "I saw some lupine blooming this morning at Such-and-Such Pass," or "We know there's a large herd of elk in the meadow right now, if you want to photograph them before sunset." I often find myself in long conversations with rangers, discussing what their job is like, what mine is like, other parks we've been to, the great coffee at the diner in town, what kind of dog we have at home ... and suddenly they're telling me about their favorite secluded places in the park. In Grand Teton, I was looking for lakes to use for photographing reflections of the mountains; a ranger told

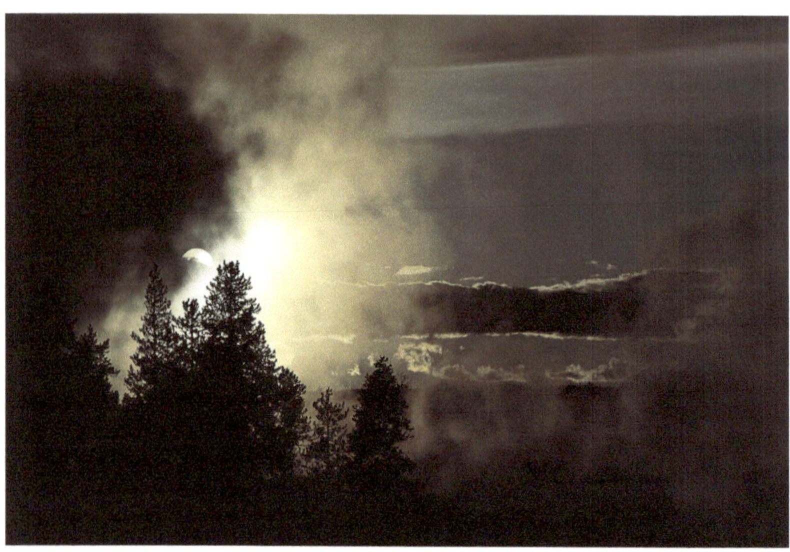

Yellowstone National Park

me not to bother, because bad weather was due and would kick up waves before I could get anywhere worthwhile—but to definitely follow her directions to an isolated spot the next morning. I did, and it's now one of my favorite locations in the park. And, incidentally, I used the bad weather to photograph some landscape scenes I would have missed had I been wasting time looking for placid lakes under a storm front.

Though they rarely offer time for photography, also consider joining a ranger-led hike. The information relayed during these can be helpful to your photography later, such as tips about the behavior of local wildlife, or locations of rare wildflower species. This is an excellent way to learn more about the area, and is a productive means of whiling away undesirable midday light.

Of course, other people can be helpful, too. My brother worked in Yellowstone for a summer, and spent two months collecting invaluable location tips for me, including an off-trail route to a spectacular view of Grand Prismatic spring that few people would self-discover. And when I was in Everglades one winter, I decided to try to photograph the barred owls at Mahogany Hammock; I was on the trail for only two minutes before someone saw my camera, guessed my intent, and showed me where he and his wife had just spotted two of them.

As I'm doing all of this—talking to people, browsing the bookstore, driving around—I constantly record notes on my map or in a notebook. I'll circle locations I want to photograph later in the trip, along with the time of day I'd like to be there, or the type of weather I'd like to photograph them in. I'll also write down general information that may help me in the coming days, such as sunrise and sunset times, or the times for high and low tide, or the date of the full or new moon. I like to have a breakdown of all the places I want to be in certain conditions. Then when those conditions happen, I can reference my list rather than waste time wandering around looking for chance opportunities. For example, suppose I'm visiting Redwood and I see a stunning rhododendron that interests me, but the background is too busy. I can make a note to return to that spot when some fog rolls in.

I never want to find myself in great light and not know where to go. Moreover, I want to have so many notes and ideas that I can't attend to them all. At the end of the trip I would rather have ideas I haven't had time to explore than have to spend the last day or two not knowing what to do.

When I go to bed at night, I use my notes to make two plans for the morning: a sunny plan and a cloudy plan. My destinations and the types of photos I work on would surely be changed by either scenario. Yes, I do look at weather predictions, but I don't blindly expect them to be accurate. This way, instead of having to reevaluate a morning strategy while still groggy from a night of sort-of-sleeping in a tent on hard ground, I already know my options.

Again, this doesn't mean I can't improvise. I've done so countless times. I won't ignore a moose wading in a misty, aspen-lined pond at dawn just because my notes say I wanted to be somewhere else. Sometimes serendipity can be a powerful creative tool, and lots of fun, too. But having a plan—knowing what you want to do and when you want to do it—will keep you focused and productive.

CHAPTER 2

LOGISTICS

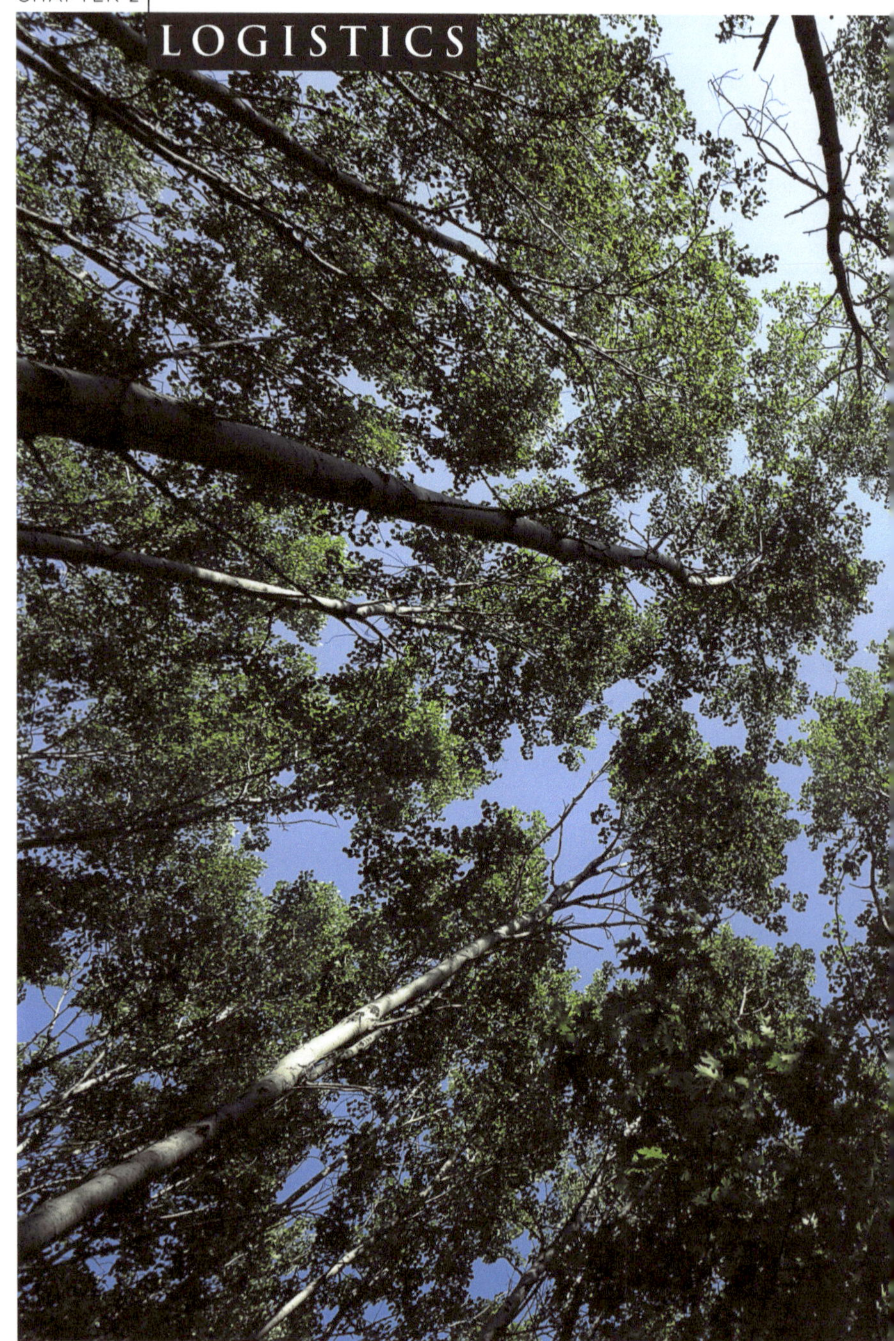

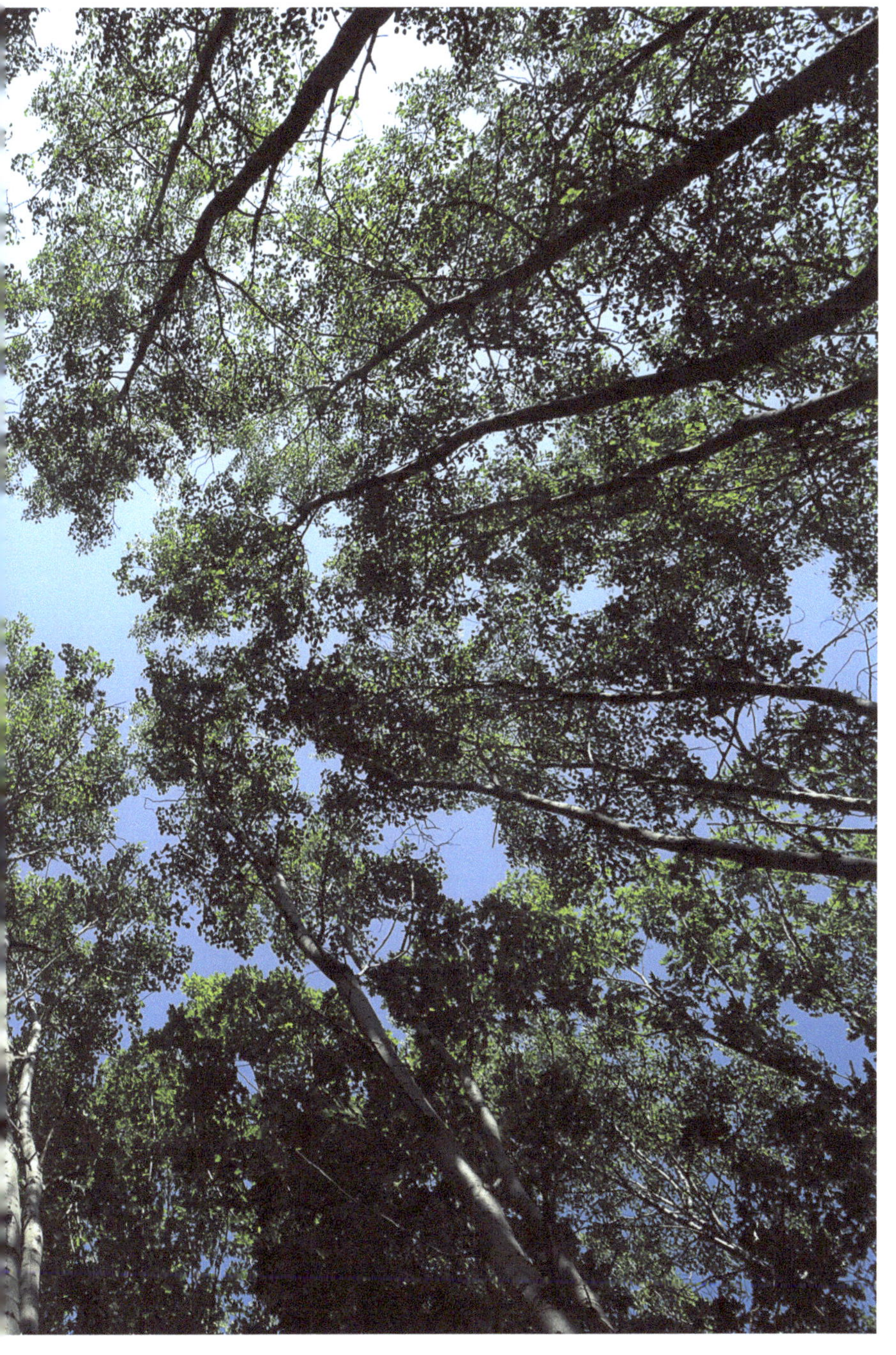

Birches, Acadia
National Park

THINGS TO PLAN

TRAVELING is traveling, and we've all done at least some. But traveling to a national park is different than traveling to a resort for a wedding or to New Jersey for Christmas. Travel is also a bit different when it involves cameras and tripods, big heavy bags and an itinerary that involves alpine lakes more than heated swimming pools.

The logistics of a park shoot don't require an advanced degree, and there certainly is no "correct"—or even "best"—way to plan and execute a trip. But there are a few ways to maximize the experience. The discussion offered here represents some best practices, or at least some good habits, that I've learned over 20 years, through experience, research and conversations with other people.

FEES

Most of the national parks charge an entry fee. But not all of them. In fact, the most-visited park in the U.S., Great Smoky Mountains, is free. The largest park, Wrangell-St. Elias, is also free, as is the smallest, Hot Springs. Acadia, which charges for most of the year, is free in winter. To access the interior of Grand Teton, you must pay an entrance fee, but you can drive the length of its John D. Rockefeller Jr. Memorial Parkway—one of the most scenic roads in America—for free, including visits to any of the park's overlooks or historical sites along the way.

Even when an admission fee is charged, the price is always reasonable—$10 or $15 is normal, and it usually covers you for at least a few days, but details do vary from park to park. Also, parks that charge always have fee-free days throughout the year, such as on President's Day and Independence Day. Check the National Park Service's website for dates and more information about when you can access the parks sans money.

I mention the free ways to get in because many of us have a budget, whether we're on assignment, traveling on a personal project, or photographing for fun. Money does usually matter. However, I believe it's also important to remember that money matters to the parks, too. They are not fully funded by the government. Entrance fees help bridge some of the financial gap, and most of those dollars and cents are appropriated right back to the individual parks that collected them. All this money is used to keep the parks open and healthy. It pays for visitor

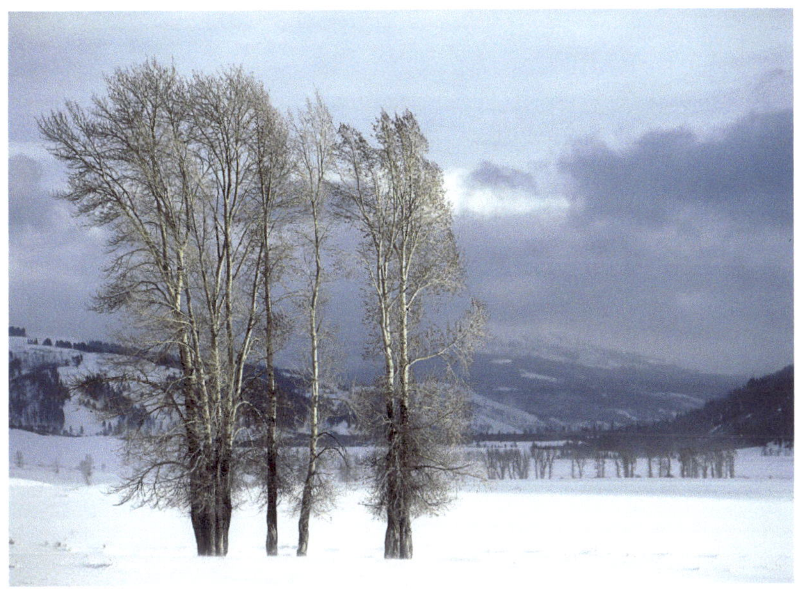

Yellowstone National Park

centers, trail maintenance, historic-site repair, exhibits, restrooms, potable water, campgrounds, staff salaries, etc. For us photographers, that money is used to sustain and preserve some of America's most stunning landscapes that we get to aim our cameras at.

So while getting around for free is fun and budget-friendly, I also like the idea of supporting the efforts behind preserving these lands. If you frequent a certain park, look into purchasing an annual pass for it. If you travel to a lot of parks, consider purchasing an Annual Federal Recreation Lands Pass, which affords access to every national park, national wildlife refuge, national forest and national grassland in the U.S. The math may work in your favor—it tends to quickly—by saving you money well before the end of the 12 months. But even if you don't save cash with the pass, you can at least feel good that you're helping the entire system stay healthy.

Incidentally, you can get an annual pass for free if you are a member of the U.S. military or a dependent, if you are a U.S. citizen or permanent resident with a permanent disability, if you are a parks volunteer with who has met an hours threshold, or if you win or place in the "Share the Experience" photography contest (see page 22). Also, seniors—defined as at least 62 years old—may purchase a lifetime pass at a very substantial discount; in 2015, the one-time fee was only $10.

SHARE THE EXPERIENCE

Take a look online at the annual passes that the National Park Service has issued over the past several years. The photos on the passes are pretty good, right? Ever wonder where those images come from? Each year the National Park Foundation sponsors a photography contest, with the winning photo used on the following year's Annual Federal Recreation Lands Pass.

Professional photographers are barred from entering, but amateur photographers have a lot to gain. There is prestige and publicity that comes with winning this contest, and the prizes are good, too. During the year, weekly winners are named and subsequently featured on the website.

For more information, visit www.ShareTheExperience.org.

PERMITS

One of the most common questions photographers have about working in the national parks is whether they need a permit. Rangers sometimes have this question, too, which is why it's imperative to know your rights.

Permits can be expensive just to apply for. If one is granted, the photographer could then incur even more fees, depending on the type of work he or she is doing. These fees are not meant to bilk photographers, but rather are designed to recoup the costs of ensuring that commercial shoots do not compromise the environment. And that word "commercial" is the key. People enjoying making photographs in the wilderness, whether for hobby or even for assignments, are very unlikely to need a permit.

The rules are slightly more complex than this, but basically, if your work meets these two conditions, then you do not need a permit:

1. ***Your shoot involves only one or two people, including you.*** This does not mean you can't travel with three buddies to backpack and photograph cinder cones in Lassen Volcanic. It only means that if you're traveling with a lighting assistant, wardrobe master and makeup artist while producing images for an outfitter, then you are now a four-person production crew that may be taxing the resources of the park for commercial gain.

2. ***You are using only cameras and tripods and other standard photographic equipment.*** If you are instead using props, models, etc., then you are considered part of a commercial activity.

If you are in the park just working on some photography—even if you intend to market those images as stock, or to sell them as prints, or to publish them in a book—then you are very unlikely to need a permit, as well as unlikely to be questioned accordingly.

However, there are some instances when you may want to apply for one, even if your intent is not commercial. One of the written stipulations for needing a permit is accessing an area, or engaging in an activity, that the park disallows to the general public. Carlsbad Caverns does not allow people to photograph the nightly exodus of thousands of bats from the cave entrance—but you can with a permit. Petrified Forest actually closes between sunset and sunrise—so if you want to drive into the Painted Desert to photograph dawn skies, you may want to apply for a special-use permit to be there off-hours. (Or you can get a free permit for backcountry camping and just sleep out overnight.)

If you have concerns about whether you would need a permit for what you want to do and where you want to do it, check the website for the park you're visiting, or just ask a ranger. If it's a slow day, a ranger might let you have some special access just for being nice.

LODGING

WHILE on a trip to a park, your choices about where to sleep will affect your photography experience. In some places, your options will be limited. For example, Gates of the Arctic has no lodge, no campgrounds—no public lodging infrastructure at all. If staying overnight, you're either camping or renting one of a few private cabins. But most of the parks have myriad ways to spend the night either within or nearby, with varying levels of comfort and convenience.

The following is a breakdown of different options, along with the pros and cons of each. None of these options are right or wrong, but the advantages of some may not be important to your needs, and the disadvantages of others may hamper your photography efforts. You may even want to move between one option and another during the trip. (For example, I usually camp, but might opt for a hotel if the weather forecast is predicting overnight rain, or if I need a good night's sleep in the midst of a rough trip.)

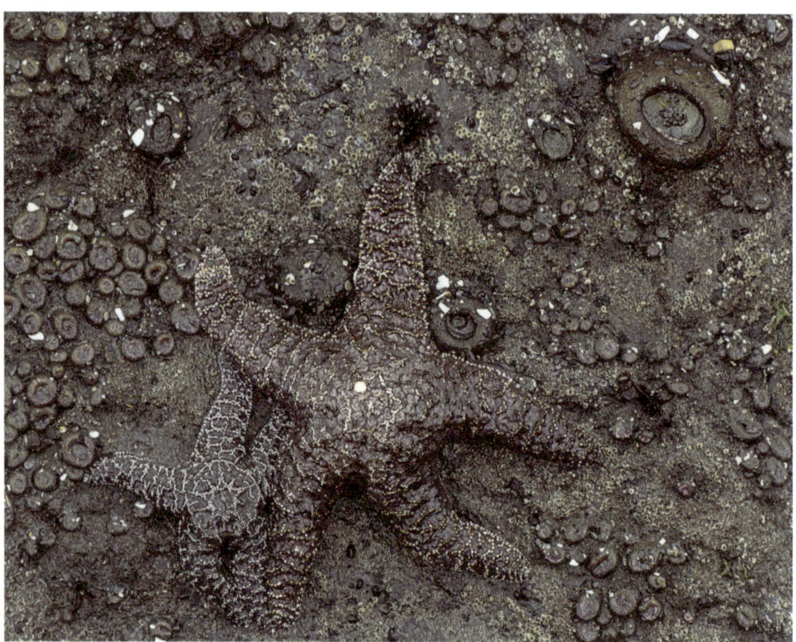

Olympic National Park

PARK LODGES

Some of the national parks have lodges within park boundaries, and they tend to be very nice facilities, many of them with charming, rustic designs. Some examples include the Many Glacier Hotel in Glacier National Park, The Ahwahnee in Yosemite and Big Meadows Lodge in Shenandoah.

Renting a room at a park lodge will keep you warm in winter, cool in summer, and dry anytime of the year. Lodges provide electricity, which is critical in the digital photography era, when just about every tool we use contains batteries that need to be recharged (see "Power" on page 59). Lodges have showers, so you can clean up after a day in the wilderness. Also, because lodges are in the park, staying in one can give you relatively easy access to your photo locations in the morning. Lodge employees often live in the park seasonally, and therefore know some "secret" spots; being friendly with these folks can yield some useful location information.

One of the downsides of park lodges is that they tend to be expensive. This can be a detriment if you're budget-conscious, whether because you're on assignment and the client has given you little funding for logistics, or because you're on a personal trip and want to spend your money in other ways. Also, the parks that do have lodges tend to have just one or very few, and they tend to be large parks. So while staying in a park lodge may position you relatively close to where you want to shoot in the morning, it will likely still leave you some distance away. If you're aiming to photograph in dawn light atop a mountain, you'll be doing some early-morning traveling in the dark. Also, lodges tend to have just one or two dining facilities, so while you can get some fresh, hot food, you'll have to settle for whatever is on a limited menu.

OFF-SITE HOTELS

Many of the national parks are flanked by small towns that cater to park visitors. For example, Acadia has Bar Harbor, Great Smoky Mountains has Gatlinburg, and Zion has Springdale. These boundary towns tend to have a decent selection of hotels and motels to fit various budgets and comfort needs.

Like park lodges, off-site hotels can keep you warm or cool, and will keep you dry overnight. They also have electricity and showers, and hotel employees can probably give you good tips on photography locations that aren't in the books you've read. Park-side towns also usually have at least a few restaurants, so you'll have different options from day to day. Also, off-site hotels tend to be more moderately priced than in-park lodges.

However, the one big disadvantage to overnighting outside the park is this: You're outside the park. If you're planning to photograph at first light, you'll have extra travel to do in the morning; and if you want to photograph night skies or moonlit landscapes, you might be a long way from your bed when you're done and tired.

RECREATIONAL VEHICLES

A common sight in the parks, recreational vehicles (or RVs) combine some of the advantages of hotels with some of the advantages of camping. You don't need to own one—many companies rent them for road travel, or for people visiting the local area.

Aside from the cost of rental and fuel (which can be considerable, especially if you're driving many miles), RVs provide a relatively inexpensive means for sleeping under a roof. They have a shower, a toilet and electricity, and space for a lot of cargo (i.e., camera bags and such). Many park campgrounds allow RVs in certain areas, which means you can place yourself relatively close to where you want to shoot in the morning.

But perhaps the most unique advantage of using an RV is this: It gives you a high vantage point for photographing landscapes, or whatever else you might be pointing your camera at. Most RVs have a ladder that allows you to climb on top, giving you an elevated angle. That can make a huge different in landscape photography. For proof, look to Ansel Adams, who installed a platform on top of his truck for exactly this reason.

The primary disadvantage of RVs is that, as alluded to before, they can be pricey. Their gas mileage is notoriously low, and, as expected, they are more expensive to rent than a car. They also handle differently than a car—there's a learning curve for driving them, and bringing them on primitive or windy roads is often not prudent or safe. (To work around the latter issues, you could tow a car with you and use it for excursions.) Furthermore, not all campgrounds allow RVs, and few parks allow overnight parking at overlooks, so your location options are relatively limited.

CAMPING

Not everyone is comfortable sleeping in the great outdoors, but if you are, it's a great choice when on a photography trip.

Camping is certainly the most budget-friendly option. The campgrounds in the parks are almost always less expensive than what the market bears in the surrounding area. In some parks, camping is even free, particularly at remote campsites or when roughing the backcountry. Sleeping outside can also make you feel more "at one" with your subject—which I suppose could be thought of as the method-acting of the photography world, but is an important part of the process for some photographers.

The best benefit of camping is that it can put you very close to your morning destination. For example, if you need to be up before dawn to photograph the sunrise from atop Mount Haleakala, staying in the campground at Hosmer Grove will put you an hour closer to the summit than would the closest hotel. Likewise, if you want to photograph a sunset in the southwest Everglades, you might prefer following the experience with a night of backcountry camping rather than hiking back to Flamingo for a couple of hours through prime alligator habitat in the dark.

Sleeping in a tent does have its drawbacks, however. Cold, hot and wet weather will certainly affect the experience. Showers, toilets and electricity are not available at every campgrounds, and are never available in the backcountry. Also, you want to be cognizant of potential wildlife issues. Animals very rarely bother campers, even in remote remote areas. But they might be interested in your food. Special precautions may be wise, or even required. For example, the parks in Alaska have some of the most stringent food-storage guidelines in the park system, due to the active population of hungry grizzly bears.

LOCOMOTION

NATIONAL PARKS are big places. Even the smallest, Hot Springs, is almost nine square miles. And that's tiny. The largest, Wrangell-St. Elias, is 15,000 square miles. Getting around in an efficient and productive way requires flexibility.

The trick is that you want to get out of the car. That may seem obvious, and perhaps it is to people who are passionate about nature photography; after all, we tend to like nature, so we tend to like walking away from the road. But in parks with roads, people often don't venture far away from the blacktop. For example, Yellowstone has reported that over 90 percent of its visitors don't make it past established roadside stops. Locally it's known as the "2 percent" rule: only 2 percent of tourists leave the road, and the road reaches only 2 percent of the park. While many of the roads were planned and built to maximize access to the best scenery, the parks were also intended to maintain the wildness of an area. That means that in almost every case, a pronounced majority of a park's best scenery is "out there" somewhere.

Moreover, when we photographers are shooting, we're striving to make portfolio-grade images pretty much every time out. We know we usually won't, but we are trying. If we're not trying, we have to question your passion and goals. So if you're putting the time and money into a trip to a national park for the purpose of photography, then at least part of you must be aiming to match or improve upon your best work. And you can't do that by making five-minute stops at turnouts and overlooks.

So, how do you get to the best spots?

AUTOMOBILES

First, you probably do want to have a car, or a truck. (That is, if the park has roads. A few, such as Kobuk Valley, do not.) You can drive your own auto to a park, or you can rent one.

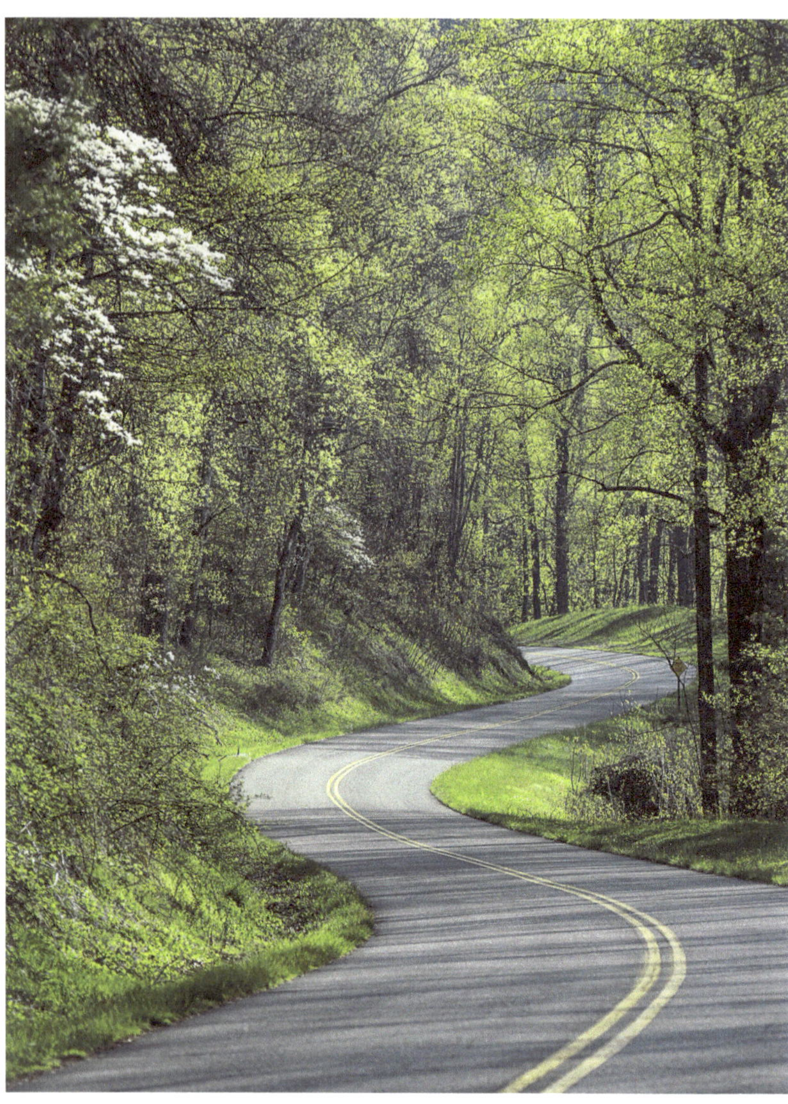

Blue Ridge Parkway

If you're visiting a park with a lot of primitive roads (such as Death Valley) or that allows winter driving in the mountains (such as Great Smoky Mountains), you may want to rent a four-wheel-drive vehicle, at least for a day or two, so you can drive to more remote areas. When renting a car, one thing I always try to avoid is a windshield that is tinted along the top. While that feature is great for reducing sky-borne glare while driving, it's not so good for location scouting; it darkens your perception of the sky, and therefore alters your assessment of the surrounding tableau. Also, if you plan to leave any camera gear in the car while you hike, get a car with a trunk—preferably one that cannot be opened from inside the car.

In addition to being useful for locomotion, cars also serve well as a blind when photographing wildlife from the road. Animals that might be startled by the sight of a human will often ignore an automobile. The first time I photographed at Grand Canyon, I was in the car with my camera aimed out the passenger-side window. My target was a deer grazing at the edge of the South Rim, with the canyon opening up in the background behind her. I didn't like the angle, so I opened the car door to get out, and the deer that was absolutely content beforehand darted away into the woods.

Using a car as a blind can be good for safety, as well. Another time, the reverse happened. I would never approach a bison, but early one morning in Yellowstone I was parked at the side of a short road to nowhere, still sitting in the driver's seat, when a small herd of them ambled up the road right toward me. I didn't want to spook them by starting the car, so I just stayed put while they walked alongside. But I also wasn't going to sit there idly, so of course I raised my camera and made a few close-up images while the bison passed only several feet away from me. I otherwise never could have safely gotten that close to a bison, nor would I try to; but being in the car while they wandered by gave me a unique photo opportunity, not mention a memorable experience.

BIKES, BOATS, ETC.

In researching a park beforehand, see what other modes of transportation might be permitted that could ease your experience. One of my favorite things about visiting Acadia is that bicycles are allowed on the packed-stone carriage roads, which can accelerate the process of reaching a location. For example, I could spend 45 minutes walking to Hadlock Falls, or I could cycle there in 10. Maybe I would prefer the quiet walk on nice fall day, or maybe I would want to get there quickly because I know the fog is about to burn off. Either way, it's nice to have the option.

Another useful tool to have in some national parks is a boat, particularly a canoe or kayak. At parks with water, you can almost always rent one either within or nearby. Personal watercraft are excellent for reaching some of the remote areas

GETTING AIRBORNE

National park landscapes can be superb locations for aerial photography, and in many nearby communities you can hire helicopter or small-plane pilots to bring you up. All likely offer predetermined tours, but if you explain that you're a photographer, most will cater to your needs. If you want to fly during specific light, you should call ahead and schedule that arrangement.

When photographing from the air, shoot out an open window if you can. If not, wear dark clothing, which won't reflect in the window (and ruin your photo) as much as light colors. Also, look at the window before flying; if it's dirty, ask the pilot if he or she can clean it quickly before leaving the ground. Also, the aircraft will have inherent vibration. To counteract it, use a faster shutter speed than you normally would in the same light (at least 1/500), and refrain from using the frame or window to brace your hands, elbows or camera.

A photo flight might end up being the most expensive part of your national park project, but in most places short trips are reasonably priced. And it could lead to some of your best photographs of the park.

of Everglades, which has an established network of water trails. At Lake Clark, a foldable kayak can be carried in a backpack and used to explore lakes and ponds on a backcountry trip. In Denali, carrying a packraft can allow for easier river and stream crossings. In a few national parks, a boat is nearly necessary. In Biscayne you can't do much without out one; in Kobuk Valley it's one of the most popular means of getting into the park; in Voyageurs, many visitors use houseboats for transportation *and* lodging. But a caution: Photographing from a canoe or kayak is difficult on a day with even moderate winds. You need to be able to sit still in the water to have time to frame and execute your photos.

Another example of alternative transportation is a snowmobile (also known as a snow machine, in some areas). While many parks prohibit them, several do allow snowmobiles in winter, with varying restrictions. Acadia allows them on the loop road, but not the carriage roads; Mount Rainier allows them in some sections; and Yellowstone allows a limited number per day. This can be a great way to access some otherwise hard-to-reach winter landscapes.

HIKING

The best way to see the best stuff is usually to walk to it. The means of travel mentioned so far can get you to some great spots, and sometimes they can even get you to perfect spots. But without fail, in every national park you can find a better location, or a better angle, by walking somewhere. You can also find more solitude, which can be good for photography. Maybe you walk only a hundred feet, away from the constructed viewpoint, away from the tripod holes of the hundred-thousand photographers who came before you. Or maybe you hike 20 miles into the backcountry to explore parts of the park that only the smallest percentage of visitors ever get to see. Either way, your feet can be a very valuable photography tool.

A great example of this is seen in Grand Teton. The park's scenic roads offer some of the most stunning vistas in the park system. Ansel Adams' "Tetons and Snake River" photograph—one of his most famous images—was made at the side of the road. Still, even here, more beautiful off-road locations abound. Short hikes can bring you to alpine lakes, meadows of wildflowers, and placid river bends reflecting the snow-capped peaks. A weeklong 36-mile hike on the Teton Crest Trail could be the greatest photographic adventure of your lifetime.

Just be sure to venture out prepared. Especially in the backcountry, and definitely if going solo, items such as a GPS receiver, water purifier, compass and map should be considered mandatory equipment.

FOOD

DURING my first day of a national park trip, I find a grocery store and stock the car. Even if the area has great restaurants (and if they do, I'll be at them), I still want food with me. I have three reasons for this, all revolving around the philosophy of flexibility:

1. ***I don't want to have to leave a good photo location for something as avoidable as hunger.*** When I'm shooting a park, I want photography to be my priority. Anything else is secondary, including the timing of my meals. If I have found a great extended photo opportunity in the middle of the wilderness, I'm not going to leave it just so I can have dinner. Knowing that I have food in the car, or in my camera bag or backpack, allows me to linger. It allows me to put my photography first.

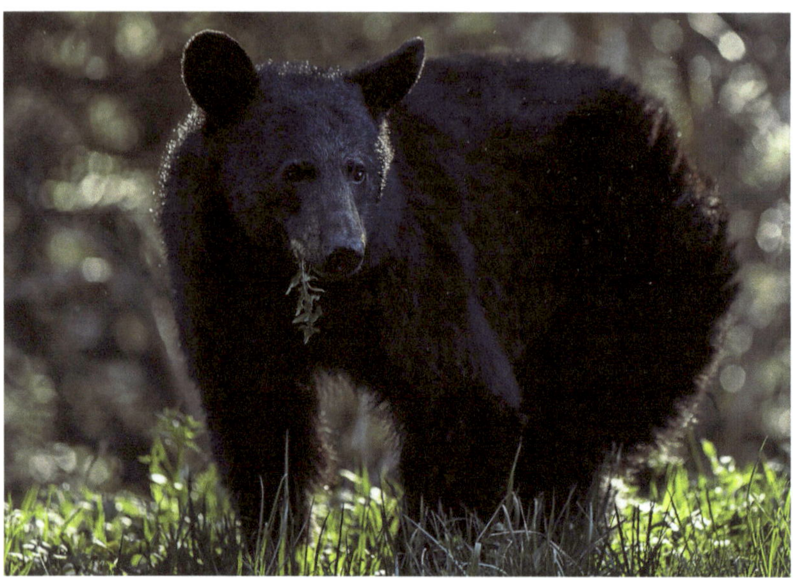

Great Smoky Mountains National Park

2. ***I can eat while I'm waiting for the light to change.*** When I'm working, meals often become an activity of opportunity. In other words, I eat when I notice that I have time to. Often my biggest meal of the day will be lunch, when the harsh light has probably pushed me off the landscape. But I have to eat at other times of day, too, and sometimes that happens when in standby mode. For example, I might arrive at a location early for a sunrise shoot; I get set up in the dark, and then might just end up sitting there for 30 minutes waiting for dawn. That's a great time for breakfast. Or if I'm photographing in the woods but have to wait for clouds to cover the sun, that's a great time for a snack or small meal. With food in the car or in my pack, I can just eat right there.

3. ***I will have food for emergencies.*** As careful as I am, there's a chance that I could get stuck somewhere. I could get hurt or lost. Perhaps the car breaks down, or a storm surge keeps a river crossing impassable for a couple of days. Having a small stock of supplies could keep me fed while I wait for help or a way back to civilization.

So I make a grocery run. I get just two or three bags of items, depending on how long I'll be in the park, and I'll buy either non-perishables or food in sealed containers. Keeping the basics of sustenance and energy in mind, I'll choose items such as granola bars, trail mix, beef jerky, graham crackers, juice boxes, Fig Newtons, freeze-dried fruit and unsweetened fruit cups. I'll also buy some quart-size sealable bags, and I'll double- or triple-bag anything with an odor I'd like to keep contained. For backcountry camping, the grocery list changes, as you'll need to sustain yourself for as many days as you'll be away from the civilized world.

I also buy a lot of water—usually four or five one-gallon jugs, or one for each day I'm planning to be on site, plus a couple of smaller bottles that are easy to carry. I can refill the gallon containers when I have access to potable water, such as at a visitor center. But I always want more water than I need. Again, I'm thinking worst-case scenario; I don't want to get stuck without enough water to keep me alive.

One problem that all this food introduces is that if it's not stored properly, it could attract undesirables—as in hungry, wild creatures of the night. I like to see bears in a stream 50 yards beyond the end of a 500mm lens, but I don't like them in my campsite. Every park has its regulations for guarding food from animals, particularly bears. In some parks, keeping the food in a hard-shell cooler in the car is sufficient. Other parks require using bear-proof storage lockers in the campgrounds, or portable bear-resistant canisters in the backcountry. Other parks require hanging your food from a tree 100 yards from your campsite, or lodging it under rocks downhill and downwind from the tent. In Glacier Bay, you're advised not to even prepare food unless you're below the high-tide line, so that the incoming saltwater can wash away the smell. Check the website for the park you're visiting, or ask a ranger.

As I mentioned before, all this food hoarding doesn't prevent me from indulging in hot meals at restaurants. When I can, I love to get a good brunch or lunch from a mom-and-pop establishment, from a greasy spoon in the non-touristy small town just outside of the less-visited edge of the park, or perhaps from the restaurant in a park lodge. The more rural or sincerely rustic the eatery is, the more I like it; I enjoy meeting locals, learning how people live in different cultures of the U.S., and maybe even picking up a tip or two about "secret" locations in the park. Stopping for a meal gives me time to unwind from a morning of work that probably began an hour before sunup; time to read guides or brochures, to review my notes, to strategize my next locations; and time to recharge my camera and laptop batteries. But most important of all, it gives me time to drink coffee.

WARDROBE

When I was younger, I would venture into nature with just jeans, a cotton T-shirt and a pair of sneakers. My boots were from a discount store, and my poncho was a free promotional gift (and worth every penny of that) from my auto-club membership. These days, I put more thought into my attire.

CLOTHING

Knowing the climate is important for knowing what clothes to bring. In hot weather, cotton-polyester blends work well for allowing airflow and not trapping perspiration. If I can stay comfortable doing so, I wear long pants, either jeans or khakis, because they offer protection from minor hazards such as thorns and ticks. They also protect the knees a bit when getting on the ground for low-angle photographs. I often wear a light-colored hat in the sun, to help keep my head cool and the sun off my face. Additionally, I carry a breathable rain jacket when the weather might turn the wrong way. (Or the right way, depending on what I'm shooting.)

In moderate seasons, dressing in layers is prudent. When working in Acadia in the fall, I have started some mornings in jeans, a sweater and a parka, then gradually shed clothing until I was wearing shorts and a T-shirt at midday. When temperatures change that drastically, wearing layers eases the transition in insulation throughout the day.

Layers are important when working in cold weather, too—but the layers are heavier. For a base layer, I have come to love Under Armour's ColdGear line of leggings and tops. My outer layer is comprised of pieces of ski outerwear, which are designed to fulfill the same needs that photographers have: They are flexible, relatively lightweight, wind-breaking, and warm but breathable. That outerwear is so effective that I usually find I don't need anything else. In very cold temperatures I might insert a layer of jeans and a sweater.

That might not sound like much, but good ski clothes are very good at what they do; the outfit I just described was enough to keep me comfortable at -20 degrees Fahrenheit during winter in Yellowstone's windswept Lamar Valley, while maintaining my mobility. And you don't want too many clothes on—with all the effort to move around and work in the snow, you can easily start to perspire, and that's when be-

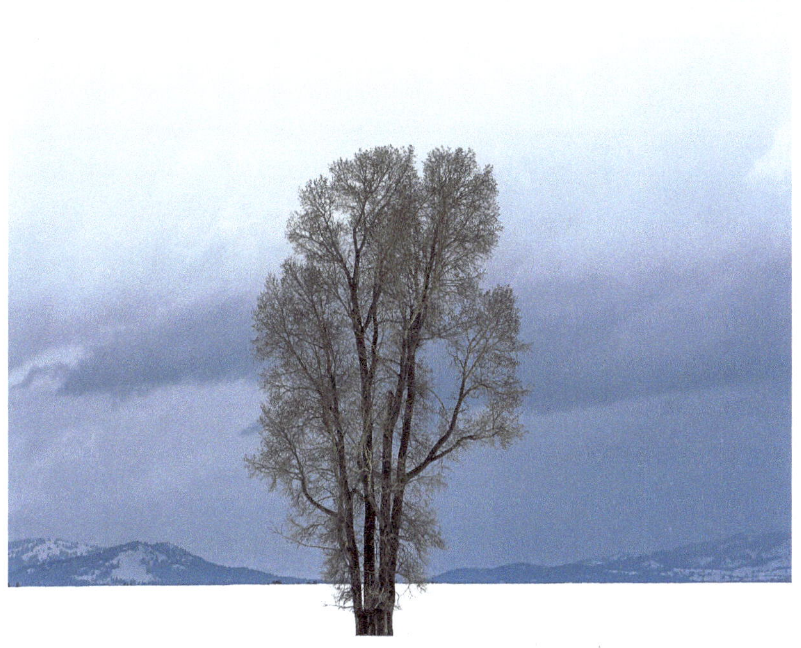

Grand Teton National Park

ing out in the cold gets dangerous. It's better to be a little cool to prevent sweating. I also use ski gloves, which are flexible, wind-and water-resistant, and have good palm and finger grips. For head coverage, I'm usually happy with just a standard wool cap, but in extreme conditions I might add a balaclava.

FOOTWEAR

One of the most important concerns while hiking is your feet. They're the first and last line of defense between you and the ground. And when you're photographing a national park,

KEEPING HANDS HANDY

Photographers use their hands a lot. From lifting and carrying gear, to swapping and focusing lenses, to adjusting tripod legs and swapping memory cards, our hands are secondary only to our eyes as anatomical tools for getting our work done. Therefore, we want to take care of them. Here are a few items I keep handy when traveling in a national park:

• Moist wipes are great for cleaning sunblock and bug spray off my hands (I don't want either getting on my camera gear) when a sink and soap aren't available.

• Moisturizer helps keep skin pliable in cold weather, when hands can dry out quickly. If they crack and bleed, they can become a detriment.

• Gloves are essential in cold weather just to keep my hands warm and the blood flowing. If they get cold, they get stiff and fine motor skills diminish. Then handling and controlling photo gear becomes more difficult. I like ski gloves because they're light, but warm and wind-proof. I also like fly-fishing gloves designed with rubber palm and finger grips, and with a flip-back finger that can momentarily free my fingertip for direct contact with the shutter release. Some companies market the exact same idea as photography gloves.

• Liquid bandages never took off as a popular first-aid product, but they can be useful out in the field. For example, if I get a cut on my index-fingertip, a traditional bandage would hamper my touch on the shutter release. But a liquid bandage is almost undetectable.

whether making long hikes or simply short jaunts from the car, you'll be on your feet often. So you want them to be comfortable, and you want them to be stable.

Always select proper footwear for the terrain and weather you're walking in. In recent years I have become avid about trail-runner shoes. (In particular, I very much like the top-of-the-line models made by Vasque and Salomon.) I generally travel with two pairs: a breathable pair with mesh uppers for regular wear, and a Gore-tex-lined pair to wear around water or in dew-covered grass. When shopping, select shoes that are comfortable and light, and that your feet don't slip in.

Also, look for shoes with a wide sole designed to reduce ankle-rolls, and with an aggressive tread that minimizes slippage even in slick conditions. Those latter points are important for protecting not just your body, but also the thousands of dollars of camera gear on your shoulder or your back. Falling on talus or a rocky shore could mean a broken arm or a broken telephoto lens—and most of us probably aren't sure which we'd be more upset about. So think of good shoes as a form of equipment insurance.

If you aren't sure what to buy, visit a quality, service-oriented outdoors store and have a knowledgeable salesperson help you choose. My favorite stores for this type of purchase are REI and L.L. Bean, because neither has ever made me feel like they were upselling me, and both back up their products indefinitely. Other national chains and regional stores offer the same level of knowledge and service, and are great options for buying such an important piece of gear.

For additional foot protection, consider gaiters, which cover the tops of your footwear, preventing snow, dew, dirt and such from getting into your shoe-tops and on your lower pant-legs. Gaiters are useful for working in shallow snowfalls, rainy meadows, etc. If you're going to be working in extended wet conditions, you might also consider rain boots. Glacier Bay National Park actually recommends that visitors pack them as standard equipment.

The criteria for good footwear changes when the weather grows cold. For me, off come the trail-runners and on go the hiking boots. I'm very particular about my winter trail boots, because an inferior pair once caused me to fall and damage an expensive lens I had borrowed from a friend. I look for boots that are warm but breathable (a tall order for heavily insulated shoes), that are relatively light and have an aggressive tread. The one fallback to that last point is that aggressive tread can get clogged with ice and snow, which subsequently causes the shoes to be more slippery; but that's why I'm going to recommend pullover traction on page 77. A final consideration with winter hiking boots is that the sole be flexible. Rubber can stiffen in cold temperatures, and a stiff sole won't flex around inconsistent surfaces—for example, a pointy rock—which could cause you to slip or lose your balance.

Between those good feet and good shoes should be some good socks. Recently the common wisdom has been that wool is the best material for backpacking socks—even in warm weather. In particular, merino wool is the magic fabric. It is softer than many of its cousins, and therefore does not itch. Wool does not retain moisture, so it remains dry even when you perspire, and it dries quickly even after getting soaked. Thin, mid-weight and thick wool socks all maintain a cushioned quality, while still being cool or warm, depending on the density and thickness. Lightweight wool socks are best for warm conditions, while mid-weight and heavy-weight are best for cold.

A final note about socks: It is the one piece of clothing for which I always ensure I have a spare. I can cope with anything else getting wet. But regardless of how soaked the rest of my clothes are, I always feel better when wearing dry socks.

SAFETY

WHETHER walking 50 yards from the car or 50 miles into the backcountry, nature can be a bear—quite literally. Real danger is uncommon (you're more likely to get hurt while traveling to a park than once in it), but there are aspects of working in the wilderness to be wary of and prepared for.

MANDATORY BASICS

If there's one thing you absolutely need to have when traveling in nature, it's water. Don't go anywhere without more than enough to last until you can get back to some facilities.

As mentioned earlier, I always buy some gallon jugs of water on my first day on-site—usually before I even get to the park, on the way from the airport or from wherever I'm traveling. I also buy or bring a few small bottles, which are for toting on a short walk. For longer hikes, I can put water in a canteen, or in a hydration reservoir that straps to the side of my photo backpack. Reservoirs are ingenious rubber devices that store your water somewhere on your person—in or on a backpack, in a waist-pack, etc. A drinking tube, capped with a bite value, extends from the reservoir; you clip or wedge the tube onto or into a strap, or a belt, or wherever it's convenient to grab when you want to drink. Hydrating becomes almost effortless. I keep the gallon jugs in the car and use them for refilling the smaller containers.

Though not as mandatory as water, one other product is at least urgently advised: sunblock. I'm not going to lecture about skin cancer—that's what your dermatologist is for. I'm more concerned with safety. Being out in the wilderness can expose you to more sun damage that you're normally accustomed to.

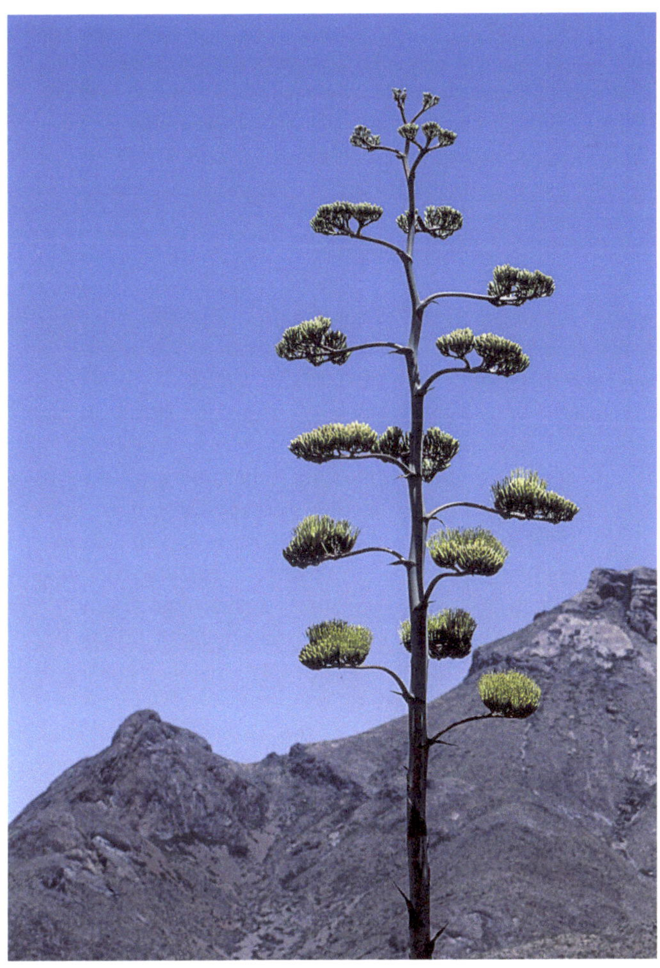

Big Bend National Park

You may just be outside longer than usual, or perhaps you didn't realize that ultraviolet rays are stronger in high elevations. Or maybe you get lost and your sunblock-free one-hour stroll turns into an all-day skin-blistering nightmare. Sunburn not only affects your comfort, but also your health: It accelerates dehydration and can lead to a compromised state of mind when making important safety decisions in the field.

SOLO TRAVELING

While photography as an activity can be social, the actual process of creating an image is internal, and thus many of us prefer to work in solitude. If you choose to work without a companion, and if you also choose to work in the backcountry, that means you'll be solo hiking, or perhaps solo boating. Wandering the wilderness alone does not necessarily increase the probability of an accident, but it does mean that if something does go wrong, you won't have anyone to help. If you're normal, being in the backcountry unaccompanied does involve some trepidation.

Despite this, countless people solo hike every day, even in areas where they are almost certain not to encounter another human for weeks. How do they do this? First, they are prepared with knowledge and supplies, just as they would be if traveling in a group. Second—and this is critical—they know not to accept any unnecessary risks. A group might try to ford a river they're unsure about, but a solo hiker never should. If someone in a group gets hurt, the others can help; if a solo hiker gets hurt, his or her safety is dramatically compromised.

Also, note that some of the national parks require you to obtain a permit for backcountry hiking. Sometimes the reason is to reduce impact on sensitive areas by limiting the number of people who traipse through; but usually the impetus is safety. When you register your itinerary with the rangers, they will know when and where to look should you become lost or injured. That greatly increases the odds of extracting you while you're still alive. Finding you quickly is good not only for you, but for anyone else who might need help, too—the faster a search is concluded, the sooner the rescue resources will be fully available to respond to another emergency. For these reasons, filing a hike plan with the park is good practice even when a permit is not required.

Also, alert someone you know about your plans—someone who will notice if you're missing. When I hike in the backcountry for even just part of a day, I usually send a text message to a family member: "FYI, I'm hiking Beech Mountain Trail and will be descending after sunset. If you don't hear from me by 10:00, please call the park." (I always add some hours onto my estimated time of arrival because I know I'm apt to stop for unplanned photos.) Choose someone who is responsible but doesn't worry easily.

You can also leave an itinerary in your car at the trailhead. Just don't leave it somewhere visible from outside, or you'll be advertising the length of your absence to every passerby. Put it someplace that would be looked through during an official search for you—in the glove box, perhaps.

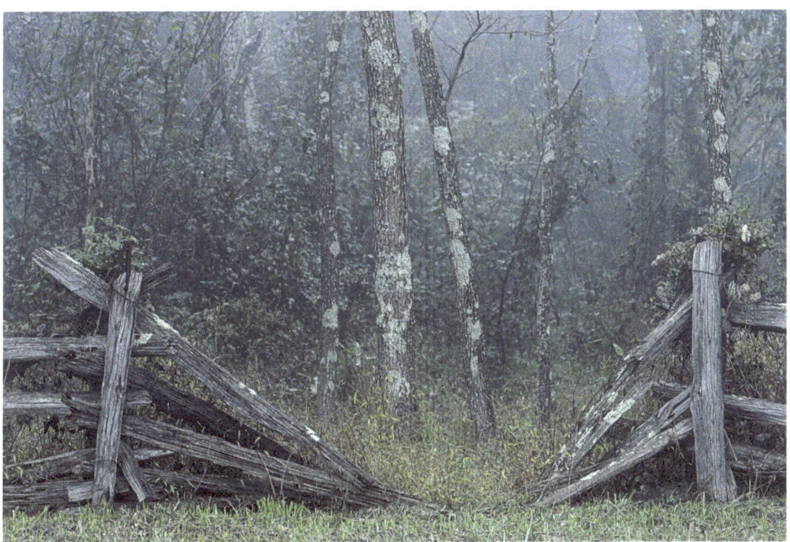

Shenandoah National Park

WILDERNESS SURVIVAL

The following notion is common among people spending time in nature: "I'm hiking for only two hours, so all I need to bring is a bottle of water. It's not like I'm spending a week in the Alaskan mountains."

That's a dangerous thought. The reality is that most people who get in trouble in the wilderness are those who go out for a short walk, because they're the most likely not to be prepared for an accident. The important thing to remember is this: The first step in wilderness survival is to go beyond preparing for the ordinary, and ensure that you're prepared for an emergency. Know what you're doing, and know what to bring. Then, if you do happen across trouble, you'll be more likely to get out of it.

This doesn't mean that every time you walk into the woods, you need to bring 50 pounds of survival gear. A key part of wilderness survival is explained perfectly by survival expert Cody Lundin in his book *98.6 Degrees: The Art of Keeping Your Ass Alive*: Even in the worst backcountry emergencies, victims are almost always found and extricated within three days. So you likely don't need the skills or supplies to survive for an entire summer. You don't need to haul a week's worth of food for a three-hour trek, you don't need to carry collapsible crutches in case you sprain an ankle, and you don't need to bring an ax so you can fell trees and build a log cabin to live in for months on end. You need enough knowledge and supplies to keep yourself alive for just three days.

A complete survival kit can be small enough to fit in the side pocket of your camera bag. Mine is a small waist-pack that is easy to strap on when I hike off on a whim, and easy to unbuckle and leave behind if I'm just momentarily walking around an overlook. A good kit contains items such as a compass, bandages, antibiotic, water purifier, a whistle, matches, snacks, etc. For a more complete list—and the knowledge of why and how to use the items—I highly recommend reading a book like Lundin's. Also, think about how some of your photography gear might be useful in an emergency: A camera lens focusing sunlight can ignite kindling, and a monopod can double as a crutch.

Another critical piece of preparedness is knowing how much water to bring. You need either more water than necessary for your planned itinerary, or you need a way to purify water you find in the wilderness. Keep in mind that you may need more water per day than when you're in your home environment. Hydration requirements can be affected by factors such as humidity, altitude, heat and the difficulty of the terrain you're hiking. If you have any doubt about how much water you'll need, a ranger can relay the best practices for that area.

REGIONAL HAZARDS

Every park has its own set of stuff to watch out for. For example, Big Bend has a harsh summer sun. Rocky Mountain has altitude sickness. Yosemite has alpine lightning storms. Yellowstone has some really cranky elk. It's prudent to research these things before you start walking around an unfamiliar place. A perusal of the park's website or a stop at the visitor center should alert you to anything you need to be wary of.

Sometimes, the cautions may surprise you. For instance, many outsiders think that the most notorious animal in Yellowstone is the grizzly bear. It's not. Bison are the leading agent of wildlife-related injuries in the park. For visitor safety, each park has its rules for viewing wildlife, tailored to the particular species that inhabit the area and the common behaviors they're known for. A trait that many animals have in common is that they really want nothing to do with people; in most encounters, they would prefer to just flee. With that in mind, a good practice is to be cognizant of an animal's escape route, and don't block it. Also important is knowing the signs that wildlife

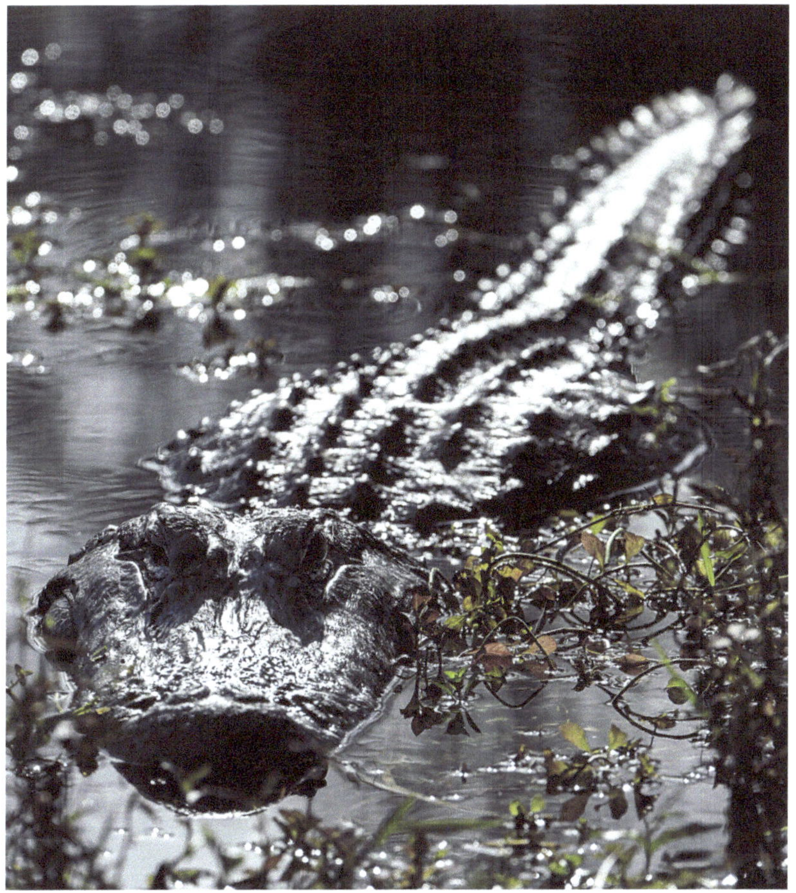

Everglades National Park

is nearby, such as recognizing fresh scat. And any park with bears will recommend that backcountry visitors carry easily accessible bear spray—it's standard equipment in places like Glacier and Denali. Threatening encounters with wildlife are rare, but harmless encounters are not. Knowing how to prevent the latter from becoming the former is what keeps everyone happy, including the animals. Knowing how to deal with the former is what keeps everyone healthy.

Also, some wildlife isn't dangerous—it's just annoying. Parks will have information for dealing with those critters, too. For instance, Denali's website is clear about advising not to visit in midsummer without mosquito repellent.

Some of the wildlife regulations are less about health and safety than about managing the stress on the animals caused by proximity to humans. A common best practice is to avoiding getting close enough to an animal to change its behavior. Sometimes this can make photographing it more of a challenge, but that's the price we pay for being responsible citizens of the places that protect the wilderness for our benefit. You can sometimes work around the problem by learning the behavioral tendencies of the wildlife you'd like to photograph. This can make the animals more comfortable with your presence, improving your chances for a closer encounter. For instance, deer tend not to worry much if you just sit still; and seals are naturally curious, so if you wait, one will probably approach you. However, baiting is strictly prohibited in all of the parks, because it can lead to animals becoming dependent on or too comfortable around people. If you want to use a blind for photography, check with a ranger to see if it's permitted in that park or in the area you want to erect it.

Another piece of nature to be knowledgeable about is toxic plants. Poison ivy, poison oak and poison sumac are common throughout the park system, and some parks have local plants you may be unfamiliar with. A good example of the latter is poisonwood, a tree in the Everglades with sap that can cause a rash worse than poison ivy. An outsider might never know to beware of it, or what it looks like, without the educational display in the visitor center.

LEAVE NO TRACE

WHEN I was a kid, I frequently went on camping trips with my dad. On the last day of these campouts, we would be cleaning and packing, and Dad would inevitably say the same thing: "Always leave the campsite cleaner than you found it." We had to pick up any piece of trash we saw, whether or not we were responsible for it being there.

That sentiment is worthy of any trip into nature. As a group, we owe this to the National Park Service, we owe this to the volunteers in the parks, we owe this to our wilderness, and we owe this to the photographers and the tourists who will arrive in our wake: Help keep these places pristine. Anyone who walks onto protected land is responsible for conserving it for others.

In that spirit, the National Park Service has widely embraced the mission of Leave No Trace, a member-driven organiza-

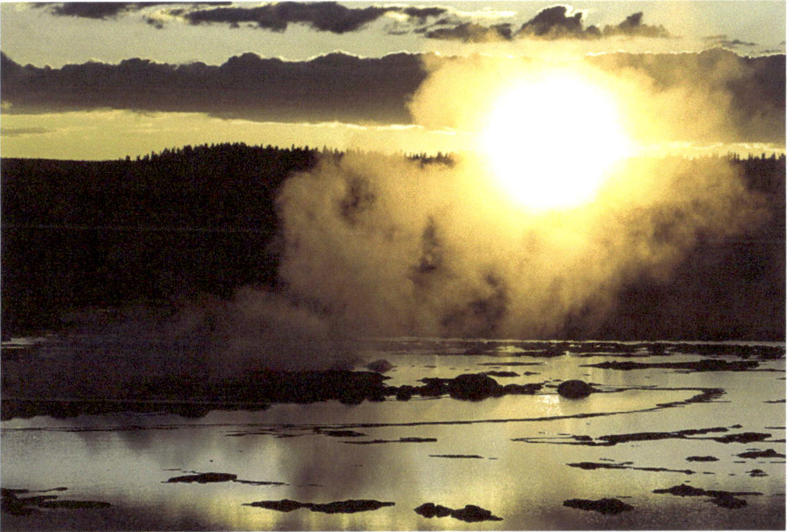

Yellowstone National Park

tion that teaches outdoor ethics. The message is essentially this: When you leave the wilderness, leave no evidence that you were there. The Leave No Trace mantra encompasses seven principles:

1. Plan Ahead and Prepare
2. Travel and Camp on Durable Surfaces
3. Dispose of Waste Properly
4. Leave What You Find
5. Minimize Campfire Impacts
6. Respect Wildlife
7. Be Considerate of Other Visitors

An important aspect of respecting this mission is heeding the regulations and guidelines set by individual parks. Some parks permit off-trail hiking; others don't, keeping some areas off-limits because they're sensitive or hazardous. I have little sympathy for the philosophy of "I'm a photographer—I had to break the rules to get the shot." The needs of the wilderness come first.

CHAPTER 3

TOOLS

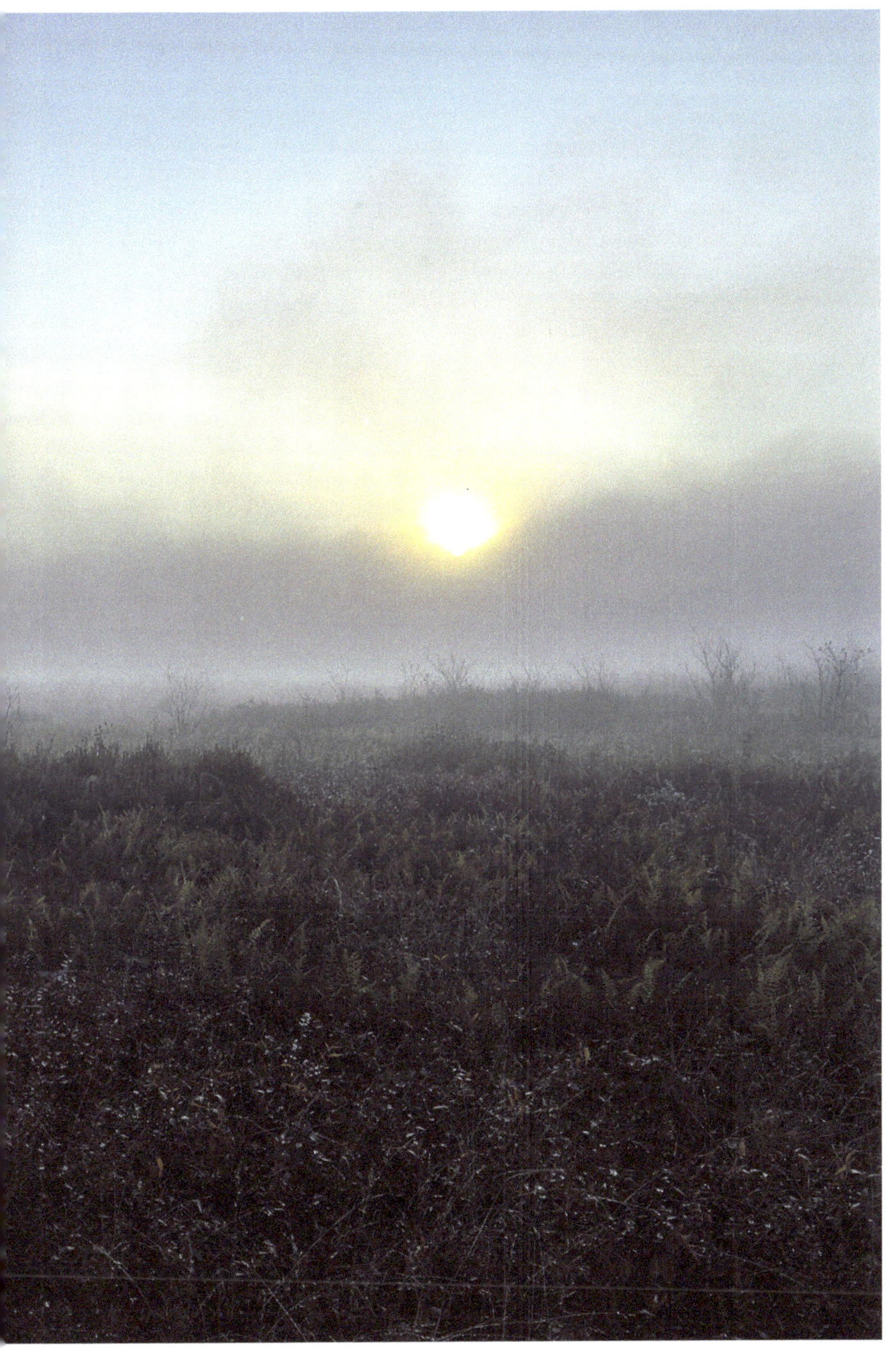

Meadow, Shenandoah National Park

THINGS TO USE

ONE OF THE great things about being a photographer during the past two decades has been seeing how quickly and dramatically camera technology has evolved. The entire industry of image-making changed within a few short years, and it continues to change every year, in ways large and moderate—but seldom small. Confusion and massive learning curves accompanied that shift, but so did excitement about the ability to make better-quality photographs. I imagine this was the way our predecessors felt about box cameras, and 35mm film, and then color photography. This is an exciting time to be in this business.

This is also an era of high flexibility in the choice of gear for pursuing photography, whether as a pastime or profession. We can't even refer to the DSLR as the king of cameras anymore, because it's the best choice only for certain types of photographers. Other sensor formats—including APS-C and Micro Four Thirds—are justifiably preferred by many.

Choosing between the types of cameras involves gives and takes, decisions about which factors are more important to the type of photography you're doing or for how you like to work. Every technology has characteristics that are better than—and inferior to—those of the alternative technologies. Crop factor, size and weight, noise, resolution, dynamic range, file size, shutter lag, depth of field capability—all of these vary from one technology to the next. Some specifications may be important to you, and others may not.

I won't delve into the pros and cons of every type of camera, and I won't assume that I know your preferences. I also won't recommend camera types that are good for me, because they may not be good for you. I have a friend who photographed a magazine assignment with a point-and-shoot. Another friend owns $20,000 of professional gear, but always says his favorite photos come from his camera-phone. I shoot my daughter's birthday party with the same $6,000 camera-and-lens combination that I used to photograph the cover of this book.

I once hiked to the top of a mountain in Olympic National Park in early morning. One other photographer was there. He was using a Micro Four Thirds camera that he had carried in a hip pack; I had 25 pounds of DSLR gear in my backpack. We were both happy, as was the tourist who arrived an hour later and used the built-in flash of his point-and-shoot to take

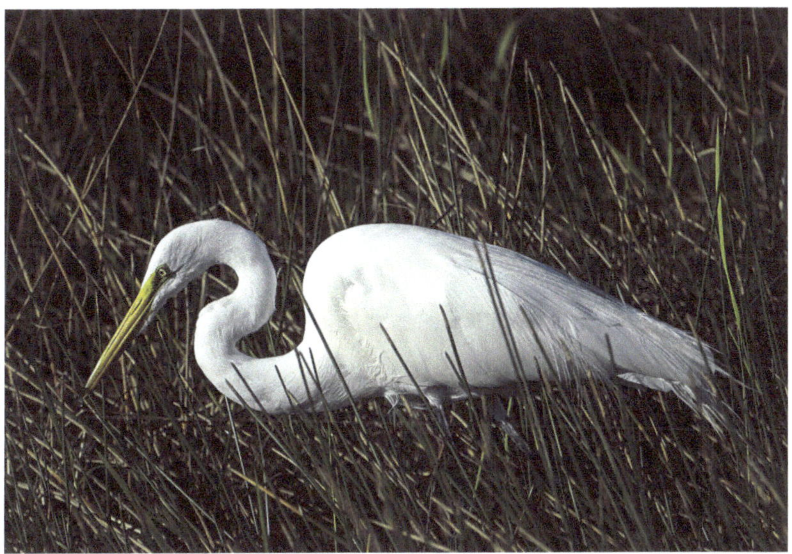

Everglades National Park

pictures of the Strait of Juan de Fuca 12 miles away. Three different equipment strategies all yielded the same result: a satisfying photography experience on a beautiful morning with a gorgeous view.

The previous 438 words all lead to this: The most important considerations for choosing a camera are that you are comfortable working with it, and that it helps you produce images that satisfy your creative needs.

LENSES

Whether using interchangeable lenses or a fixed-lens camera, the focal lengths available to you will be important to the types of photography you can do. I recommend having a flexible selection, because every national park has a wide range of subject matter. Even if you're primarily interested in wildlife photography, I'm not sure it's possible to visit Mount Rainier in midsummer and not want to photograph wildflowers.

I recommend having the capability to shoot at wide-angle, normal and telephoto focal lengths, and also to have macro capability unless you're sure you won't want it. I'm still young enough not to mind some weight on my back, so I still travel with a full cache of lenses, from 14mm to at least 300mm (and often a 400mm or 500mm), plus a 105mm macro and a teleconverter. I very rarely finish a national park project without using every lens I packed.

The detriment of this approach is that when you travel with a lot of gear, you need to carry a lot of gear. So don't bring more than you're willing to hike with, or more than you're willing to leave in the car when you're somewhere else.

FILTERS

Digital photography has made most filters obsolete, because their effects can be achieved more effectively, with greater control, and with more ease, in post-production software. The two exceptions to this also happen to be the most used filters in nature photography: the polarizer and the neutral density.

POLARIZER > A polarizing filter removes reflections from surfaces. This has multiple uses in the field, as reflections alter our perception of color in ways we don't like. A polarizer can remove glare from leaves, making them appear more green (or more red, yellow, orange or purple in fall); it can remove the shine from water particles in the atmosphere, revealing a deeper blue; it can remove the reflection of the sky from the surface of a lake or river, exposing the water's true color in the landscape. A polarizer is required gear in a rainy forest, or for restoring the muted color of foliage in overcast conditions. The cost of this improvement is one or two stops of light, but that is easily compensated for with the excellent high-ISO capabilities of today's cameras.

Visualizing the effects of a polarizing filter can sometimes be challenging. We are so accustomed to seeing the world's vast collection of reflected surfaces that we might not always realize when better color is just one filter away. We can see the effect by just putting a polarizing filter on the lens and looking through the camera, but that might not be a convenient option if all your gear is packed on your back.

To more easily see the terrain the way a polarizing filter would, wear polarized sunglasses. Wherever you look, you'll get a preview of how the scene would appear if you photographed it with a polarizer on the lens. Tilting your head left or right will increase or decrease the effect, and you'll see changes in the sky, on leaves and on the surface of water—just like when you rotate a circular polarizer.

NEUTRAL DENSITY > A neutral density (ND) filter reduces the amount of light entering the camera without altering the color temperature. The intent is almost always to enable slow shutter speeds for blurring motion. The most common application is to blur moving water, such as surf or a waterfall—other possibilities are blurring clouds or windblown flowers. A more advanced use of an ND is to reduce incoming light for the purpose of using a large aperture to achieve shallow depth of field in bright conditions.

Neutral density filters can be stacked to cumulate their effect. For years I have been carrying a 1-stop and a 2-stop ND filter, which I could use separately or stack for a 3-stop reduction. (I can also stack them with a polarizer—which I'm almost always using anyway, especially around water—for a 4- to 5-stop reduction.) However, I seem to always stack those two ND filters, so I will likely start carrying just a 3-stop filter soon. ND filters are also available in the 10-stop range, which is almost black glass. A 10-stop obstruction of light enables blurring motion even in bright sunlight.

READY FOR WILDLIFE

At large national parks with long roads, you can spend many hours just driving from location to location. Along the route, you may often observe wildlife in places where you can pull over and perhaps have an opportunity for a nice photograph. However, as mentioned in Chapter 2, getting out of the car can spook wildlife. What's the point of leaving the car if your subject just runs into the woods?

My approach to that conundrum is this: Whenever I'll be driving for a while, I keep one camera mounted with a telephoto lens on the floor in front of the passenger seat. If I curb the car for a wildlife sighting, all I need to do is pick up the camera, and I'm ready for an out-the-window shoot.

This is one of the few times I will hand-hold a camera, because obviously I can't use a tripod from inside the car. (Though once in Great Smoky Mountains I did lower my monopod from the car window.) I usually just brace my elbow on the armrest for support, or I may lay the lens on a folded jacket or sweatshirt atop the window frame.

Several companies manufacture beanbags for this purpose. They cushion the lens, absorb vibration, and protect car and camera from the metal-on-metal contact. I have also seen camera mounts that clamp to the window, but have never felt comfortable applying the combined weight of a professional DSLR and telephoto lens to the glass.

A variation of the neutral density filter is the graduated-ND, which reduces light in only a portion of the frame. A graduated-ND (or GND) is used most often when part of a scene calls for a different exposure than the rest. A classic example is a landscape with a sunset sky. The ground will be much darker than the sky, so a GND filter is placed in front of the lens with the transition along the line of exposure variance, resulting in an evenly rendered scene.

Fewer photographers carry graduated-ND filters now because the same effect can be achieved in post-production with HDR techniques. The method can be as simple as stacking two exposures of the scene and using a graduated mask to differentiate them appropriately. Doing this digitally actually introduces more control over the result, because you can either adjust or abandon inadequate attempts. (See "Exposure Stacking" on page 99.)

EXPANDING THE TOOLBOX

The photographic opportunities at a national park can often be more varied than the equipment we own. But when you're investing the time and money to travel to a park, you shouldn't sacrifice your photography options just because you lack a key lens, or a second—or even third—camera body. These days gear is expensive, but many resources are available to obtain temporary access to equipment:

- The internet has made gear rental a more viable business, so many such companies have launched in recent years. The cost of securing a lens or body for a week or two is not excessive. Also, many of these companies will ship to your destination, so you don't have to travel with the extra weight.
- Similarly, a few web-based services have arisen that enable renting gear directly from other photographers, which can result in a cost savings.
- If you are affiliated with a manufacturer's professional association, one of the privileges may be to loan gear for special assignments and projects.
- If you are feeling lucky, you can browse online auctions or classified ads for used equipment. Buy what you need, then resell it (perhaps for a profit) after your trip.

With any of these options, best practice is to add the extra gear to your professional or homeowners insurance policy. Or, if renting equipment, consider purchasing any insurance option the retailer may offer.

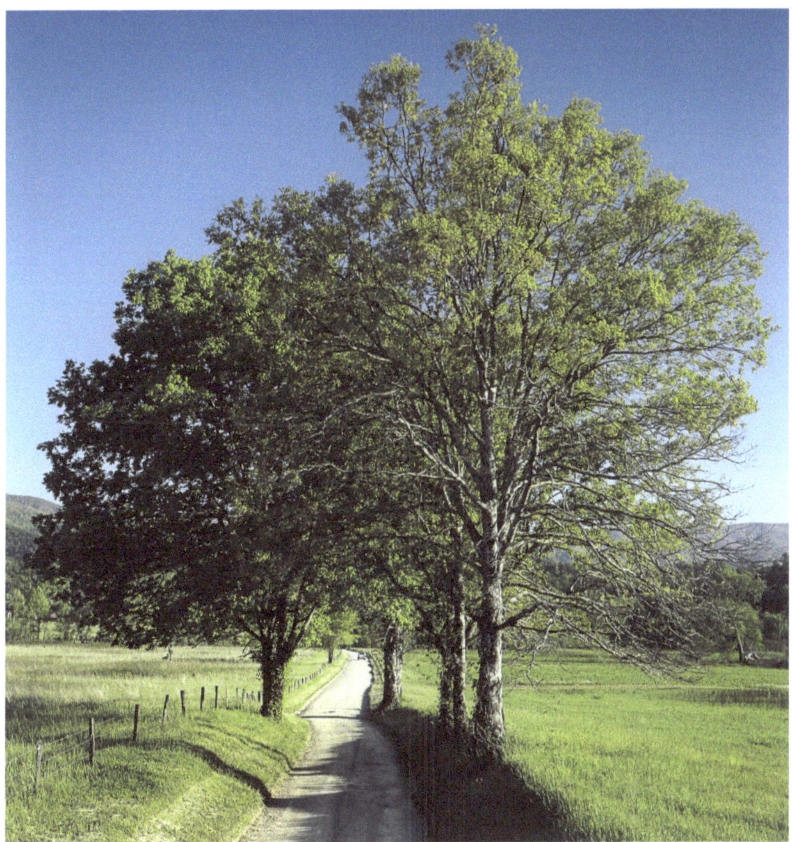

MEMORY

Great Smoky Mountains National Park

THE MOST important consideration with memory is only this: You need to have enough of it. How much is sufficient? You need either enough memory cards to store everything you shoot on the trip, or the capability for dumping your cards and backing up the data in the field. Ideally, you want both.

Even after all these decades into the computer revolution, memory drives still crash. Cards don't fail often, but they do fail if used long enough. Moreover, they could go lost. They could also get damaged—for instance, by falling into water, or being eaten by an alligator. (The former is more common.) And just about all the photographers in the world would rather lose their gear than their work. Therefore, having two copies of your data is safe; having three is safer.

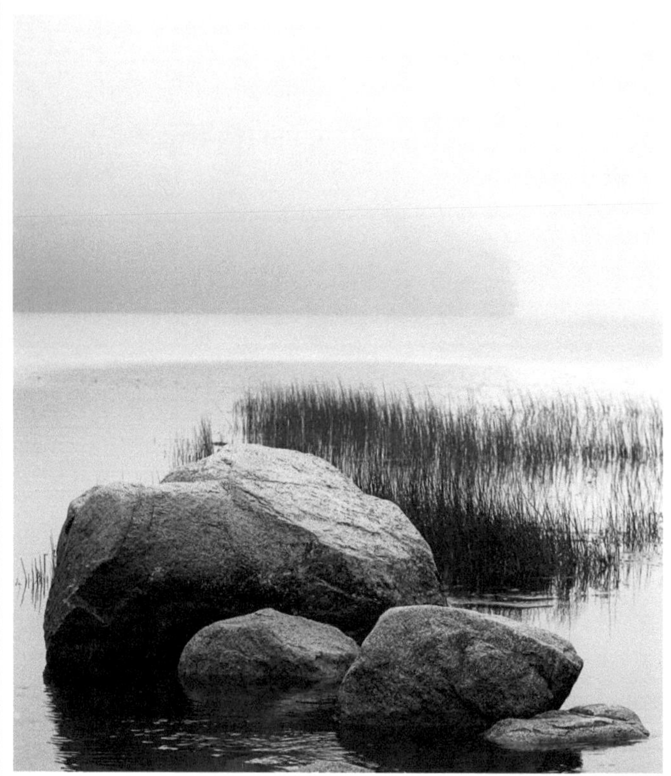

Acadia National Park

Best practice with memory cards is to bring more than you think you'll need. If planning a weeklong project, and if you normally shoot 100GB in a week, then bring maybe enough cards to store 150GB or 200GB. Additionally, travel with two backup receptacles for your data—perhaps a tablet and an external hard drive, or a laptop and a portable storage device that accepts your card type. One of your backups could even be an extra set of cards; if your camera has two card slots, you can record to them simultaneously, so the second card contains automatic backup files. (If your itinerary includes long periods in the backcountry, backup devices may be ill-advised because you'll have nowhere to recharge their batteries and they'll add weight to your pack. In that case, just bring extra cards.)

When you have your two backup copies, store them in different places. You could perhaps keep one in the car and the other in your camera bag. At the end of your trip, if you fly home, keep at least one backup in your pocket or elsewhere on your person.

BAGS

WE NEED something to carry all that gear. Actually, I recommend having two things to carry all that gear: A backpack large enough to stow everything you might want to bring on a photo-oriented hike, and a smaller bag that fits just a few items you might need for quick jaunts.

For example, when photographing at Bryce Canyon, if you're planning a daylong hike into the basin, you may want all your gear with you so you're prepared for different types of opportunities, plus some water and food, along with a way to haul it all easily so you don't need a chiropractor when you return home. But if you're spending a morning photographing from overlooks along the scenic drive, you probably know that you'll keep using the same lens or two. There's no need to carry everything you own plus ancillary supplies in a big, heavy bag that you need to lug out of the car every time you take a 100-yard walk. That's when the small bag is useful.

For the big bag, I like backpacks better than traditional bags because they distribute the weight around the torso. My shoulder is grateful for that. Backpacks don't allow for quick access to the gear, but I'm not usually working quickly when on the trail anyway. If I'm in a situation where I think I'll need to react rapidly, I can always carry one camera on my shoulder, ready to be flung into action. I can also carry the camera mounted to the tripod, but when I do, I always make sure to have a grip on the camera strap in case the mount fails. One option I consider undebatable is the ability to strap accessory pockets onto the sides of the backpack, where I can stow water and food (which I never want in the main compartment with my cameras), or an ultralight tent, gloves, etc.

For the smaller bag, anything that can hold a couple of lenses and a few accessories is great. Many designs are available, including sling and messenger bags, and packs with an optional hip strap.

The selection of camera bags available today shows a lot of ingenuity, and a lot of thought about how different photographers like to work. Many features are available in different configurations, including padding, repositionable compartments, water-tightness, stowable rain covers, tripod straps and laptop pockets.

When carrying a bag into the wilderness, even if not far from the road, it will likely collect a fair amount of dust, dirt, twigs, leaf bits, etc. Keeping these away from your gear long-term is a good idea, so when you get home from a trip, use a vacuum cleaner hose to suck debris off and out of the bag.

VESTS

An alternative to a small bag is a photography vest. With its many and large pockets, it can keep a lot of gear accessible.

However, you can't easily put a vest on the ground while you're working, like you might with a bag—if loaded up, they can get heavy and uncomfortable, especially in hot weather. Also, I found vests more useful in the film days, because the big pockets were so easy to grab a fresh roll from and to discard a used roll into. In the digital era, I might change cards once in a day, and I certainly wouldn't just toss them into a pocket.
I no longer use my vest often, but I still travel with it because it's convenient for carrying items through airports and on a flight. Also, my vest was a gift from my dad a few years before he passed away, so I like to have it with me.

SUPPORT

In my philosophy, any photograph worth making is worth using a tripod for. Yes, sometimes setting up the tripod can be a hassle, an unproductive delay between having an idea and executing it. And yes, sometimes I'm tempted to just pick up the camera and shoot. But when I defer to the temptation, the photo almost always ends up in the trash—not necessarily because it was visually soft, but because it was conceptually soft. If the idea was good enough, I would not have been tempted to rush through it.

Sometimes, of course, setting up the tripod is not practical. If something unexpected happens—a fleeting moment that will be lost in five seconds—then you have to just shoot and see what you get. But more often than not, the moment will still be there a minute from now. And almost always, camera support will make your photos better. This is true even with high shutter speeds—just do a test and see which is sharper at 1/500, a photo made on a tripod or one hand-held. Moreover, using a tripod simultaneously allows and enforces more precision in composing an image.

For anyone serious about photography, support should be the second highest priority when spending good money for good quality. (Lenses are the first.) Use a light but sturdy tripod (carbon fiber is the contemporary industry standard) that is rated to support about double the weight that you think you'll put on it. If you intend to photograph wildflowers, make sure your tripod legs can extend to 90 degrees, so you can photograph from ground-level. Buy a quality ball head with a quick-release clamp, and get quick-release plates for all your cameras and for every lens with a tripod collar. If you want to save some dollars, one feature you can skimp on is a center column; I don't advise using one anyway because when extended even a few inches, it will lessen stability.

Many accessories are available for tripods, a few of which can be helpful when working in a national park:

• A strap that attaches to the head and a leg will enable you to sling the tripod over your shoulder for easy carrying.

• A leveling base helps you level the camera quickly, ensuring straight horizons for landscape work or multi-frame panoramas.

• Instead of a standard quick-release plate for your camera(s), consider an L-plate, which allows you to quickly change from horizontal to vertical framing, or vice versa.

• If you plan to use large telephoto lenses, such as a 400mm f/2.8 or 600mm f/4, it will be easier to maneuver on a gimbal head than a ball head.

Another option—that is not as stable as a tripod but is more stable than hand-holding—is a monopod. I have a history in sports photography, where a monopod is standard equipment, so I'm accustomed to having and using one. Therefore, a monopod is always in my tripod bag, even when I'm doing nature photography. A monopod offers a few stops' worth of support while being fast to set up and easy to move around with. A monopod can be good for photographing a moving subject; for example, butterflies can move around so much that constantly repositioning a tripod becomes a chore, while using a monopod enables you to reposition yourself and the camera more efficiently.

REMOTE RELEASE

When photographing from a tripod, using a remote shutter release will further reduce vibration, which is essential for long exposures. A remote release also allows you to keep your hands off the camera, which helps maintain critical positioning when using a telephoto or macro lens, or when shooting multiple

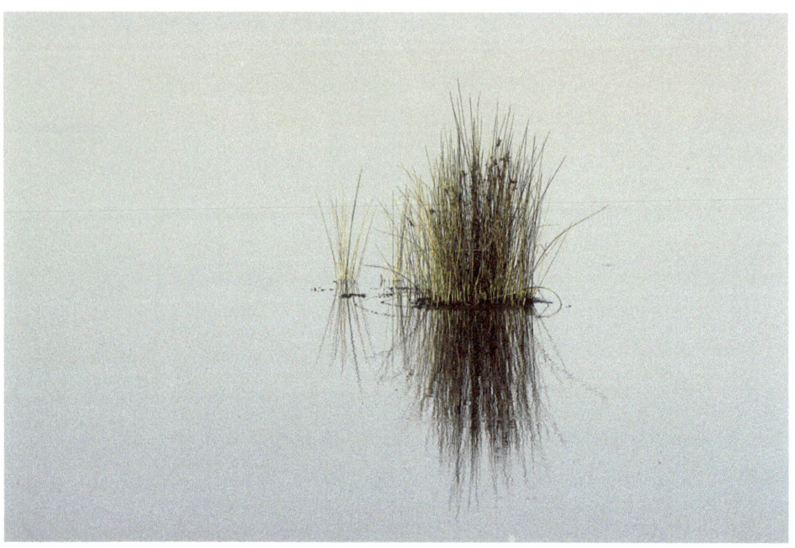

Merritt Island National Wildlife Refuge

frames for double exposures, focus stacking or HDR. This little piece of equipment is so critical to the way I work that I carry two of them, just in case one breaks or disappears.

The most common remote is a cable release, which ends at an apparatus as simple as a button or complex enough to operate advanced camera functions. Wireless remotes are also available, which can be useful for firing the shutter from a distance. An application of that would be if you were trying to photograph a prairie dog emerging from its den; if it won't come out because of your presence, setting up a wireless trigger can allow you to photograph from someplace it can't see you. A wireless release also allows you to be a subject in the composition without having to run back and forth to the camera to set the timer. Also, several smartphone and tablet apps offer the ability to operate a camera remotely; some are even advanced enough to allow you to use the display for live-view focusing.

ANCILLARY ITEMS

ALSO IMPORTANT to consider is all the "stuff" that helps execute a national parks photo project. Cameras and lenses are the tools for actually making the photos—they're the engine that makes the project move. All the supplementary gear is the oil that makes the project run smoothly.

POWER

If there's one aspect of nature photography that the digital revolution made more challenging, it's keeping cameras and peripheral gear running. The batteries in my film cameras would last months. Some cameras, such as my old Nikon FM2, didn't even require batteries to take a picture. Now I have a wealth of gear that needs to be powered. On a standard trip I'm recharging batteries for each of two to four cameras, a laptop, tablet, GPS logger and cell phone.

If staying in a hotel or RV, that's not too hard. Just plug everything in at night, and you're back to 100 percent power by morning.

If camping, electro-life starts to get more challenging. Some campgrounds have electricity in campsites, but this is less prevalent in national parks than at outside establishments. My preferred solution is to plug an inverter into the lighter outlet in the car. I like an inverter with multiple outlets for three-prong plugs and USB, and that shuts itself off if the automobile battery drains too low. If the car's electrical configuration allows for it, I keep the inverter on the floor of the backseat along with all of my chargers. Then I have a mobile charging station available to me anytime I'm driving. In urgent cases, I might ask to plug in at a restaurant while eating lunch. (Which is also an excellent place and time to dump cards and run backups.)

On multi-night trips through wilderness, all those options are moot. There is no outlet beside the boulder 20 miles across the tundra. Also, due to the remote location of some parks, no power may be available anywhere—you won't be plugging anything in at places such as Kobuk Valley or Channel Islands. When away from electricity for long periods of time, you just need to bring enough batteries to sustain your gear. But for a very long unplugged trip, look into the option of carrying a solar recharger. This technology is yet not up to ideal performance levels for a full pack of camera electronics, but in the right circumstances, it could be better than carrying pounds of pre-charged batteries.

Lastly, most contemporary cameras use custom-sized batteries, but plenty of other types of gear use standard sizes, such as AA or AAA. After supporting the disposable-battery industry for years, I finally switched to rechargeable in 2012. They come with a higher entry cost, but savings are quickly realized after only a few recycles. Shop for quality—this investment has a good return.

GEOTAGGING

Depending on your impetus for photographing national parks, geotagging can be important, interesting or needless. For me it's the first two. Geotagging helps me know where I made all my photos, which also helps me keyword them, both of which subsequently teach me more about my photography subjects.

Geotagging can be accomplished several ways. Some cameras have built-in capability to embed the appropriate GPS coordinates into the metadata of each photograph made. Some other cameras can accept an attachment that does the same job. Alternatively, a separate GPS (or "geotracker") can periodically record your location and write it to a text file; later, that data is matched to the image files based on their timestamps. (In order for that to work well, synchronize the clocks on your cameras to GPS Time before you travel.) Alternatively, you can use one of many smartphone apps that do the same thing.

Though many photographers like using an app for geotagging, I find that a phone's GPS function drains the battery too quickly. I have the same concern with an external GPS unit that attaches to the camera; though I love the efficiency of the coordinates automatically writing to the image file, the

RETROACTIVE GEOSYNCING

If you forget to sync your cameras to GPS Time before using an external geotracking device, you can still accurately match the timestamps. All you need to do is use software to correct the "capture time" in your image files' metadata. Adobe Lightroom and Photo Mechanic provide this capability, as do some other photography programs. You can also find third-party apps that specialize in changing metadata.

How do you know what time to sync the camera to retroactively? You don't want to benchmark it with Universal Time, because GPS Time is different. The former accounts for anomalies such as leap seconds, while the latter is constantly chronological.

Once home, the procedure is simple: Search online for "GPS Time" and you'll find various websites that display it to the second. With each camera you used on your trip, take a picture of the screen. Load those files into your photo-editing software, then compare each timestamp to the GPS time pictured. Subtract one from the other, and that's the time difference you need for adjusting the metadata.

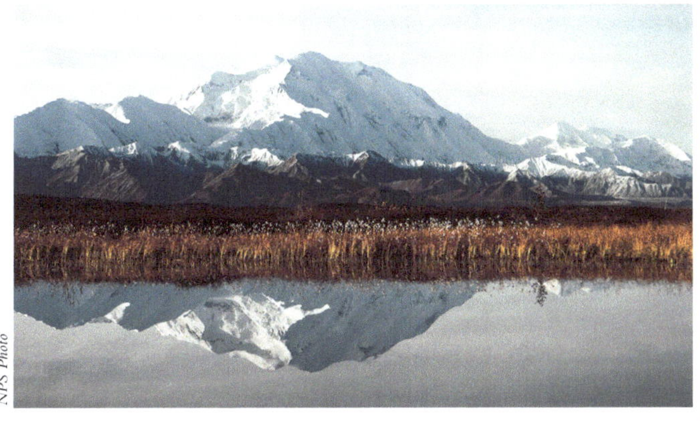

NPS Photo

Denali National Park & Preserve

unit cuts my camera's battery life to less than half. Also, these devices each attach to just one body, so you end up with data for only the photos made with that camera. Any backup or secondary camera you use will need its own dedicated unit, or you will not have coordinates associated with its photos.

The option I prefer is an external geotracker. I can turn it on in the morning, clip it to my belt, vest or backpack, and forget about it until I stop working that night. Every 10 seconds it records my location in the world, creating a virtual track of where I spent my time. A set of AAA batteries lasts a little more than one day—so I keep a few sets charged, and then I can cycle through them during a trip, starting with a fresh set each day. Because the GPS data is kept separate of any particular device, it essentially covers all the cameras I may photograph with, including my phone and tablet. When my trip is over, I can load all the photos from every camera and device into Adobe Lightroom and match them to the coordinates in my tracklog.

One of the great applications of this data is that Lightroom's map feature uses it to show exactly where a photo was made. To dig even deeper, I can copy the coordinates into Google Earth, which will help me identify any mountains, lakes, rivers, etc., that may be in the photo.

APPS

The age of the internet and computers that fit in our pockets has brought us tools we couldn't have imagined a generation ago. A wide variety of apps for tablets and smartphones allow you to access information in the field that can dramatically improve your location scouting.

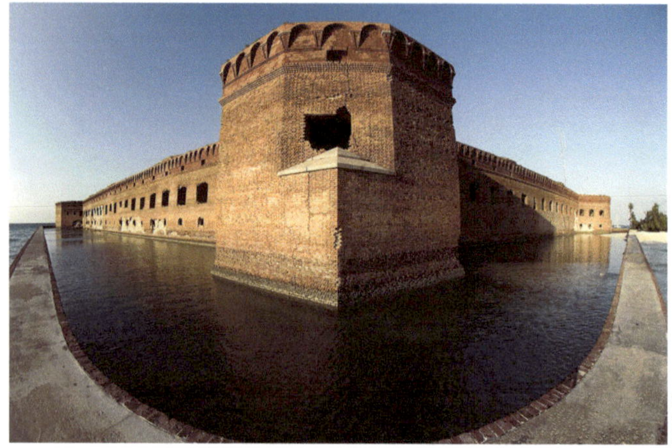

NPS Photo

Dry Tortugas National Park

One of my favorite apps is The Photographer's Ephemeris. I used it as desktop software before the proliferation of PDAs and smartphones, and these days I have it installed on my Android phone and my iPad. The app shows a map of your current location (or any other spot you pick) along with a graphical representation of where the sun and moon will rise and set, and the times for all those celestial events. No more guessing, "Will the sun set beside that sea stack?" With The Photographer's Ephemeris, you can know it will. Other, newer apps provide similar information. A particular one to note is Photo Pills, which also works in reverse—if you want to photograph the sun setting beside that sea stack, it will tell you what days of the year that will happen.

I also like apps that tell me what stars I'm looking at, because other than the obvious few (such as the sun), I have no idea. When I'm doing night photography, I like to know some of the planets, constellations and notable stars that may appear in the composition. Using a stargazing app, I can point my tablet or phone at the sky and it will label every celestial body I'm seeing.

If you're working along the shores of a coastal park—such as Redwood or Kenai Fjords—an app that reports the times and heights of the tides will help you plan photos around those events. Especially in more northern latitudes, the tides are so extreme that they can dramatically change the appearance of coastal features. In Acadia, knowing the tides can let you plan a hike on the land bridge to Bar Island or Little Moose Island. In Olympic, knowing the tides can keep you from being dangerously trapped below cliffs.

ACCESSORIES

As the years come and go, so does the minutia I carry in my bag and in the car. Gone are my film-leader retriever, my laminated exposure cheat-sheet and the manual for my Nikon F5. They and others have been replaced by the following:

- ***Sensor cleaner.*** Even for a camera that self-dusts its sensor, this can be a critical item when working outdoors, especially in dusty areas such as forests or springtime meadows. Many types and brands are available. I have heard promising things about gel sticks, though I use chemical-treated swabs.
- ***Silicone jar opener.*** These are flat rubbery discs designed to loosen stuck jar lids. They're also great for loosening jammed lens filters.
- ***Solunar wristwatch.*** Definitely for the landscape photography geek, this is a watch that tells you the times of the sunrise, sunset, moonrise and moonset, the phase of the moon, and the time of solar high noon.
- ***Two-way radios.*** If I'm shooting with someone, I like to be able to stay in touch, and cell phones don't always work in the center of 2,000 square miles of wilderness. Having a radio allows photography partners to communicate to help coordinate timing, or perhaps to call in scouting reports about new locations. They can also help in emergencies, or if someone gets lost.
- ***Flashlight.*** I always carry a small but powerful flashlight. I don't often use it for walking at night—I prefer to do that in the dark, to keep my night vision sharp. Rather, the flashlight is helpful when trying to focus on features of the landscape at night. (See "Moonlit Landscapes" on page 91.)
- ***Cap light.*** This is a small LED flashlight that clips to the front of a hat brim. Using one allows both hands to be free for setting up a camera and tripod in the dark, such as when photographing star trails, or preparing for a sunrise photo. Some photographers use headlamps for the same purpose.
- ***Knee pads.*** Donning these will save your knees when spending a lot of time on the ground, such as when photographing flowers. They're also useful when working on wet ground, on shores of barnacle-encrusted rocks, or in the desert around cactus needles.

CHAPTER 4

ENVIRONMENTS

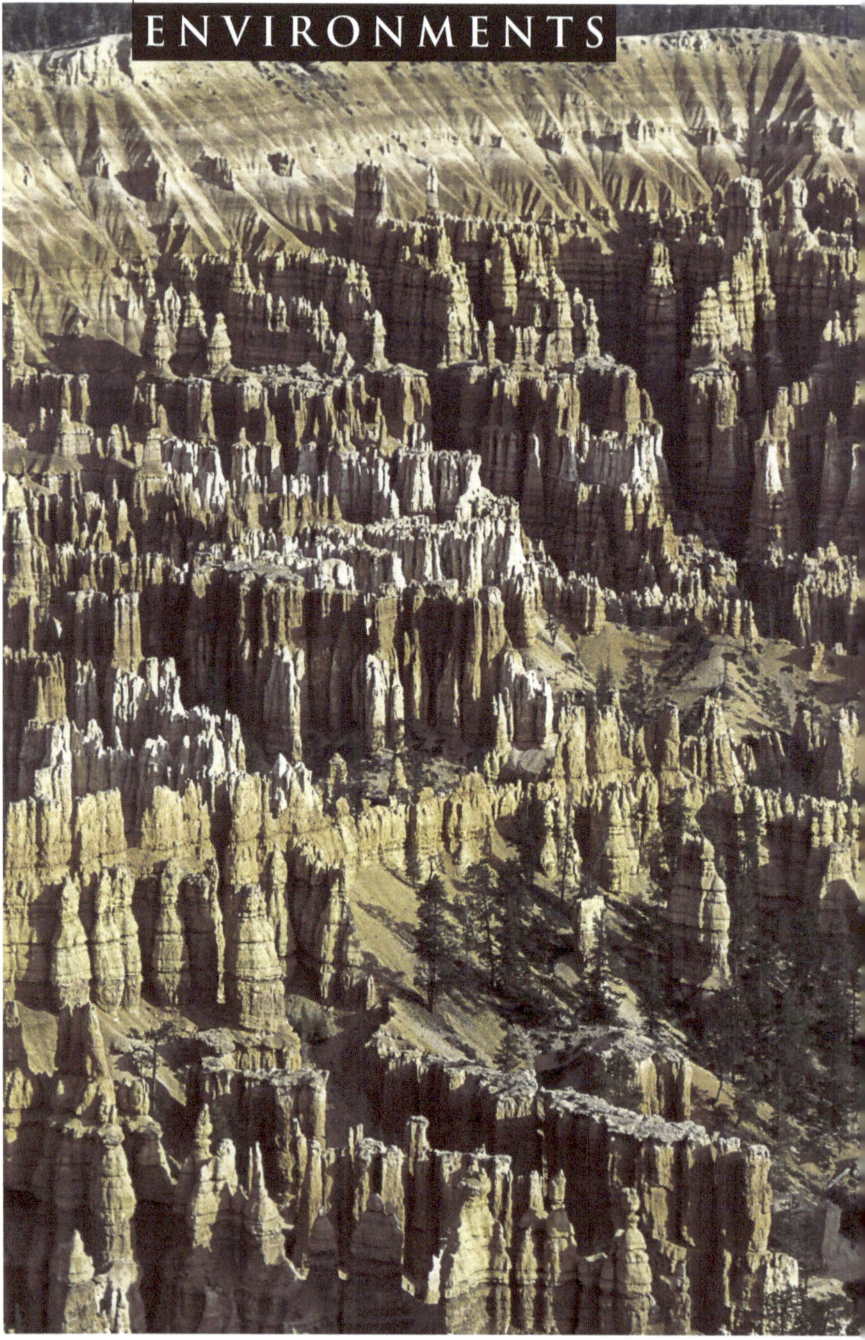

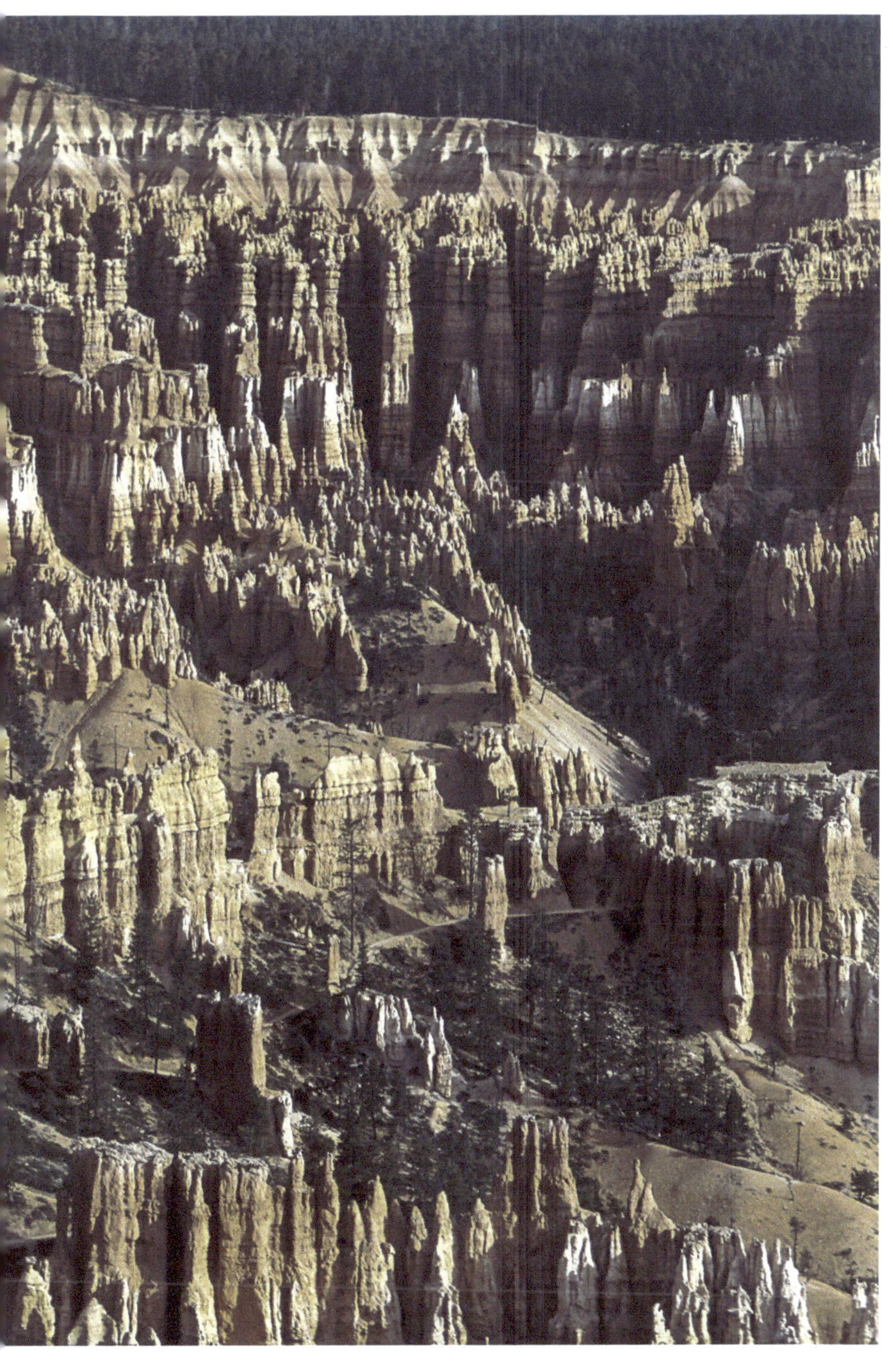

Hoodoos, Bryce
Canyon National Park

THINGS TO SEE

PART OF WHAT I LOVE about the American national parks is their variety of landscapes. For a nature photographer, the options can never really get stale. If you tire of photographing mountains, then travel to the ocean. If you're weary of desert, visit the grasslands. If bored of the surface of the earth, explore some caves. Every type of terrain in the country is represented in at least one of our national parks. We have plains and plateaus, birch groves and rainforests, lakes and rivers, tundra and prairies, coral reefs and kelp forests, and so on and so on. The variety of topography and ecosystems is almost difficult to fathom.

All of these types of places are beautiful, but some present unique challenges to photography, either from a technical or workflow standpoint. This chapter explores a few of the issues you're likely to encounter while photographing in some of the scenarios common to our parks.

MOUNTAINS

OF ALL THE types of topography in the park system, mountainous regions might be the biggest widespread star. Spectacular mountains are found in many parks, including Rocky Mountain, Kings Canyon, North Cascades and Glacier.

The first issue to be aware of when working in mountain country is that if you're not accustomed to the altitude, then you should allow a few days to acclimate before trying anything strenuous. The thin air can cause fatigue and dehydration more quickly than usual, and the sun can cause skin damage faster, too. Finding yourself exhausted and sunburned after a just a three-mile hike into the wilderness can ruin your day—and maybe your entire trip—rather quickly. When working in the mountains, bring more water than you normally would, wear sunscreen and a hat, and allow plenty of time to move around on foot.

Mountain regions contain a wide range of artistic opportunities. The mountains themselves can be used as a primary subject, as a setting, or as a background. You can use a wide-angle lens to encompass a range of peaks into one tableau, or a telephoto to compact the layers of the landscape. Many mountainous regions contain lakes and ponds, which, when placid, can

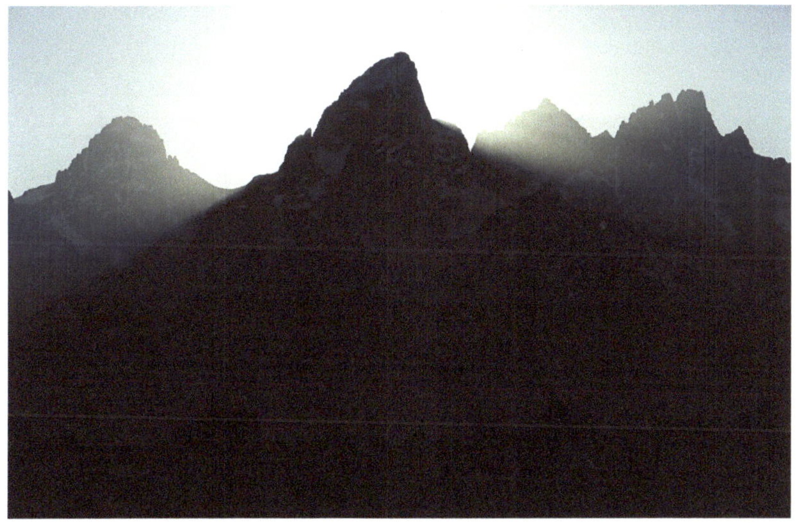

Grand Teton National Park

be used to photograph reflections of the surrounding scenery. And wildflowers are often found in alpine meadows, providing a scenic foreground.

Weather plays an important role in alpine photography. An overcast sky is generally too boring for mountain scenes. A blue sky is usually better. But a blue sky with clouds is best, because they add depth to a composition. Winter lasts longer at high altitudes, which is good, because snow-capped peaks are almost always more photogenic. And storms tend to be more dramatic in high altitudes, bringing lightning and dark clouds that are excellent for photography if approached safely. (See the Appendix.)

An alluring phenomenon to look for in the mountains is alpenglow. This is the pinkish light sometimes seen on peaks minutes before sunrise. Alpenglow is not caused by sunlight directly striking the mountains; rather, in the right conditions, the light is refracted by water and ice particles in the atmosphere and "bent" onto the scene. The effect is stunning—and fleeting, so be ready ahead of time, and shoot quickly.

Also, the light around and in alpine terrain tends to be dynamic. Due the nature of peaks and valleys, the juxtaposition of light and shadow changes constantly during the day, presenting different creative opportunities. The downside of this is that, again, due to the nature of mountains, golden-hour light does not make the same impression, because usually you can no longer see the sun when it's that close to the true horizon.

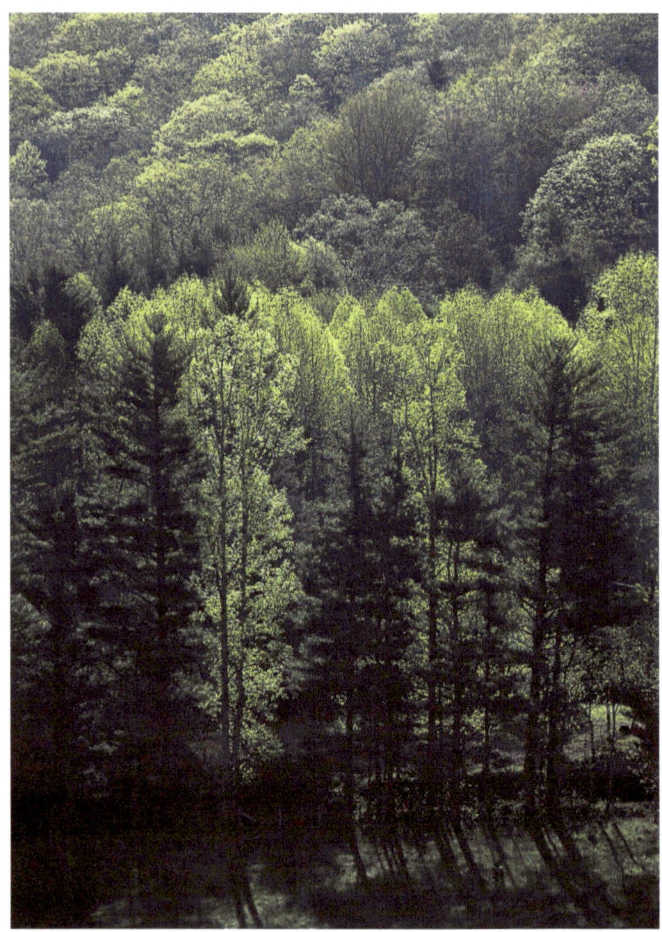

Blue Ridge Parkway

FORESTS

THE NATIONAL PARKS are full of forests. Whether a tall grove of redwoods or a sparse landscape of Joshua trees, forests are probably the most common landscape element throughout the system. And while single trees can be easy to photograph, unfortunately forests can be tricky.

The first challenge is light. Strong, direct light is rarely ideal, because it creates too much contrast beneath the trees—too many hot spots and deep shadows. In the forest, dappled light can be pretty to look at, but not to photograph. If your view is from the outside—such as facing a tree-covered mountainside from the other side of a valley—then you can use whatever type of light best fits your goal. But if you're photographing from within the trees, then you almost always want flat light, such as the soft, diffused light from an overcast sky.

Generally, two circumstances can break that rule. The first is when the light is coming directly from the side, such as immediately after sunrise or before sunset, creating horizontal layers of light in the forest. The second is when fog or mist is present; then the direct sunlight can create smoky crepuscular rays that radiate through the trees, or that perhaps highlight an interesting subject on the forest floor. (This effect can also sometimes be found in Yellowstone, when the steam from fumaroles mixes with surrounding stands of pines.)

Three photography tools are just about critical to good forest photography: a tripod, a remote shutter release and a polarizing filter. The first two are needed because exposures under a tree canopy almost always call for slow shutter speeds. As for the filter, that's for removing glare from the greenery. The glare might not be apparent to the naked eye, but it's always there—subsequently, a polarizing filter will almost always improve the color of a forest scene. Polarizing becomes even more important when shooting in a rainforest, or in any forest that has recently been rained upon.

Incidentally, in many cases the best time to photograph in the forest is during or immediately after a rainfall. All that water coating everything brings visual life to the scene. Working in the rain can be uncomfortable, but if we were looking for comfort, we'd be lounging on a sunny, sandy beach in the Caribbean instead. Also, forests can also be beautiful in snow, and of course during the fall foliage season (if the right species are present).

A popular strategy for photographing a grove—particularly of picturesque aspens or birches, such as those found in Great Basin and Voyageurs—is to frame a stand of trunks so that they create a pattern of parallels across the composition. This is harder than it looks. The first problem is finding a grove that is dense enough to frame a set of trees together, but not so dense that you can't find clean patterns in the clutter. (Much of forest photography is exactly that: finding visual order in chaos.) When a good grove is available, the next challenge is finding a pleasing composition, then working (usually tediously) to inch the camera in different directions, and to adjust focal lengths, to avoid having any trees overlap each other—in other words, the best compositions usually have space between every tree trunk.

Also remember that forests contain subjects other than trees. Within them we find ponds, moss, fallen leaves, wildflowers, mushrooms, waterfalls, birds and other wildlife. Look for paths and streams, as well, which can be useful as leading lines in a composition.

COASTLINE

THE COAST can be a magical place for photography. People have been drawn to the side of the sea throughout human history, both as a place to build civilizations and as an inspiration for art. The sounds of waves crashing and gulls crying, the smell and taste of salty air, the sight of water meeting land in all the visual configurations in which they come together—all of this arouses creativity.

Coastline can vary considerably. It can be sandy or rocky, and it can be composed of vast expanses of level land, or the water can crash into the bottom of sheer cliffs. Coastline can extend straight away in both directions, or weave in and out of inlets and headlands. It can be barren, or covered with plant life such as forests of coastal mangroves. The sea can be smooth as glass, or turbulent with whitewater or rolling waves, and it can be dotted with sea stacks or icebergs. And however the scene appears, it will look different every few hours, as the tides move in and out. Seascapes are always changing.

Coastlines present several sorts of photography opportunities. In addition to a straightforward landscape approach, you can also seek its wildlife, in the form of seabirds in the air, or crustaceans, mollusks and such on the shore or in tide pools. Coastal details await macro lenses, such as shells and sand dollars, rockweed and seaweed, sea glass and patterns in wet sand. And the ocean always has at least one true horizon, which means you get unobstructed views to a sunrise or sunset, as well as access to all the great light that comes immediately after or before.

But working amidst this does present challenges. The biggest problem along coastline is that the environment contains two of the worst enemies of photo gear: sand and water. Cameras and lenses don't like either of them. Tripods also aren't too fond of sand, and though carbon-fiber models do okay with fresh water, if one contacts saltwater then you'll certainly want to rinse it off later.

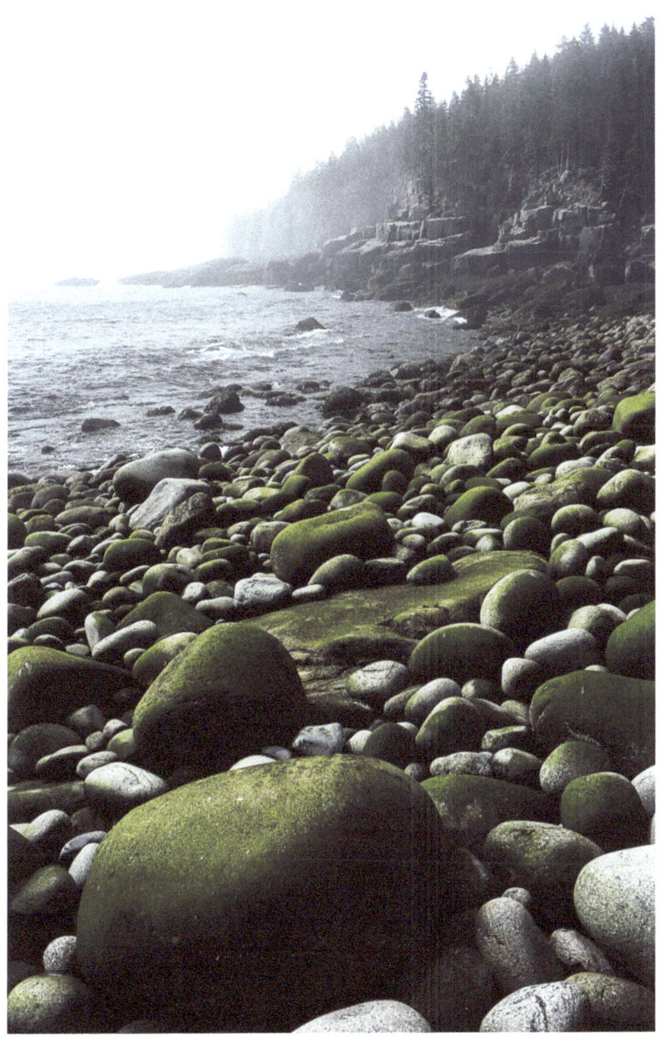

Acadia National Park

This means that utmost care is required when photographing along the coast to ensure that no gear ever falls anywhere. Always buckle your bag closed, even if you think you'll be digging through it again soon. That's just good practice, to ensure that you never absentmindedly lift the bag while it's not clasped shut and thereby spill its precious cargo. Also, if a bag falls in water just momentarily, that closed zipper can keep liquid out for a few seconds and save all your gear. (I once fell while crossing a stream in Great Smoky Mountains. I was amazed at how little water seeped into my closed backpack.) As for your tripod, when setting up it up, double-check that it's stable and that all the legs are tightly locked. Some photographers use specialized tripod feet when working on the beach—common preferences are either spikes that dig into the sand or round "shoes" that rest on top.

Aside from avoiding tumbles, just generally keep gear off the sand. Don't put a camera down on the beach—ever. If you want to be especially prudent, work on a towel or blanket. Another product to investigate is a sandless beach mat, made of material specially designed for sand not to stick.

Proper footwear is also helpful for keeping yourself—and thus your gear—off the ground. Rocks on the shore can be wet and covered with slippery algae or seaweed. Even dry rocks can present issues with footing; barnacles can be dry or brittle, and may disintegrate under your foot while you're stepping from rock to rock. When working around any water, I always want shoes with the best traction, regardless of whether they're waterproof. Even then, I make every step with care. (Except, apparently, for that time in the Smoky Mountains.)

Lastly, always watch the tides—not just for envisioning how a scene will look later, but for safety as well. You don't want to discover that your route back is under 10 feet of water. Similarly, be aware of regions that commonly experience sneaker waves, which even on calm days can suddenly and momentarily swarm the beach. They can knock down people—and camera gear—and pull them into the ocean.

DESERT

As harsh an environment as a desert can be, it can also be beautiful. Life grows among lifelessness, light dances around dunes, rock formations rise from the sand.

Most desert landscapes look downright inhospitable—and inphotographable—during midday. The light is just too harsh, and comes from too high an angle to accentuate the subtle textures of the terrain. But in golden hour, all the drab desert colors transform into warm tones that soften the scene. The same happens in blue-hour light, albeit with cool tones. If you do want to photograph at midday, look for opportunities for sunbursts (see page 90), or use shadows as your subject. Deserts also tend to be interesting locations at night, whether photographing the stars or moonlit landscapes.

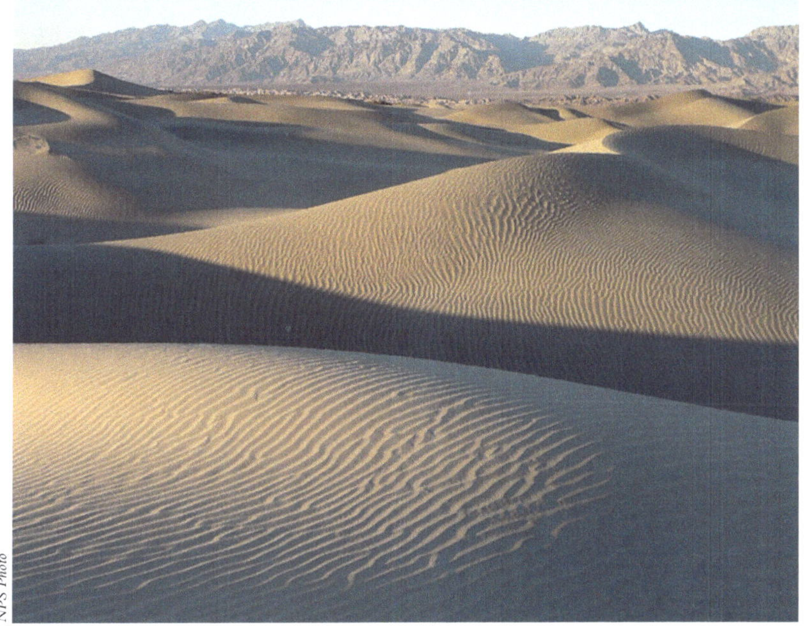

NPS Photo

Death Valley National Park

When we think of desert photography, the first mental image is usually of sand dunes, and there are plenty of those to be found in the national parks. Photogenic expanses of them are found in Death Valley, Kobuk Valley, Guadalupe Mountains and (of course) Great Sand Dunes. But other subjects are in the desert, too. Look for wildlife, such as lizards, tortoises and hares. And desert wildflowers—such as the many blooming cacti in the country, most notably prickly pear—serve nicely as portraits of life in a desolate environment.

Sand is an adversary in the desert, especially when it becomes airborne. When you are not actually using your camera, keep it in the bag or otherwise covered. Even in your bag, gear isn't always safe, as at least a few sand particles will certainly infiltrate. For extra precaution, some photographers put lenses and bodies in plastic bags before stowing them in their pack. And because sand spreads so easily, I never put my bag down in it. I either hang it on my shoulder, lay it on a rock or piece of clothing, or I keep my gear in a photo vest.

When actually using a lens, always attach the hood—just that little bit of protection can help in an unexpected gust. You can also consider using a UV filter on the lens as protection against sand. And if wind is blowing, don't change lenses—keep the camera closed, to avoid sand being blown inside. If you want to work with two different lenses, best practice is to use two cameras, each dedicated to a lens. For this same reason, zoom lenses are good for desert work because they give you a range of focal lengths without having to change lenses. And if you're working with a compact camera that has a retractable lens, be especially careful because one grain of sand can jam it.

Another issue to be aware of is that loose sand can present a challenge to stable tripod footing. Just like at the beach, you'll probably have better stability if using tripod shoes designed for sand and snow.

Photographing in the desert might compel you to carry some gear you otherwise might not pack. If you'll be working on the ground near cacti, then knee pads, a tarp or a folded jacket will help protect your knees from needles. Just in case they fail, have some tweezers available to pull the needles out of your skin. And, of course, you'll want plenty of water, sunblock and a hat.

Finally, hiking in sand is different than hiking on more solid ground. More physical effort is required when your foot is sinking a bit with every step, so a route will take longer to complete (and you'll dehydrate faster). This is especially true on dunes, where gravity can pull you back a pace for every two forward you make. The most secure (and least strenuous) footing is usually found along the ridges of the dunes; hiking along them lengthens your route, but the ability to maintain momentum should amount to a more efficient hike.

No matter where and how you walk, try to avoid making footprints in any sand that you might want to photograph either soon or later. Once the footsteps are there, they're visible until the next sandstorm.

SNOW

None of the U.S. parks are under complete permanent snow cover (other than a few snow fields in some alpine regions), but many offer pristine winter scenery. Crater Lake, Yellowstone and Yosemite are a few that are well-known as highly photogenic places to visit in winter.

One of the first lessons a photographer learns when photographing in snow is how the expanses of white fool a camera's meter. The camera tries to make everything match "middle

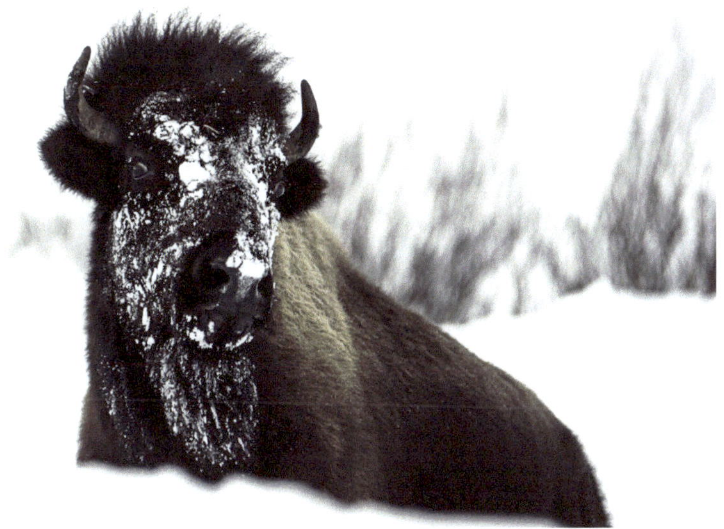

Yellowstone National Park

gray," so when the whole scene is white, the exposure algorithm darkens it. To correct for this, the photographer needs to proactively address the error—either by adjusting the camera's exposure compensation feature (usually by one to two stops), or by setting the exposure manually.

For landscape photographers, an advantage of working in winter is that golden hour generally lasts much longer than an hour, because the sun makes a very slow ascent from and descent to the horizon. In some areas, literally all winter daylight hours are excellent for photography. Winter landscapes are also ideal for shooting under moonlight, because so much illumination is reflected around the scene. Moreover, nighttime photography is easier to schedule in winter; because the days are so short, you can photograph in utter darkness and still get to bed at a decent hour.

When you're working in falling snow, one issue you may encounter is flakes collecting on your lens. Do not blow it off—your breath will condense on the glass, and you'll be out of commission until it dissipates. Instead, use a bulb-blower to remove the snowflakes. To minimize snow hitting the front element in the first place, use a lens hood. The drawback is that flakes will collect in the hood, but you can remove it and shake out the snow. Also, if the snow is blowing, know that you don't want the camera to be facing upwind, or your lens will get hit directly from the front.

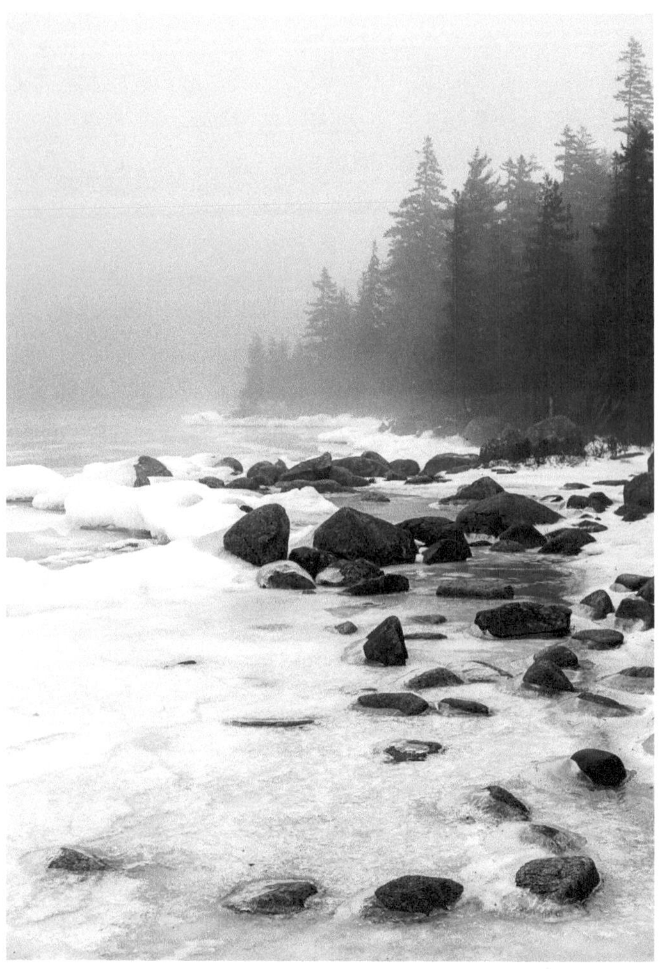

Acadia National Park

Snow is similar to sand in some regards: You don't want to walk in it until you're sure you don't want to photograph it. When snow is falling, try to avoid opening the camera to change lenses, so that you don't end up with droplets on the sensor. And to prevent your tripod from sinking in the snow, replace the feet with specialized shoes. Also, if your tripod is aluminum, consider buying foam wraps for the legs, because you will not want to touch them with bare skin in deep-freezing temperatures.

After working in cold conditions, when you enter a warm environment (either indoors or in a heated car), condensation can form on your camera and lenses. To avoid this, wrap all your gear in a large plastic bag, and remove it only once it has warmed to room temperature. The cold can also cause your batteries to weaken. Carry a spare or two, and keep them warm in your pants pocket; then you can rotate warm batteries into the camera as needed.

Moving around in snow presents some difficulties, particularly when it's deep. Some of the parks allow snowmobiles, which can be a relatively easy way to access remote locations. But most don't allow them, or they permit them only in very limited locations. However, almost all the parks allow cross-country skiing or snowshoeing. For me, snowshoes are standard equipment for a winter shoot. They make traveling over snow much easier compared to wading through drifts or through deep snowy fields.

Another essential tool for me in winter is ice-traction attachments for the soles of my boots. A few designs are on the market, but all do essentially the same thing: pull-on metal treads grip into ice and prevent you from slipping. They're like tire chains for your feet, but much less conspicuous. I've used these during winter shoots in Grand Teton and Yellowstone, and during a week hiking icy trails in Acadia—all with pounds of expensive camera gear on my back—and I never once slipped. It's like the ice isn't even under you. (One caution, though: If the metal treads become blocked up with snow, they can lose their effectiveness. But clearing them out fixes that quickly.)

Working in winter entails some specific health risks, including hypothermia and frostbite. Be sure to know how to avoid each, and how to recognize the warning signs of either. And of course wear proper clothing for the temperatures and climate (see page 34). Definitely wear snow-resistant clothing—if jeans are your outerwear, then getting them wet will end your day quickly. If you ever start to shiver, get back to warmth; that's your body's signal that it's about done dealing with the cold.

Finally, if working in alpine regions in winter, also learn about avalanches—how to avoid them, how to spot the danger signs of them, and how to survive them.

CHAPTER 5

TECHNIQUES

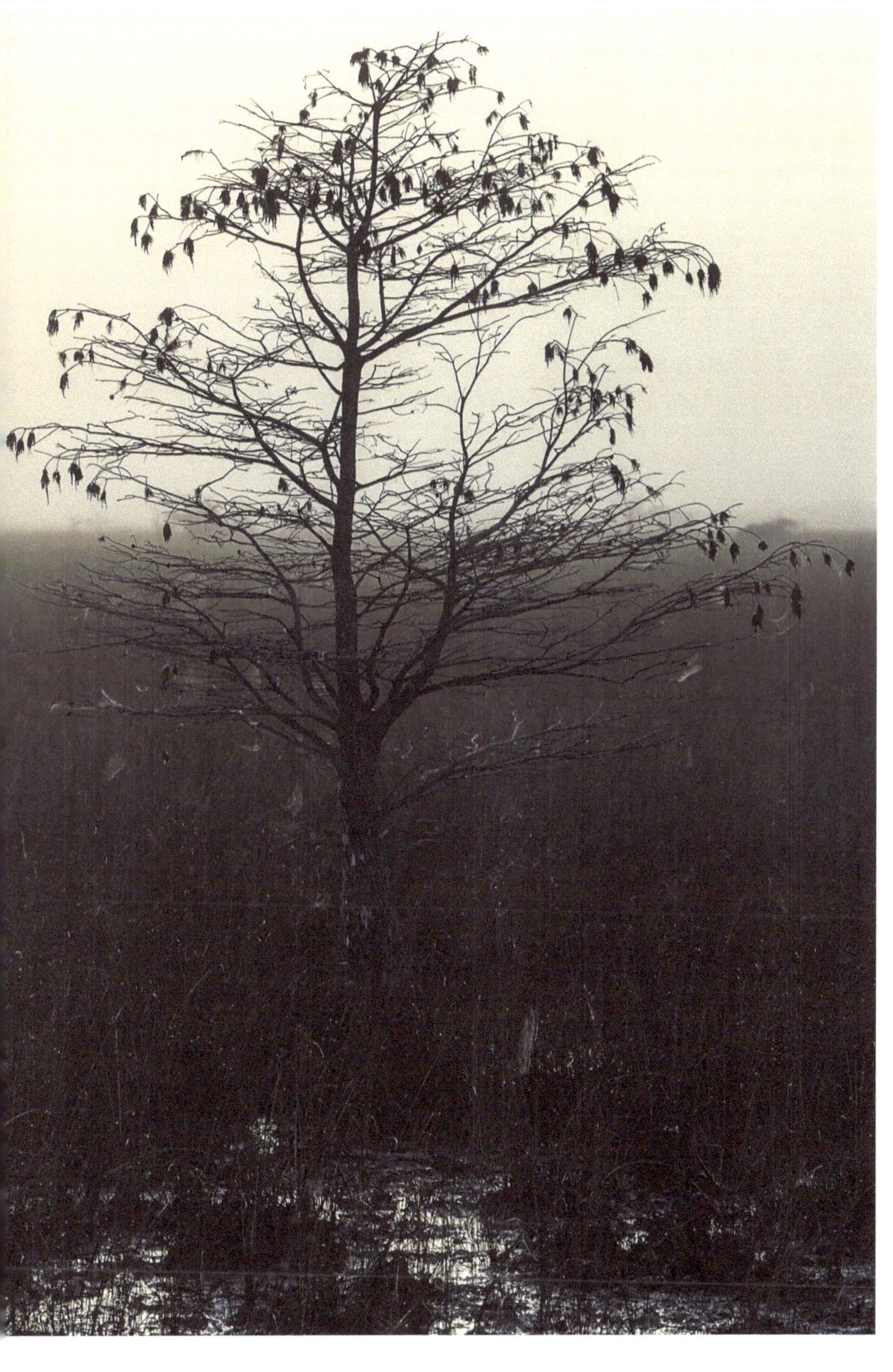

Sunrise, Everglades
National Park

THINGS TO DO

THE IMAGE-MAKING opportunities in the national parks include just about anything you could think of in the realms of nature, wildlife and landscape photography—plus, in some places, other genres as well, such as historical and archaeological photography. To capitalize on these opportunities, our cameras are only the tools. The art comes from within, and from knowing how to use those tools to exercise our creativity and vision.

Throughout this book I mention opportunities to use common photography techniques in different situations and in various specific parks. This chapter explains how many of those techniques are accomplished. It is not intended to be a complete tutorial on all the nuances of these procedures, but it does contain enough information and advice to get you far enough along so that you can start practicing these techniques in the field. Experience will bring you further, as would investigating more in-depth tutorials found in books, magazine articles and online resources.

REFLECTIONS

WHENEVER I see water, I look to see if anything interesting is reflecting in its surface. Reflections are fantastic fodder for photography, especially in nature. Most opportunities will come in the form of alpine lakes and ponds. Grand Teton, Glacier and Denali have many locations renowned for their mountain scenery reflecting in water. But other spots abound, too, such as puddles of rainwater on rock formations, calm bays on an Alaskan shore, or the shimmering sand of a beach as a wave ebbs back to sea.

GEAR

Using a wide-angle lens is a common approach, as it allows you to encompass an entire scene in the frame—and considering that a reflection essentially means you're doubling the size of the composition, much may need to be encompassed. But you may also use a short telephoto to home in on just the reflection portion of a larger landscape. A polarizing filter will often improve the colors, but be careful not to use it at full power, which could eliminate the reflection you're trying to photo-

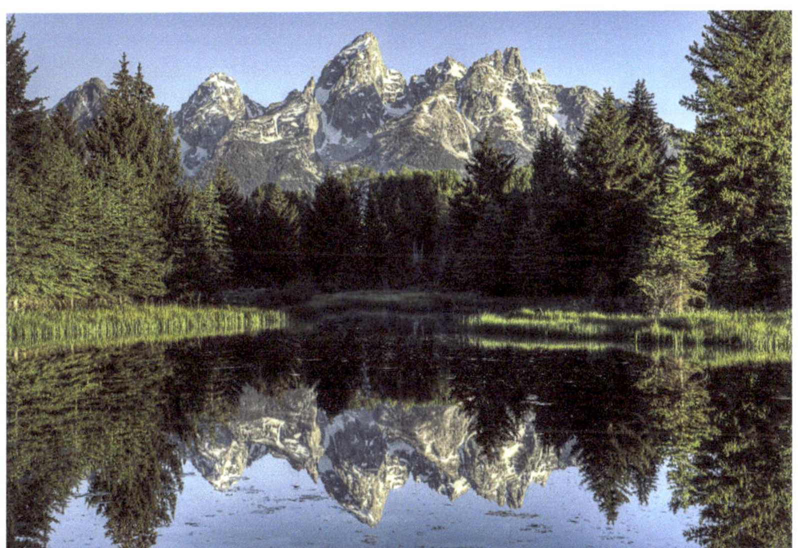

Grand Teton National Park

graph. (Some glare can also be avoided by photographing water that isn't directly lit.) Another filter to consider is a graduated neutral density; a reflection is one or two stops darker than the scenery it's reflecting, and the filter will help balance the exposure. (Or you could balance it in post-production. See page 99.)

STRATEGY

To photograph a reflection, the first requirement is placid water. Morning is usually the best time to find it. Ripples tend to start forming soon after the sun rises (the day's new warmth gets the wind moving), so you probably want to photograph in blue hour and a little beyond. Also, look for shallow water, which is less apt to ripple—shallow ponds, very flat beaches, or the water that coats melting ice. If your subject's surface is just a little ripply, using a slow shutter speed can smooth it out; the result will be a bit blurred, but at least it won't be distorted. (Distortion can be used creatively, though, so don't discount it completely.)

Just as the exposure is different in the water, so is the focus. For a sharp reflection, you need to focus on the reflected scenery, not on the water—their focal distance will be quite different. If you want them both sharp, you'll need to use a small aperture to achieve sufficient depth of field, or can use focus stacking.

In terms of composition, when working with reflections you can selectively ignore the rule about never putting the horizon in the middle of the frame. Doing so usually creates a stagnant scene, but with a reflection it can emphasize symmetry.

You can get very creative with color, too. An interesting technique is possible when the reflected scenery is directly lit but the water is shaded. That visual discrepancy places two planes in your frame with different color temperatures, a phenomenon that often renders beautifully in-camera. For instance, golden light on rock face or autumn color will be reflecting in the water, while reeds or rocks will be in cool, blue light. The juxtaposition of color creates a chance for some innovative compositions.

FOG & MIST

PHOTOGRAPHING in foggy or misty weather is almost magical. It changes the terrain, from simply altering the mood to actually improving the aesthetics. Fog can happen just about anywhere with moisture in the air, but is a common element at parks such as Acadia, Olympic and Redwood. It is commonly found in alpine areas—if you see the mountains are covered by clouds, head up and you'll be in fog.

Fog can help you improve a scene in several ways. By its nature, it obscures objects that are farther from the camera. If the background happens to be cluttered or otherwise undesirable, fog can hide it. Many times it has allowed me to photograph a location that I would have disregarded in clear conditions. Also, the farther that objects recede into the background, the more that fog masks them, which helps to convey depth in a photograph. Fog can be used to create abstract images, as well—in the right light and weather, objects in the landscape can be silhouetted a bit amongst all the gray, which emphasizes shape, and they will lose color saturation, which lends an ethereal quality.

EXPOSURE

Fog will trick your meter, and the camera will attempt to underexpose by about one stop. Compensate using your preferred method—decrease the shutter speed, open the aperture, raise the ISO or dial up the exposure compensation. Check the histogram—you want the data to appear toward the right side

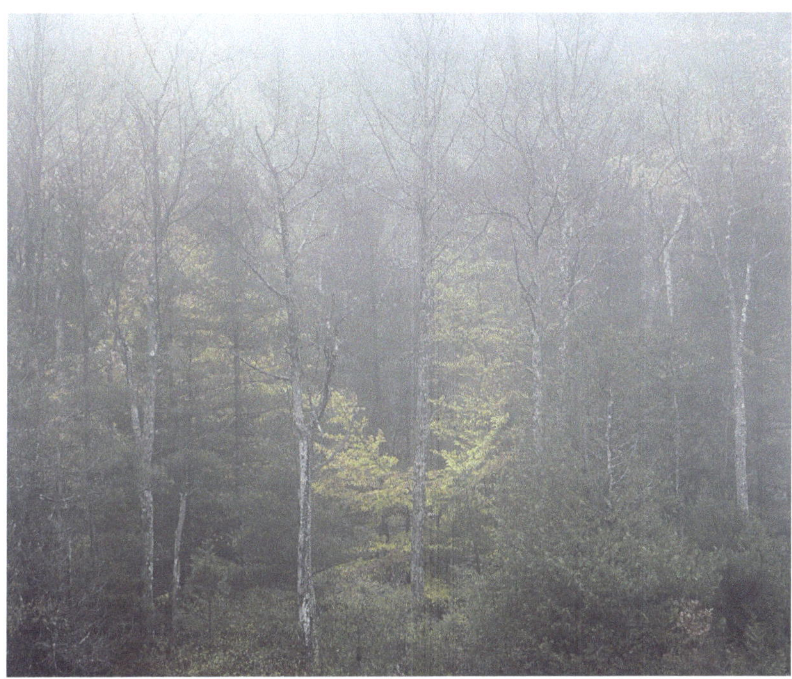

Acadia National Park

(see page 89). You will need to perform some adjustments in post-production, but the final image will be better. Also, note that the histogram will not show dark darks and light lights in the data, because a misty scene is composed entirely of mid-tones.

Another aspect of fog to be aware of is that it moves. That sounds obvious, but it doesn't always look obvious when you're in the middle of it. This is important because fog is not usually uniform throughout the cloud—its density can change from minute to minute, or even second to second. Thus, the appearance of the surrounding landscape changes. If you're planning a great photograph but the fog seems too thick or thin, be patient and see if things adjust to your advantage. Intermittent fog density will also affect your exposure, so be vigilant about continually double-checking it.

Fog can also affect the efficacy of auto-focus, because it diminishes the details that focus-detection systems use to lock onto an object. If this happens, try moving the AF target over the edge of something dark in the scene; just that little bit of contrast should be enough for the camera to focus on.

If the fog begins to look thicker through your viewfinder than with your naked eye, check the front of the lens.

Especially in thick fog, condensation can collect on the front element. Keep a microfiber cloth handy so you can wipe it off. You might also want to carry a small towel to dry the condensation from your camera.

WATER MOTION

THE NATIONAL PARKS are full of waterfalls. Yellowstone, Shenandoah, Cuyahoga Valley, Kings Canyon, Great Smoky Mountains, Yosemite, Lake Clark—together they have more waterfalls than have been counted, and those are only a few of the parks that have them.

Waterfalls come in many shapes, such as fans, curtains, cascades, chutes, funnels, horsetails, terraces, etc. And the falls are usually only part of an overall tableau. They're often surrounded by dense forest or sheer cliffs, perhaps wildflowers or lush ferns. Pools at the bottom can sometimes reflect the surrounding scenery, or a stream might be able to lead the eye in a composition. The flow of the falls can be a beautiful trickle or a thundering deluge.

Regardless of how they look, you always have at least one creative control to alter their appearance: shutter speed. Using a time exposure to blur the flow of a waterfall is an old technique, dating back to when cameras weren't fast enough to stop motion anyway. Today we can photograph with incredibly fast shutter speeds, but that rarely captures the beauty of a waterfall. The reason is that the water, when frozen by a split-second exposure, looks contrasty and jarring. That effect can be exciting, but not generally tranquil. To portray a softer scene, blurring the water—at least a bit—is often suggested. (Incidentally, this technique works for whitewater rivers and streams, too—and for surf. Try it on the coast for some creative seascapes.)

GEAR

Because you'll be working with slow shutter speeds, a tripod is required. Otherwise everything else in the scene will be blurred, too. You will also want a remote shutter release, or at least a camera with a self-timer. A polarizing filter is nearly necessary, because areas with waterfalls are full of unwanted reflections: in the plunge pool, on wet rocks, on leaves, etc. Also, removing the reflections from the surface of the still water will create more contrast with the whiteness of the moving water.

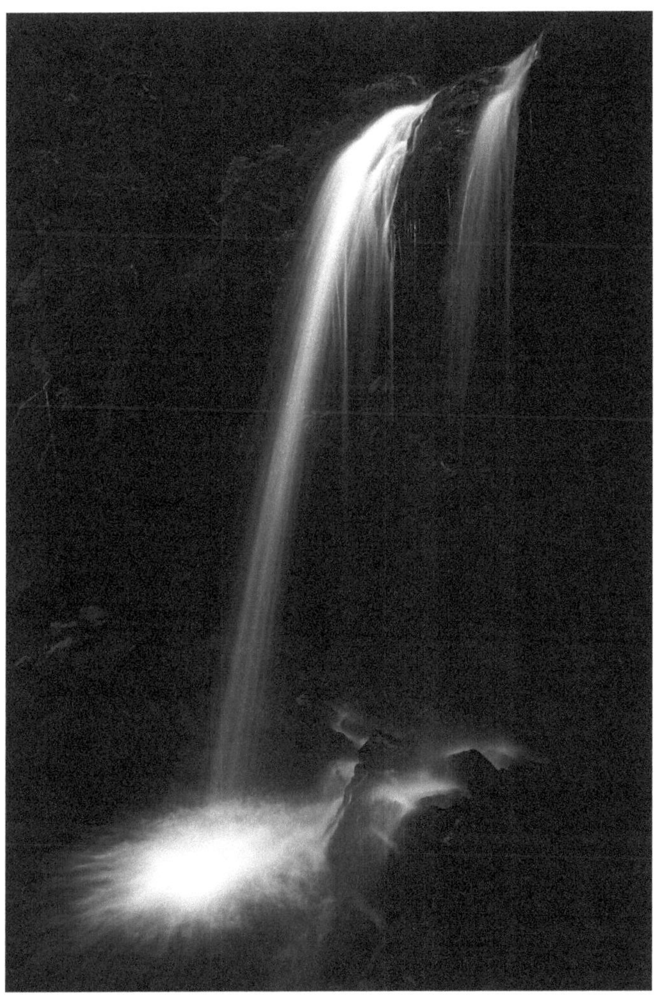

Great Smoky Mountains National Park

Depending on the strength of the light and how much of a "milky" effect you want, you may also consider using neutral density filters.

Think about your feet, too. The area around a waterfall can be slippery, and you'll be carrying costly camera gear, so take every measure to prevent falling. Waterproof shoes are beneficial; secure tread is imperative. Whenever you step on a rock, be sure it isn't loose and that you have good traction before you shift all your weight onto it. Don't cross the stream or river unless you're sure doing so is safe, and never climb the face of a waterfall.

If the falls generate a lot of spray or mist, consider wearing a raincoat, and bring a microfiber cloth and a towel for drying your lenses and cameras.

EXPOSURE

Shade or overcast conditions are usually best for photographing waterfalls, because in most cases direct sunlight creates dark shadows that contrast too much with the white highlights in the water. But don't let a sunny day get you down—if the waterfall is on a west- or east-facing slope, or in a canyon or gorge, it will probably be in shade during at least part of the day, in either morning or afternoon.

You need to achieve a slow shutter speed. But how slow is slow enough? Much depends on the particular waterfall and how much blur you like. Some photographers like a shutter speed of 1/15, and others try to go as slow as a few minutes. I like about 15 to 30 seconds. The intensity of the flow will affect this decision—less water means longer shutter speeds are needed to create the milky effect. Just remember that anything else that might move will be affected, too—such as breeze-blown trees.

That less-intense light is only the first step toward achieving a slow shutter speed. The second is using a low ISO. The polarizing filter will consume another stop or two, and ND filters will consume even more. Closing down the aperture will also slow your shutter. Experiment until the effect is what you want, and monitor your histogram to be sure the highlights in the water aren't blowing out.

MINUTIA

Remember that this technique is altering our normal perception of the scene. Try to envision how the water will look when it's all a uniform blur, and use that mental image to help build a quality composition. That flow of white will be a strong element that moves the viewer's eye around the frame—make sure it's leading where you want it to.

Also, when you're photographing a waterfall, be sure to examine not just the whole scene, but also its parts. Often wonderful photographs can be created by honing in on a small cascade or some water swirling around a rock. The opposite strategy can work well, too: Instead of making the waterfall the primary subject of a photograph, consider using it as just an element of the wider landscape.

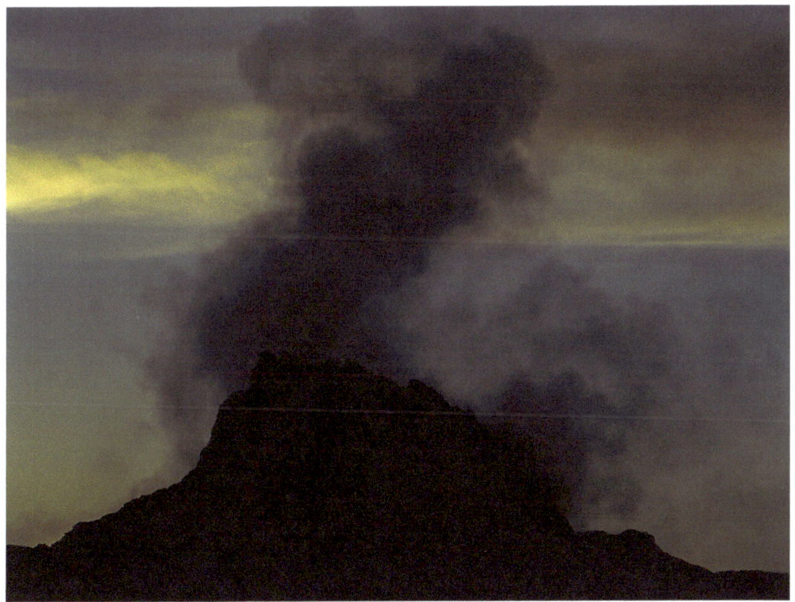

SILHOUETTES

Yellowstone National Park

THE ABILITY to photograph subjects in silhouette comes precisely from the shortcomings of camera equipment. In a sense, silhouetting is the opposite of HDR—rather than trying to capture detail throughout the image, we deliberately push all detail out of the shadows. The result is a revelation of form—we see only the outline, the shape, of our subject.

TACTIC

Silhouettes are most often made at sunrise and sunset, when they serve the composition by adding an interesting foreground to the background of sky and sun. But other opportunities exist, too—any setting that has an expanse that is brighter than the foreground can provide a chance to create a silhouette. For example, light bouncing off snow, ice or bright sand, or evenly reflecting off the surface of water—all of these can be juxtaposed with dark objects, or objects in shadow, to create compelling images of silhouettes. The background doesn't need to be bright, but rather just lighter than the foreground; for instance, a dusk sky can work wonderfully. Also, the best scenarios are often when the scene is backlit—the light coming toward the camera reinforces the effect.

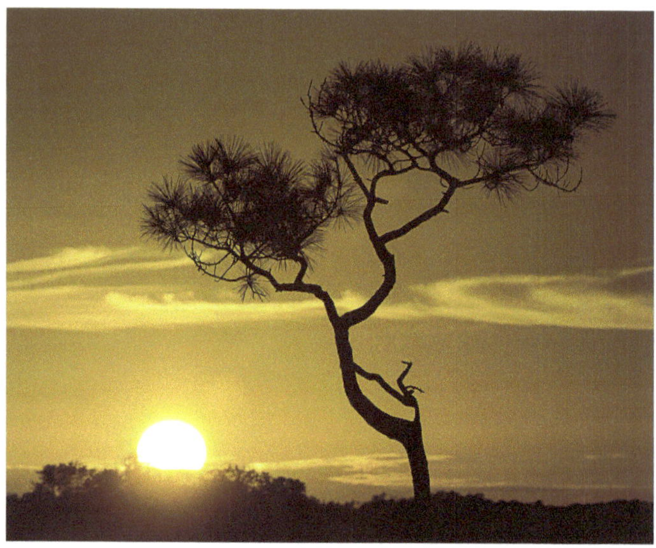

Everglades National Park

When you find an appropriate background, look for an object to silhouette in front of it. The darker the object, the better it will look in the final image. If it's in shade or shadow, that's even better. The important consideration is that an accurate exposure of the background needs to be an underexposure of the foreground. For example, if the exposure of a sunset calls for a shutter speed of 1/1000, and a tree in the foreground would need a shutter speed of 1/30, then that's a perfect situation for a silhouette. But even if you're new to this technique, you won't need to wander around metering backgrounds and foregrounds; you will very quickly develop a sense for recognizing good opportunities.

The execution is even simpler than the preparation. Just expose for the background, focus on the foreground, and shoot. Because modern cameras have such great dynamic range, you may not end up with a pure black in the silhouette, especially if even minimal light is bouncing around the foreground. If that happens, you can pull down the shadows in post-production to achieve a truer black. (Or you can leave the little bit of detail if you think it helps the image.)

Also, remember that any technique that involves the camera going against its programming will fail in auto-exposure modes. You will almost certainly need to know how to use exposure compensation or manual exposure for this technique to be effective. And if your camera has auto-flash, definitely turn it off.

CONSIDERATIONS

In refining this technique, you'll notice that a recognizable, distinct subject works best. Its outline will probably be the most noticeable component of the composition, so it should also be compelling. Bare trees, sea stacks, rock formations and wildlife are examples of good subjects. For optimal sharpness, make sure to focus on the edge of the object you're silhouetting—focusing on the middle may leave the edges soft, and because it all falls to black, you won't see softness anywhere except at the edge.

Be sure that multiple elements of the composition don't converge. Keep edges separate, because the silhouette concept is all about emphasizing form. If things overlap, their shapes combine, which creates visual confusion. Similarly, busy backgrounds will deter from the effect, so minimize depth of field accordingly. For example, clouds in a sunset sky might be distracting if they are in sharp focus; however, if set well out of the depth of field, they become a pleasing blur.

Finally, if you're using a sunrise or sunset as a background, remember to never look at the sun through your lens.

READING THE HISTOGRAM

The histogram is the light meter of the digital world. Essentially, it is a bar chart that illustrates tones, from black on the left to white on the right, with all the mid-tones in between. More often than not, an ideal exposure will be indicated by a histogram reading that begins after (or precisely at) the left edge and ends before (or precisely at) the right.

In most cases, each end of the histogram should slope down to nothing. If the chart ends abruptly at the left edge in sort of a "wall," then you're missing information in the dark areas of the scene—in other words, you're blocking up your shadows, and the image may be underexposed. Conversely, if the chart ends abruptly at the right edge, you're missing information in the bright areas—you're blowing out the highlights, and the image may be overexposed.

An accurate exposure can look different depending on what you're photographing. If the scene is predominantly dark, most of the data will be toward the left; if bright, toward the right. If the scene is mostly moderate tones (such as a large grass meadow), you'll see a bell curve that peaks in the middle.

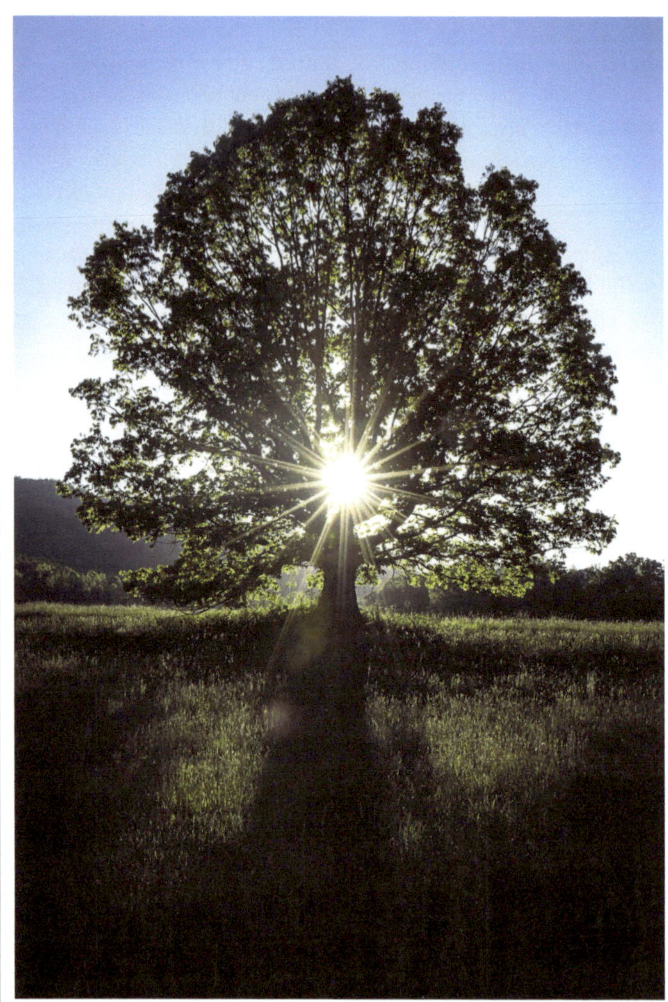

Great Smoky Mountains National Park

SUNBURSTS

A GOOD TECHNIQUE to have on standby is creating sunbursts. They can be made at any time of day (and look great at sunrise and sunset). But more importantly, they can keep you busy when you might otherwise be idle, because they're a productive use of the harsh midday light that photographers usually ignore. In addition to other contexts, sunbursts can be useful for creating compositions in barren landscapes (such as deserts and tundra) and in the monotony of dense forests, because they introduce another element to the scene.

PROCEDURE

Three things are required to create the effect: a wide-angle camera lens with a small aperture, the sun, and something between the two.

Position the camera so the sun is barely visible behind the subject. For example, if you are photographing a tree, you might let the sun appear just behind a branch. Be careful not to let the sun shine unimpeded directly into the lens, which could damage the sensor; and be especially careful not to look at the sun through the lens, which could damage your eye. I find that the best method is to block the sun completely with the subject while I compose and focus, then when I'm ready to shoot, I move the camera slightly to allow the sun to peek out a bit.

When determining the exposure, stop down to at least f/22. The smaller the aperture, the more intense the effect will be. The number of points in the star will correlate with the number of blades in the lens' aperture—an even number of blades correlate one-to-one with the light rays, but an odd number will produce twice as many. Also, modify your expectations with the histogram. This is one type of photograph where highlights will be blown out, and they should be. If you were to try to adjust the exposure to retain the highlights, you would end up with the sun shining in an otherwise dark frame. Expose correctly for the sky, and everything else will fall where it should.

MOONLIT LANDSCAPES

After the sun sets, the world is still being lit, even if only by starlight. When the landscape is under a full moon, it comes alive in a way that day-dwellers rarely see. Colors shift, and light and shadows intermingle, creating a mysterious quality to the terrain. This can all be captured by a camera.

GEAR

While moonlight is indeed light, it's not a lot of light—so you need a good tripod and a remote shutter release. The exposures can be minutes to hours long. Also, the camera needs to have excellent high-ISO capability. Carrying a flashlight is always prudent at night, but under a full moon, once your eyes adjust, you likely won't need any supplemental lighting to avoid bumping into trees. (But you still can use the flashlight for light painting if inspiration nudges you in that direction.)

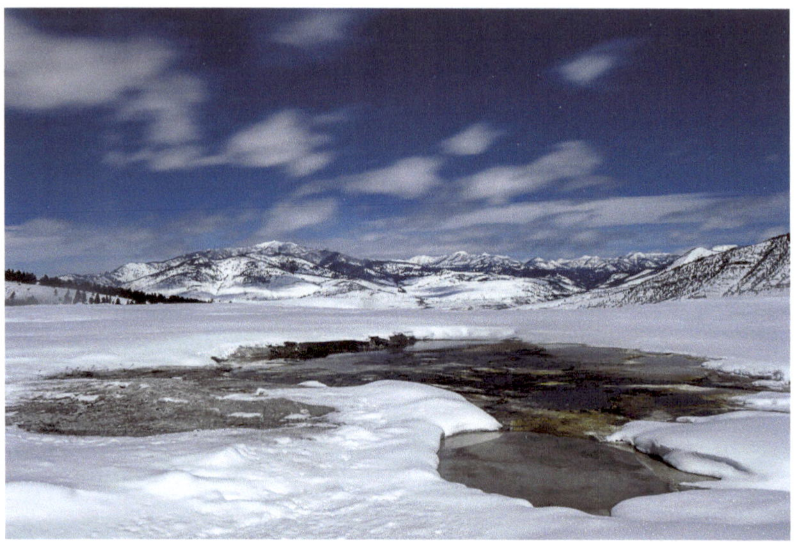

Yellowstone National Park

EXPOSURE

Photographing moonlit landscapes requires a somewhat different approach than daylight photography. You can envision a composition, but it's hard to know exactly what it will look like until you make the actual exposure. Color shifts can be unpredictable, and during long exposures the angle of moonlight changes, filling in shadows.

The exposure is hard to meter. You'll probably find the correct exposure fastest by employing trial-and-error. Just be sure not to use the camera's LCD to judge, because your eyes will be accustomed to the dark, making the display appear to be brighter than it really is. Instead, use the histogram to ensure that all the tones of the scene are being captured—then your exposure will be accurate, or at least close.

FOCUS

Finding the correct focus can be challenging in the dark because … well, you can't see. More importantly, the camera can't see either. Auto-focus will either not work or will not work well, because the camera will not be able detect enough light and contrast. But you can help it. (It's always helping you, so why not return the favor?) Use a compact, high-power flashlight to brighten an object in the composition, then the auto-focus should have something to lock onto. You can also place the lit flashlight in the scene, focus on that, and then remove it. If auto-focus still isn't working, try focusing manually using the camera's live view on the LCD.

An alternative to all these late-night work-arounds is to scout the location during the day. Find your composition, focus the photo, and write down the focal distance indicated on the lens barrel. When you return at night, you'll know exactly how to focus. (You could also tape the focus ring so it won't move before you use it, but I wouldn't do this unless positive that I didn't want to use the lens again before nighttime.)

Finding the right focus can take work, while achieving decent depth of field will just keep you out longer. Every time you stop the lens down, you double the shutter speed, and at night that adds up fast. For example, if the correct shutter speed at f/2.8 is 30 seconds, then the speed at f/16 is 16 minutes. If you are using long-exposure noise reduction (which you should), that becomes 32 minutes. That's a long time to wait to see if you like the result. So consider your depth-of-field needs and solutions carefully. Would you rather wait half an hour for a complete one-frame photograph, or would you prefer to focus-stack four 30-second exposures? Another option is to accept the noise issues inherent in higher ISOs in exchange for smaller apertures at shorter shutter speeds.

Also, when you're ready to open the shutter, use your camera's mirror-lockup feature, if it has one. Doing so will reduce minor vibrations that can diminish apparent sharpness.

CONSIDERATIONS

For best results, photograph moonlit landscapes on a clear night. Also, working under a full moon is best, or at least within a few days of it. During gibbous and lesser phases, the available light is much less intense. Four days after the full moon, the light will be two stops darker; a week after the full moon, the light will be four stops darker. Unless you want to spend literally hours waiting for one exposure to complete, work within two days before and after the full moon.

Also, just like with the sun, the angle of the moon affects aesthetics. If the moon is directly overhead, the light will be more harsh and the shadows will be short; if the moon is closer to the horizon, the light will be softer and the shadows longer.

Finally, experiment with white balance. Start with 3500, which will usually create cool tones that are visually reminiscent of nighttime. In post-production, try lower and higher settings to see how it affects the mood of the photograph.

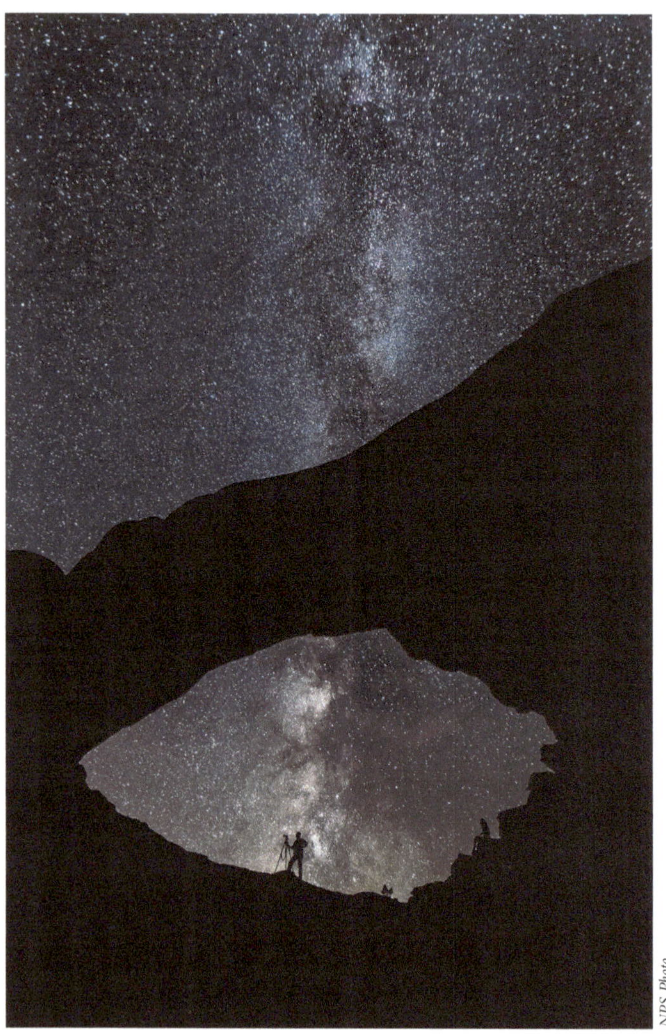

NPS Photo

Arches National Park

STARS

DIGITAL sensors have become so exquisitely capable of recording low light that the once-elite field of astrophotography has become accessible to even casual hobbyists. With a little knowledge and practice, anyone with a decent modern camera and a respectable tripod can spend an evening shooting the stars. And the park system has some great night skies to photograph, because many of their locations are far removed from the lights of big cities. Some of the best examples include

Badlands, Bryce Canyon, Great Basin and Haleakala. Furthermore, Death Valley, Capitol Reef and Big Bend are designated as gold-tier by the International Dark-Sky Association.

GEAR

If you want to get deep into astrophotography—as in, photographing deep space—you need specialized equipment, such as an imaging scope and an equatorial mount. But if you just want to shoot stars over the landscape, you probably already have the gear you need.

Astrophotography is one area where you really do want to use the best camera possible. A full-frame top-quality sensor with excellent low-light capability, wide dynamic range and minimal noise will, quite simply, perform better than the alternatives. Other formats and grades of cameras will work, but the night will test their limitations.

For lenses, any focal length will work okay, but most star-covered landscape photos are made with a wide-angle—especially if you want to freeze the movement of the stars, and if you want to fit the entire Milky Way in the frame. The most important aspects of the lens are quality (use one that is sharp when wide open) and maximum aperture (f/2.8 is ideal).

A tripod is mandatory, as is a remote shutter release. If you plan to be out for a few hours, have some extra charged batteries in the bag, because long exposures will wear them down relatively quickly. You will also need a flashlight to help assemble your gear in the dark—a clip-on cap light is my tool of choice, because it keeps both my hands free. And, incidentally, this is a good time to use a stargazing app.

EXPOSURE

To maintain the appearance of stars as points of light, limit the shutter speed to 20 seconds or less. Longer exposures will record the movement of the stars (well, of the earth, more precisely), resulting in streaks. (Of course, if star trails are the objective, reverse that advice.) Also, 20 seconds is approximate. To determine the precise maximum shutter speed in seconds for a particular lens, divide 400 by the focal length. (Some photographers use 500. Experiment and choose, or just trust my 400.) For example, 25 seconds would be the maximum for a 16mm lens.

Even with a shutter speed that long, the light is just barely adequate. To maximize it, we need to use a wide aperture.

Again, f/2.8 is ideal. Now, with our 16mm-lens example, we are shooting at f/2.8 for 25 seconds.

To finish finding our correct exposure, we need to determine the ISO that will allow a shutter speed equal to or faster than the maximum determined above. Start at 3200, experiment with a few frames, and see what you think works best. Now you have your exposure.

TECHNIQUE

To have both the stars and an earth-based foreground in focus, obviously f/2.8 won't work. But smaller apertures will consume stops of light—we can't just stop down and decrease the shutter speed, because then the stars will blur. Therefore, best practice is to focus-stack two frames: one with the stars in focus, the other with the foreground. (See next page.) Working with two frames also gives you a chance to expose the foreground exactly how you want it, perhaps to open up details, or to play with light painting. You can also photograph the foreground at a lower ISO to minimize noise—noise may not bother you as much in the sky portion of the frame because it can blend in a bit with the stars, but it can spatter onto the dark regions in the rest of the composition. For both frames, if your camera has a long-exposure noise-reduction feature, this is a good opportunity to use it.

POINTERS

The core of the Milky Way is more visible in darker skies—both in terms of location (far, far away from city lights) and lunar phase (new moon is best, or at least when a partial moon is below the horizon). In North America, the Milky Way is visible from late winter to late fall. Between those periods it will move from the southeast sky to the southwest. It is due south in midsummer, which is also when it's highest off the horizon. The best conditions for photography are perfectly clear skies in dry weather. To find the Milky Way in the sky, you could use a stargazing app—but if the conditions are right for photography, you won't need to.

When constructing a composition, waiting for a 20-second exposure to complete so that you can move the camera an inch and try again—over and over—can consume a lot of time. Instead, set the camera to a very high ISO that will allow you to make shorter exposures. The photos will be very noisy, but they're serving only as a temporary reference for your creative

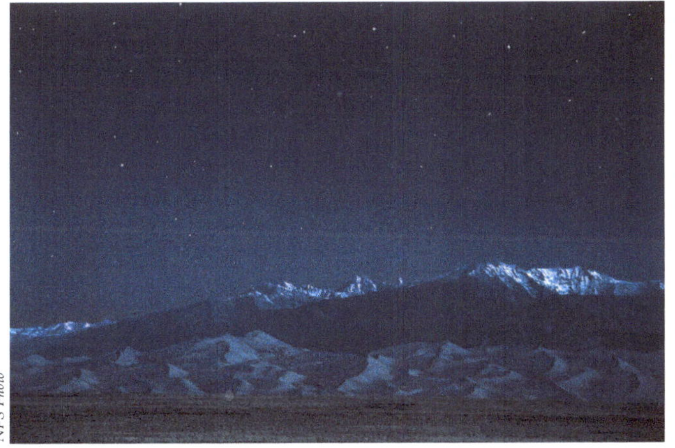
NPS Photo

Great Sand Dunes National Park & Preserve

process. Once your composition is set, return the ISO to where you want it for the final exposure.

Again, attaining accurate focus in the dark is challenging. To ease the issue, refer to the tips mentioned for photographing moonlit landscapes. Another difficult task in the dark is finding your tripod again if you walk too far away from it. Keep the flashlight in your pocket.

IMAGE STACKING

STACKING encompasses two techniques mentioned frequently throughout this book: focus stacking and exposure stacking. Both involve using multiple frames as layers of a final image, and masking the flawed areas to reveal the desired replacement pixels. They achieve different effects, but involve a similar workflow.

FOCUS STACKING

Focus stacking creates the appearance of greater depth of field without having to use a small aperture at initial capture. The impetus could be to avoid long shutter speeds, or to curtail diffraction—or just because the depth of field required for a scene is greater than the capability of the lens. This strategy is common in macro photography, but can be advantageous for landscapes, too.

The procedure in the field is to focus on your foreground and capture the image, then focus on the background and cap-

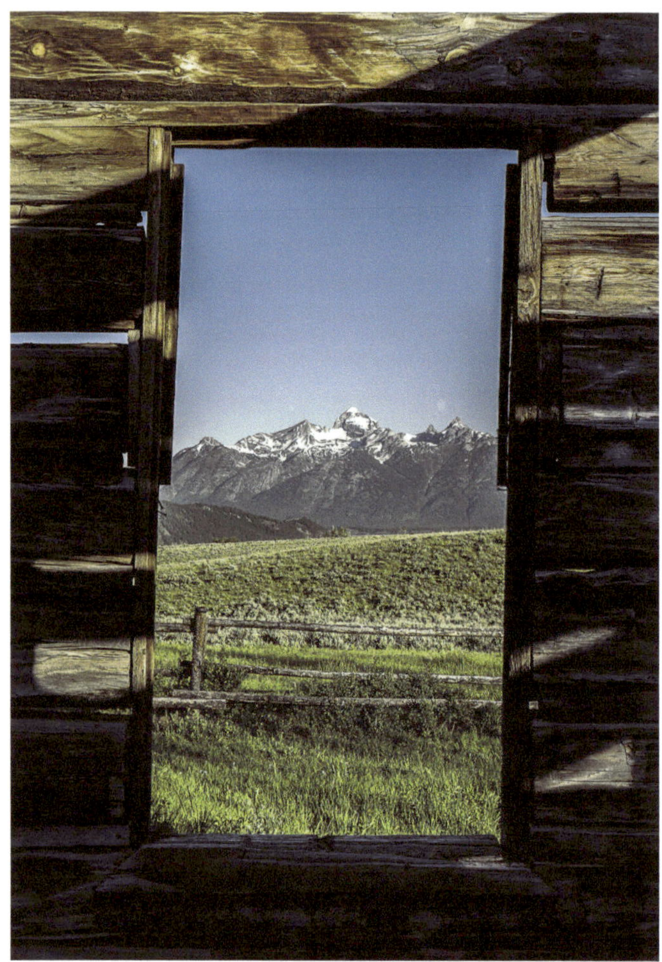

Grand Teton National Park

ture that image. You are not limited to two frames; you could also shoot intermittent frames that focus on different portions of the middle-ground—whatever is needed to produce the overall sharpness you want. If the scene has a distinct foreground, middle-ground and background, then three frames would likely be needed to achieve the sharpest effect. Using a tripod is mandatory to ensure that the individual photos align as closely as possible.

In post-production, you essentially build a file with each frame you photographed as a separate layer, then create layer masks to hide the out-of-focus portions of the image and to reveal the in-focus pixels below. In practice, the process is usually automated. Adobe Photoshop has a "Photomerge" feature that will use selected files to create a layered and masked version. Helicon Focus is specialized software that accomplishes the same task.

EXPOSURE STACKING

If you don't work with a graduated neutral density filter but still want a balanced exposure of an unevenly lit scene, you can stack two exposures to create an evenly lit composite image. This is essentially a very simple HDR technique. And while this does involve more work than using a graduated filter, it provides greater control over the result.

Though scenarios vary, the need for this approach usually arises when the sky requires a different exposure than the landscape—particularly near the beginning or end of the day, and especially when the sun is part of the photograph. Another common application is when photographing a reflection, because reflected light is almost always dimmer than the remainder of the scene. (See page 80.)

In the field, determine the desired exposure for both portions of the frame. The difference will rarely be outside the range of one to three stops. Using a tripod to ensure alignment, shoot two frames, one at each exposure determined beforehand. In the example of a landscape and sky, in one frame the sky will be properly exposed and the ground dark, and in the other the sky will be blown out and the ground properly exposed.

In post-production, create a file with both frames as individual layers. Then, using the gradient tool, apply a mask to the top layer. The mask should cover the improperly exposed portion of the photograph, thereby revealing the properly exposed portion underneath. You might need to undo and retry, using different expanses of gradient and varying angles, before achieving a perfect effect. (This is where the extra control is apparent versus using a graduated filter in the field.) If the delineation between exposures is not a straight line, you can customize the shape of the mask using other tools, such as the paintbrush (which is also not possible with a physical filter).

You can also use HDR software to combine the two exposures. But for such a simple application, doing this manually might actually be easier, and would definitely allow more control. Also, when determining the two initial exposures and editing them later, keep reality in mind. There is a natural tonal relationship between the sky and the earth. If your adjustment reverses that—if the sky ends up being darker than the ground—then the result will not look believable.

Incidentally, you could use just one photograph of the scene and apply a graduated adjustment in post-production to lighten or darken half of the frame. However, because of the light conditions that create problematic exposures, this method will often degrade the adjusted part of the image by introducing noise or blowing out highlights—especially if the exposure difference is more than one stop.

HIGHLIGHT PRIORITY

WHEN PHOTOGRAPHING a scene with very wide dynamic range—with true blacks and extremely bright highlights—common wisdom is to either expose for the middle of the range and deal with the imperfections in post-production, or use an HDR technique.

Here's another option: Use an exposure that will render the highlights as normal, and let everything else fall to black. You might think of this as the converse of creating a silhouette: The properly exposed highlights are the subject, while the negative space is dark.

While sometimes this produces a file that is difficult to pull a useful image out of, other times I have been very pleased with the creative effect. The more successful images are usually those with few mid-tones—that is, scenes dominated by darks and lights, and more of the former than the latter.

TECHNIQUE

The opportunities for this approach are particular: A little light falling on a minimum of the scene, with a lot of dark elements of the composition in shadow. For illustration, here's a real-life example:

I was photographing at Little Long Pond in Acadia and found some lily pads backlit by dappled late-afternoon light, and the surface of the dark water was otherwise in deep shade. First, I put a polarizing filter on the lens to remove the reflections from the pond surface and most of the glare from the floating leaves.

To the naked eye, the pads were very bright—almost too bright to look at, because the reflection was intense and my

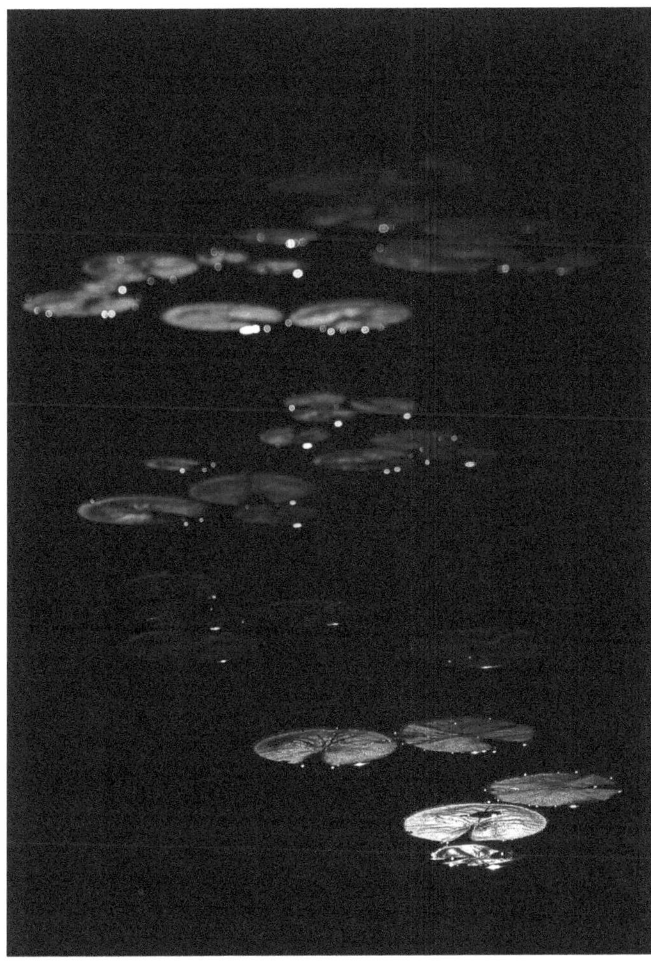

Acadia National Park

eyes were adjusted to the heavy shade. To the camera, they were severely blown-out highlights—the kinds of highlights that continue to be blown out even as you get aggressive with the exposure. I sped up the shutter almost as fast as my camera allows, until the leaves alone were properly exposed. Everything else was rendered a detail-free black. It was exactly what I wanted: a high-concept, low-key image.

I have used this same technique to photograph white ibis in the shadows of Big Cypress National Preserve, sunlit fumaroles at Yellowstone, a backlit forest tree line along the Blue Ridge Parkway, backlit alligators in Everglades, and partially lit flowers just about everywhere.

HDR

THE TECHNIQUE of high dynamic range is perhaps the most divisive issue in contemporary photography. Some people love the creative possibilities it offers. Some like its ability to reconstruct components of light to create a realistic reproduction of a landscape. And some dismiss it as mere photographic trickery that violates the integrity of the medium.

For a long time my philosophy has been that, for my work, I'm not interested in any digital manipulations that could not have been produced with established darkroom techniques in the film age. Therefore, HDR is absolutely acceptable. When we were working with film, dodging, burning, contrast masking, split filter printing and so on were used to create what were, essentially, HDR photographs.

However, HDR is only a tool, and as my dad always said, "Use the right tool for the job." We don't use a screwdriver to pound a nail, nor a lens cloth to wipe dirt from a tripod, nor a telephoto lens as a step stool. (And we certainly don't use a telephoto lens to pound a nail.) For the purpose of nature photography, I use HDR only when it is necessary to emulate a scene the way I see it in person. If the extremes of the light are spread too far apart for a camera sensor to capture, then I need to choose between tools and techniques that can compensate: I could use those extremes of light creatively, perhaps to produce a silhouette, or I could use HDR to record it all and reconstruct it naturally on the computer.

The problems with HDR come from abusing its power, creating images that are so far beyond reality that they look cartoonish. Of course, that's not a "problem" if it's your artistic goal. But most photographers prefer to depict the world somewhat realistically—if not how they really see it in the field, then at least how it could be seen. Therefore, unless you have a good reason otherwise, use HDR judiciously, sparingly and responsibly.

OVERVIEW

The components of an HDR image are multiple frames photographed at different exposures, all with a tripod to ensure that the compositional elements align. One frame should capture all the highlights without losing any of their detail. Another should do the same for the shadows. The remaining frames (however many you decide are appropriate) capture vari-

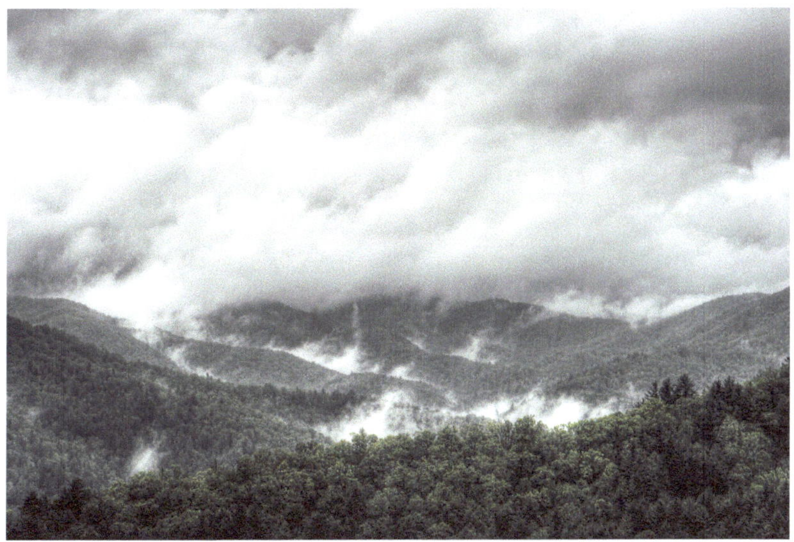

Great Smoky Mountains National Park

ous concentrations of mid-tones. I find that when I employ HDR, I rarely need more than three frames spaced two stops apart (that is, exposures at -2.0, 0.0 and +2.0)—though some photographers prefer five frames at one or two stops apart. Best practice is to change the exposure by adjusting only the shutter speed (while ensuring that it is fast enough to avoid blurring any motion). The reason is that varying exposure by ISO can introduce inconsistent noise, and varying by aperture will introduce inconsistent depth of field.

In post-production, software such as Photoshop, Photomatix or HDR Efx Pro will analyze the set of exposures and create a composite image that—in simple terms—includes the best samples of all the light. Presets are usually available to help you choose among different adjustment algorithms, which can be your final image or your starting point for fine-tuning the photograph. You can also generate a 32-bit composite image that you can manually tone-map in your preferred image-editing software.

CHAPTER 6

THE PARKS

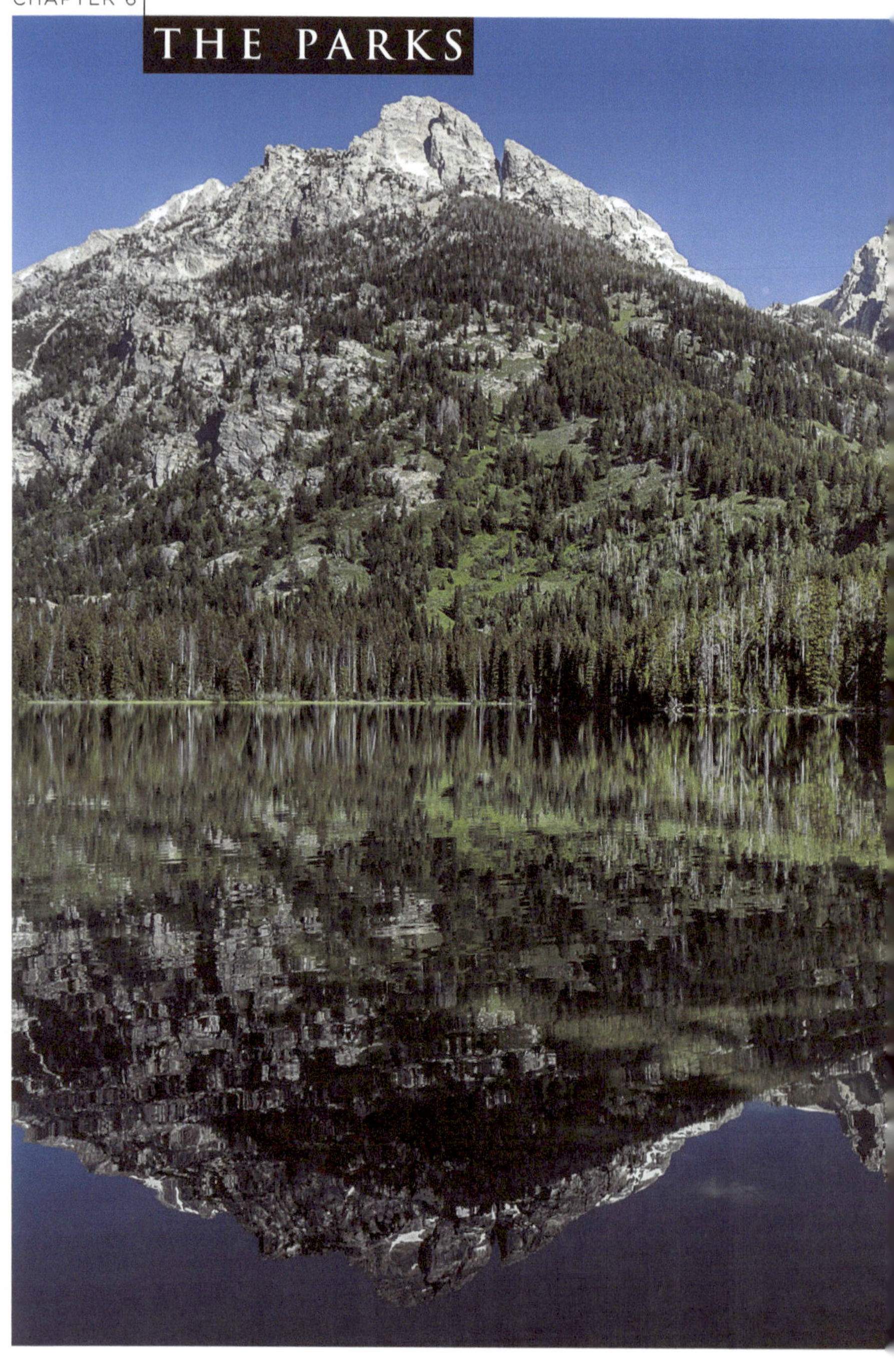

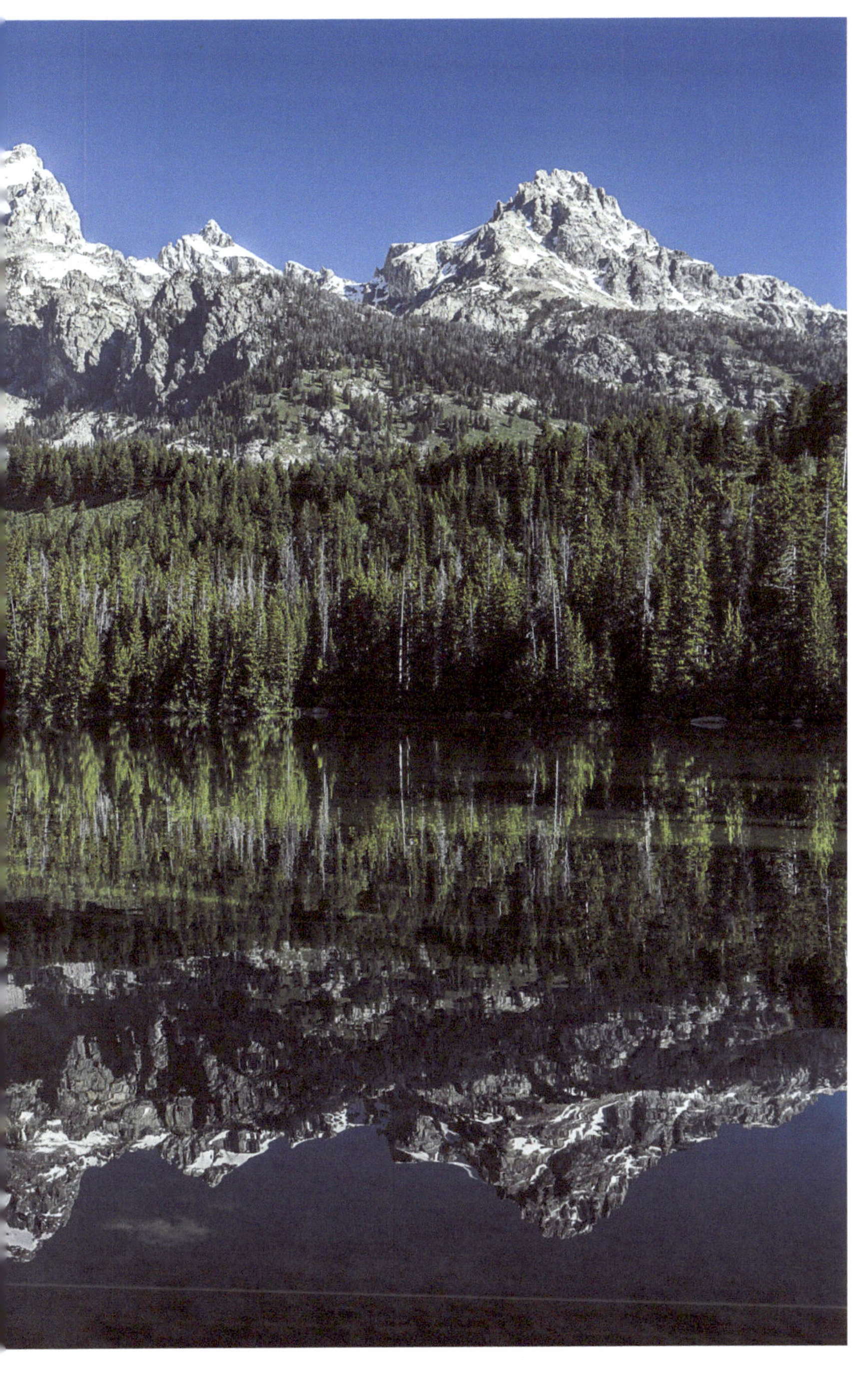

Reflection, Grand Teton National Park

FROM ACADIA TO ZION

I only went out for a walk, and finally concluded to stay out till sundown, for going out, I found, was really going in. – John Muir

THE 59 national parks of the United States preserve some of the country's very best wild and scenic spaces. This is, of course, a boon for photographers, particularly in an era that has seen so much of nature lost to development and progress. The national parks are slices of the world the way it once was, before humans began altering both the landscape and the way other creatures live upon it. From the nature photographer's perspective, the parks allow access to the wild parts of our planet, and to borrow its beauty to exercise our skills, to practice our craft, and to fulfill our creative needs.

The list of cumulative items that the parks protect represents a wide spectrum of subjects for photography and other visual arts. Almost any natural topic you could center a photo project around can be found within the park system. Subjects of earth, air, water, weather, history, archeology, fauna, flora and more await our lenses and our imaginations. They range from below sea level to the highest point in the nation, from deserts to rainforests, from grassland to forest, and they are available at every time of year, and every time of day or night. The seasons change them constantly, as seen in the spring blossoms on the plants, in the autumn color of the trees, in the winter ice on lakes and waterfalls, in the migration routes of enormous herds of mammals.

The following pages relay what each park offers to the photographer. Some parks are similar to others, but they are all distinct—even those that are neighbors. They're not just the same experience with different scenery. Every park has its own dynamic that makes visiting and photographing a unique adventure. I encourage you to explore.

ACADIA NATIONAL PARK

Maine

ACADIA NATIONAL PARK is fringed by Maine's quintessential rocky shores, serving as a final crashing point for waves that have come from distant places in the Atlantic Ocean. The

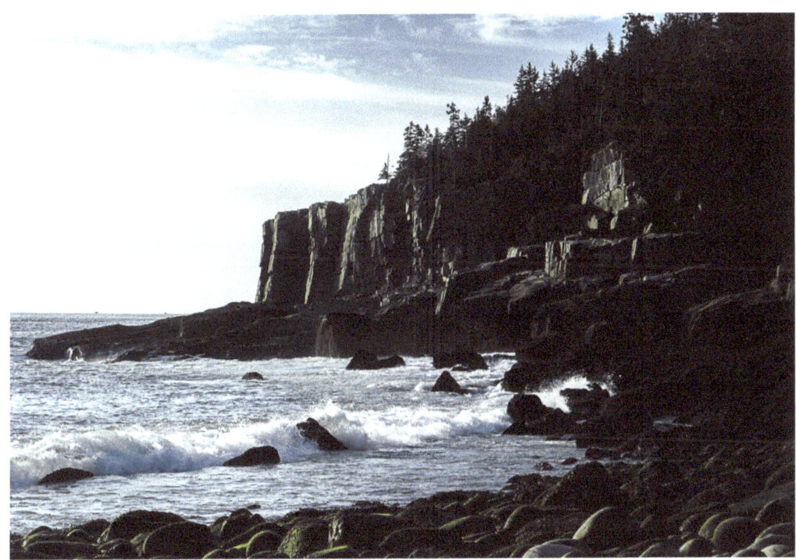

surrounding bays and open water are home to picturesque lighthouses and harbors of lobster boats, as well as seals, whales and sea birds (including the distinctive Atlantic puffin, that while elusive on the mainland, is easily photographed from permanent blinds on Machias Seal Island).

The majority of the park is on Mount Desert Island. With its unrestricted views east and west, you can find great spots for sunrises and sunsets. By climbing to the uppermost peaks, you can access unrestricted views of the coastal islands, and of Somes Sound, the fjord-like body of water that separates the east and west sides of the island. Acadia is large enough to find locations where you feel relatively isolated, but 45 miles of crushed-stone carriage roads make remote spots easy to reach via walking, biking, snow-shoeing, etc. In addition to being useful for transportation, the carriage roads and their 17 bridges (each uniquely designed) are an excellent photography subject, particularly in the forest.

Acadia is a wonderful place for photography any time of year, but perhaps shines best in autumn. New England's famous fall foliage has few better stages than in the region's only national park. Even in below-average years for autumn color, Acadia's varied elevations and ecosystems still offer the photographer something to focus on. Combine that with the fog that's common to the island, with the light rains that are easy to shoot in, with the many aspen and birch groves tucked in the forest, and with the ponds and trails and mountain views over Bar Harbor, and you have a perfect setting for fall photography.

LOCATION TIPS > Photograph the rocky shores at sunrise, especially along the Park Loop Road on the southeast corner of the island, where the waves wash onto the shoreline in the morning light. The top of Cadillac Mountain is also a nice sunrise spot, and offers spectacular views of the surrounding bays and islands. If you see it's obscured by clouds, head up there right away, because that indicates foggy conditions up top. Take a morning or afternoon to walk around the perimeter of Jordan Pond, a body of water big enough to offer a wide variety of photography opportunities but small enough to be pretty from pretty much any spot. Be sure not to ignore the western side of Mount Desert Island, where you'll find quieter trails and mountaintops, stony beaches with a different aesthetic than the aforementioned loop-road shores, and Bass Harbor Head Light, one of Maine's most iconic locations. One of several noncontiguous parts of Acadia is the little-visited Schoodic Peninsula, where you can experience quieter coastal settings, and where you can walk out to Little Moose Island at low tide. At Schoodic Point, large waves crash dramatically into the boulders on shore during storms and high tides.

ARCHES NATIONAL PARK

Utah

At this park in eastern Utah, more than 2,000 rock arches rise from the desert floor in just under 120 square miles, creating the highest concentration of such formations in the world. For a photographer, the opportunities for unique landscape images are plentiful. You can use the red sandstone arches as primary subjects, as elements of a wider environment, or to frame other rock formations or distant mountains.

The park also has features aside from arches. You'll find pinnacles, hoodoos, fins, balanced rocks and sand dunes. In spring, if the rainfall has been adequate, you'll find wildflowers such as sunflowers and lupines, along with blooming prickly pear and grizzly bear cactus. In fall, the weather is pleasant and clear, perfect for photographing distant views.

Arches also boasts fantastic night skies. You can shoot by moonlight, capturing the surreal landscape in surreal light, or you can use the rock formations as geometric silhouettes against a backdrop of star trails. Any season at Arches is photographable, though spring and fall are traditionally considered the best. Summer, though often oppressively hot, can bring strong storms that darken the red rock and fill the sky with dramatic clouds and lightning. Winter brings tourist-free scenery and the occasional snow-dusted landscape.

The possibilities surround you—you don't have to look hard to find them, nor work hard to get to many of them. Your primary responsibility is to pay attention to the light. Know when and where it will be best. Different rock formations will be better photographed in morning than late afternoon, and vice versa. With some you can frame the sunrise, with others the sunset. Some may be in shadow in the morning, and some may cast unwanted shadows in the afternoon.

LOCATION TIPS > The most popular arch for photographers is Delicate Arch, located at the far east side of the park. You can photograph it from a viewpoint about a half-mile away with a telephoto lens, or hike a mile-and-a-half trail to get close with a wide-angle lens. Delicate Arch is also one of the best places to photograph a sunset. If you want to stay near one spot for a day, consider working at The Windows. The loop trail there will present photo opportunities that look great in both morning and late-afternoon light, and you'll be able to play with shadows and backlight in between. One particularly popular strategy at The Windows is to photograph Turret Arch framed by North Window. To get a little water in your images, try Courthouse Wash. During wet periods, water flows into the area and collects in pools that you can use for reflections of rock face, or of the surrounding willow and cottonwood trees. Courthouse Wash is also the most reliable place for spotting wildlife. For even more water, photograph scenes along the Colorado River; you can't access it easily from within Arches, but it skirts 11 miles of the southeast boundary of the park along Route 128.

BADLANDS NATIONAL PARK

South Dakota

STROLL into Badlands in the wrong light, and you're likely to just keep on strolling. It's a harsh and rugged place that would beckon most photographer folk to find somewhere else to be. But when the right light rolls in—when the sun is

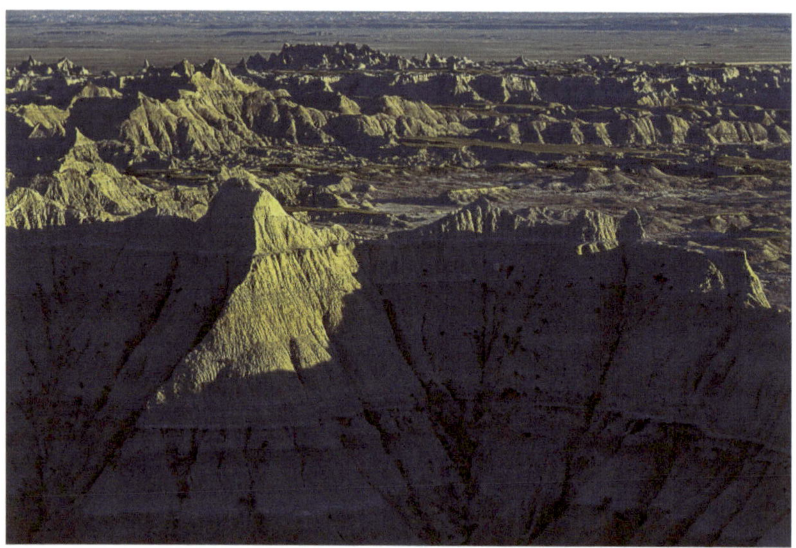

Badlands National Park

getting ready to shine or to vanish into dusk, or when summer storm clouds darken the horizon or fill the overhead sky with dramatic thunderheads—the landscape becomes a complex and beautifully chaotic collection of shadows and light, and of striations of colors from yellow to orange to red, all mixed into the same set of cascading mounds and buttes and bluffs and ridges and cliffs receding into the distance.

The photography opportunities at Badlands are mostly of the landscape variety, and the attraction has much to do with patterns—the patterns that the rock formations create when viewed from different angles, and the patterns formed by light angles changing throughout the day. These are highlighted even more in winter, when snow laces the landscape. The geologic formations themselves have patterns as well, in the colored striations of sedimentary rock layers. You'll find patterns in the cracked, sun-scorched earth, and in close-up views of the rock, and in the lichen that grows on them. A macro lens will not go unused at Badlands. Moreover, one can be especially useful for photographing the wildflowers of spring and early summer, especially in the park's other prominent ecosystem: mixed-grass prairies.

Badlands is also excellent for night photography. Flat, distant horizons permit the moon to illuminate the landscape from just about any angle, and clear, dark skies allow for remarkable views of stars and the Milky Way. If you night-hike a little off the road (or back-country camp), you can use artificial light to illuminate the rock formations as foreground elements.

Wildlife is not a main attraction for the Badlands photographer (though the park does have populations of pronghorn, bison and bighorn sheep). But one critter that does get a good amount of attention is the black-tailed prairie dog. You can find them in various places in large colonies called "towns." Though you do need a long lens to photograph prairie dogs, they're much less skittish here than outside the park.

LOCATION TIPS > Almost all visitors to Badlands tour the North Unit, specifically along the 35-mile Badlands Loop Road. This prime tourist route also happens to be an excellent concentration of the park's best features. Walking a short distance off the pavement will isolate you from just about anyone, but if you really want to ensure solitude, try the less-traveled roads of the park—particularly the primitive road to Sheep Mountain Table in afternoon and at sunset, or Route 40 fringing the western edge of the Stronghold Unit, giving grand views of Red Shirt Table. Castle Trail stretches about five miles along the northern edge of the Badlands Wall, passes through grassland and past an elevated view of Buffalo Gap through a break in the bluffs. For the best chances of photographing wildlife, explore the primitive Sage Creek Rim Road and abutting areas. Along this route you'll find Roberts Prairie Dog Town, one of the largest prairie-dog colonies in the country.

BIG BEND NATIONAL PARK

Texas

BIG BEND is nestled in the far south, hugging the Rio Grande for 118 miles. From the wetlands at river's edge, across the desert, up foothills and into the mountains, photographers will find a variety of topography that provides a broad spectrum of opportunities.

The desert is perhaps best photographed when anything is flowering. A moist spring will bring a wildflower bloom, the most notable of which are the cactus blossoms. From mid- to late-spring, pink, magenta, red, orange and yellow flowers sprout from prickly pear, cholla and the other 40-plus local cactus species. Other interesting blooming subjects include ocotillo, century plants and yucca (a forest of which can be found at the end of the primitive Dagger Flat Auto Trail).

Most photographers who visit Big Bend focus on the landscapes or flowering desert plants, but the park has varied wildlife opportunities, as well. The heat, however, does often persuade the fauna out of view until dawn and dusk. Mule and white-tailed deer, coyotes and javelinas are common, as are bunnies. Bobcats and mountain lions reside in the park, but are not as frequently seen.

Black bears, which had been missing from the vicinity for about four decades, are now living in the Chisos Mountains again—though with a population of only about one- to two-dozen, you may have to work a bit to find and photograph them. Also hard to spot, but prevalent, are lizards; the foot-long collared and leopard lizards might be of most interest to photographers. And due to the variety of ecosystems, Big Bend is also a good spot for bird photography; over 450 species have been recorded, including vultures, golden eagles, hummingbirds, roadrunners, doves, cuckoos, owls and more.

Most people will agree that Big Bend is best photographed in the milder, non-summer seasons: in winter, when the weather is most comfortable and the short days allow for non-drowsy access to spectacular nighttime photography; in spring, when rainfall can inspire dramatic wildflower blooms; and in fall, when autumn color can be found around desert springs, along river beds and in the forests of the Chisos Mountains. And the summer months? They're uncomfortably hot, but also great for storm photography and bright-red sunset skies.

LOCATION TIPS > Drive or hike anywhere in Chisos Basin for excellent landscape opportunities, but especially consider the 14-mile round-trip trail to the South Rim, thought by many to be one of the best views in the national park system. An overnight back-country campout will place you there at best light—twice. The road from Castolon to Santa Elena Canyon is flanked by beautiful views of the Chisos Mountains and the Rio Grande, and ends at one of the park's most striking natural features. Santa Elena Canyon is at once a mesmerizing and frustrating subject. It is beautiful and dramatic, but because of its orientation and steep 1,500-foot walls, the light can be challenging to work with. The entrance is in its best light at first light (especially in early summer), and can be reflected in Terlingua Creek or Rio Bravo when water conditions are right. But don't stop there—hike into the canyon (or raft the Rio Grande) to photograph the interplay of light and shadow inside, particularly in late afternoon.

BISCAYNE NATIONAL PARK

Florida

BISCAYNE IS A UNIQUE PARK because it is almost entirely water-based. Of its 172,000 acres, about 164,000 are beneath the surface of the Atlantic Ocean. Therefore, this park is a destination primarily for the underwater photographer.

A comprehensive visit to Biscayne National Park requires special equipment—most notably a boat, underwater housings for your cameras, and snorkel or scuba gear. You don't have to be an underwater specialist to photograph the park, but you should at least be knowledgeable in safe and responsible boating (or hire a guide who is), be able to read navigation and depth charts (or hire a guide who can), and be either scuba certified or very good at snorkeling. (One caveat: Photographing underwater should probably not be attempted for the first time at the edge of open ocean.)

If you do want to photograph in the wet, then the coral reefs are your best and likely destination. The reefs are home to hundreds of species of fish, plus manatees, sea turtles, sponges and much more. And because coral grows in relatively shallow water—which happens to be quite clear here—you can often photograph the environment without supplemental lighting.

Along the shores of 40-plus islands in the park you can photograph myriad wading birds (egrets, herons, etc.) and the endangered American crocodile. True horizons at all compass points mean you can capture Atlantic sunrises and sunsets from just about anywhere within park boundaries.

LOCATION TIPS > For underwater opportunities, check out the Maritime Heritage Trail, which highlights a series of shipwrecks, some of them accessible with just a snorkel. If you prefer land-based photography, you can still make use of Biscayne, particularly in two spots. The first is Elliott Key, the largest island in the park, which has a one-mile nature trail that loops near the marina, plus a six-mile trail that bisects the island. Together they are a good combination that offers access to ocean views, mangroves and maritime forests. The second is Convoy Point, which is the most accessible place in the park, as it's on the mainland. That's where the Visitor Center is, along with a short trail to the jetty, where you may spot manatees and wading birds, or dolphins swimming near shore. From there you can also kayak and photograph along the mangrove shoreline, the longest such expanse in the United States.

BLACK CANYON OF THE GUNNISON NATIONAL PARK

Colorado

In western Colorado, the Gunnison River has cut through the earth to form a gorge up to a half-mile deep and, in some places, only 1,100 feet wide at the rim. The geologic effect is so dramatic that the National Park Service describes it perfectly as a "vertical wilderness." The north and south rims, though geographically close, are different. Most tourists visit the former, while most photographers prefer the latter due to the light angles and the steeper canyon walls.

The infrastructure for touring the park—the roads, the trails, the human interaction—are at the top. Hiking to the bottom is possible, though precarious, as you don't walk down a trail so much as try not to slide while descending an 1,800-foot gully. Light at the bottom is scarce. Due to the sheer and close nature of the walls, sunlight streams directly into the canyon only at midday—by some accounts, for only half an hour. There is no magic-hour light at the floor. However, the constant shade conditions are ideal for photographing wildflowers and the moving water of the river. Also, when the sun does shine down, it creates sharp juxtapositions of light and shadow that, with some effort, can be creatively photographed.

Several types of birds can be photographed soaring above the canyon thermals. These include peregrine falcons, golden eagles, ravens and turkey vultures. Great horned owls may be observed hunting very small game near dawn or dusk. More laid-back birds in the park include canyon wrens and American dippers, as well as migratory mountain bluebirds that visit in late spring and early summer.

LOCATION TIPS > Most hiking options keep you at either the top or bottom of the canyon; the Oak Flat Trail, however, does dip below the rim for a bit, allowing for a somewhat different angle for photography, and some nice overlooks in general. Chasm View is the narrowest squeeze of the canyon, and therefore one of the better spots for photographing both walls with the river running between them. Cedar Point Nature Trail leads to a view of Painted Wall, one of the more popular photography subjects. It's a 2,250-foot sheer cliff striped with white and pink crystalline rock. It can be framed alone, or with the river on the far-below bottom. Near either the vernal or autumnal equinox, the sun will set directly in line with the canyon and the river, as seen from Cedar Point. At the North Rim, the North Vista Trail is almost a must for the landscape artist. Two points along the route are especially noteworthy: Exclamation Point affords a view into the gorge, looking straight down the flow of the river, and from atop Green Mountain you can photograph an aerial angle of the canyon dropping from the surrounding plateau.

BRYCE CANYON NATIONAL PARK

Utah

At the bottom of this arid basin is a forest unlike anything else on Earth. Everything on this desert floor exists not among a growth of trees, but at the base of thousands of hoodoos—columnar limestone formations that rise to heights of 150 feet. Weather has eroded the Paunsaugunt Plateau into other rock formations as well, including arches, fins and slot canyons.

The best place to view all of this as a whole is from the rim of the six-square-mile Bryce Amphitheater, which overlooks the heart of the park. Sunrise is the best time for photographing Bryce Canyon from the rim, and locals claim the best sunrises are in mid-spring and late summer. The very first light of day shines from over the Aquarius Plateau and flits across the tops of the hoodoos, creating an otherworldly play of light and shadow, accentuating the detail in this land of magnitude. Midday sunlight is far too harsh for such a vertical three-dimensional landscape, and it washes out the colors of the rock. Sunset light, unfortunately, is coming from the wrong direction to be useful in most areas of the park. Rainy weather is also good for photography here, because as the hoodoos get wet, the colors in the rock appear to saturate. Snow brings another aspect to the tableau, frosting the spires and hoodoos.

The other option is to hike into the canyon and photograph the terrain from ground-level. A system of interconnected trails descends from the rim and wanders about the hoodoos. From here you can make better use of the midday sun, as it backlights the rock formations. The canyon floor is a good place to be after dark, too, as Bryce has some of the most celebrated night skies in the park system.

LOCATION TIPS > To photograph the entire scene, you'll want to be along the 11-mile Rim Trail. Sunrise Point is the

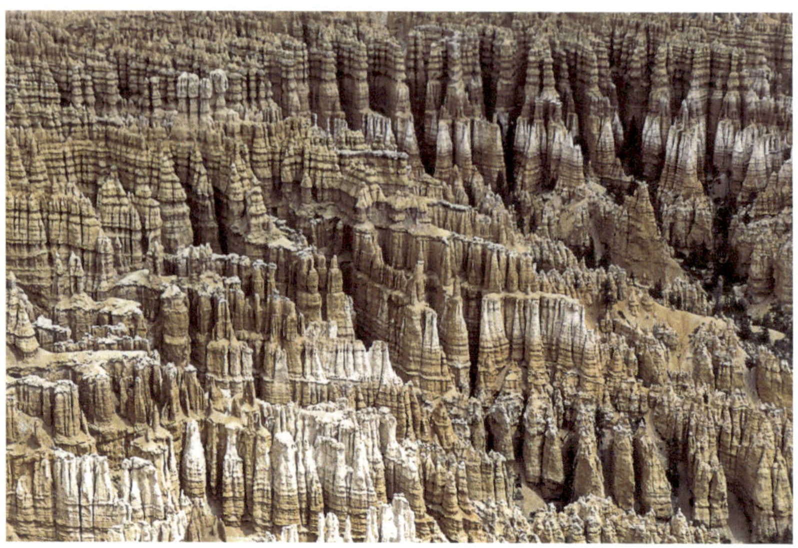

most popular spot for observing the day's first light illuminating the tops of the hoodoos, because it's from here that you'll get the most comprehensive overlook of the canyon. For a closer take on Bryce, you can hike down into the basin and among the geologic wonders it houses. The Navajo Loop Trail is one of the more popular, and it's worth hiking, especially right after sunrise, as it leads you down into the canyon in some of the best light of day. Wall of Windows is a fin located on the Peekaboooo Trail; a number of arches have formed in the rock, all of which will one day further erode into hoodoos. An especially attractive arch in the park is the 125-foot-high Natural Bridge. Viewed from above, this window of red rock frames a green ponderosa pine forest below.

CANYONLANDS NATIONAL PARK

Utah

CANYONLANDS NATIONAL PARK is a landscape photographer's desert paradise. The image-making opportunities are almost all about rock and land formations. The topography was eroded into its current state by the Colorado River and the Green River, which carved this part of the Colorado Plateau into an apparently infinite series of mesas, buttes, gorges, cliffs, spires, arches and (as you might suspect) canyons.

The main park is divided into three sections, with the rivers as the boundaries: Island in the Sky, and the Needles and Maze districts. All three offer unique photography opportunities, as do the rivers.

Island in the Sky is the most accessible region, particularly if you're not hiking and don't have a four-wheel-drive vehicle. The "island" is a thousand-foot-high mesa surrounded by canyons that can be viewed and photographed from many overlooks along the few paved scenic roads, and from the 100-mile primitive (and time-consuming) White Rim Road. The Needles District contains concentrations of colorful banded sandstone spires hundreds of feet tall, creating a unique and beautiful landscape. The Maze is the most remote district, composed of deep canyons and gorges and all sorts of intertwined land features that make land-based navigation difficult.

A fourth region, Horseshoe Canyon, is separate from the main park, located to the west with about eight miles between boundaries. It's known chiefly for rock-face panels of petroglyphs and pictographs believed to be as old as 4,000 years, though it's also home to some impressive sandstone cliffs and cottonwood groves along Barrier Creek.

All these sections of Canyonlands have remote backcountry that is accessible only by four-wheel-drive autos or by well-shoed feet. In fact, that's where most of this park is—in backcountry. Overall, the majority of Canyonlands is not a place for touring by sedan. The good news is that for the patient and prepared, hundreds of miles of primitive roads and hundreds of miles of trails lead to spectacular places.

LOCATION TIPS > Sunrise at Mesa Arch is perhaps the most famous photo opportunity in the park, for good reason: When the sun rises over the distant La Sal Mountains (as seen through the arch), the warm light illuminates the underside of the rock opening along with the towers and rugged landscape in the background. The location can be quite crowded with photographers in the morning—like a paparazzi scrum for a rock formation—even a couple of hours before dawn. If you want to photograph an arch alone, try Angel Arch (considered by many to be the most visually impressive arch in the park), which requires an overnight hiking trip to be there in golden- and blue-hour light. The flat, two-mile Grand View Point Trail snakes along the southern tip of the Island in the Sky mesa, grazing the edges of sheer cliffs and affording vistas of everything that makes this area beautiful. Though known as an excellent sunset location, Grand View has plenty of scenery suitable for any good light. At Pothole Point, depressions in the sandstone ground fill with water after a rain, producing an interesting foreground for landscape images. In Horseshoe Canyon, Great Gallery is considered the must-see spot, with large rock art as high as 12 feet. Clear mornings provide nice warm light directly on the panel, and late-afternoons provide even shade.

CAPITOL REEF NATIONAL PARK

Utah

IN THIS 378-square-mile sliver of land on the Colorado Plateau, rock formations ripple across the earth. The park's centerpiece, the Waterpocket Fold, is essentially a 100-mile buckle in the planet's crust, a geologic phenomenon that, along with millions of years of erosion, created the diverse desert landscape that exists there today. Rock domes, cliffs, gorges, slot canyons, basins, arches, monoliths and more mix and match into seemingly ceaseless combinations of scenery.

The Capitol Reef section of Waterpocket Fold is a subject unto itself. It's a visual marvel of layers of both color and texture, from the multicolored smooth surfaces at the base, to the dark tones of the talus and craggy barrier cliffs, to the light sand-tones of the jagged ridges and soft domes.

Cathedral Valley is north of the most-traveled section of Capitol Reef, but if it were situated far away, it could probably have been the geographical highlight of its own park. A 59-mile primitive road loops through the valley, passing such photogenic features as the smooth and rounded Bentonite Hills, the Mancos Shale badlands, and a long series of awe-inspiring 500-foot monoliths. Much of the topography is formed from reddish-orange sandstone that practically glows in magic-hour light. The landscape is also excellent under moonlit skies, as well as for photographing stars on very dark new-moon nights.

But this park offers so much more than big rocks, particularly in its most conspicuous historical area: Fruita, the remains of a Mormon community founded in the late 1800s. A schoolhouse still stands, as does a rustic barn in an agricultural setting, complete with a split-rail fence, backed by the red cliffs of the Waterpocket Fold. Fruita also contains an orchard of about 3,100 trees, including cherry, apple, walnut and plum. The neat, choreographed nature of the orchard provides an attractive, orderly foreground for the wildness of the rock face behind it. During the periods of spring blooms and fall foliage, the orchards add even more color and life to the landscape, as do the area's cottonwood trees.

LOCATION TIPS > The Hickman Bridge Trail is the conduit for a moderate, mile-long hike to the 125-foot-high Hickman Natural Bridge. The nearby Rim Overlook Trail leads to good views of the Pectol's Pyramid and Navajo Dome rock formations, as well as a fantastic aerial view of Fruita and the surrounding Fremont River Valley. In Lower Cathedral Valley, two of the most striking monoliths are Temple of the Sun and Temple of the Moon. Photographed together in morning light, they make a striking desert scene. Toward the southern end of the park, hike to the Strike Valley Overlook, where you can photograph the S-curve of the Waterpocket Fold receding toward the horizon. To access some attractive slot canyons, invest in the multi-day, 22-mile round-trip hike to the Halls Creek Narrows, where the water has carved a three-mile rut into the Navajo sandstone.

CARLSBAD CAVERNS NATIONAL PARK

New Mexico

At the northern end of the Guadalupe Mountains, the peaks reach 6,500 feet into the Chihuahuan Desert sky. But 750 feet beneath those mountains is what prompted the creation of Carlsbad Caverns National Park: one of the largest and most exquisite cave systems in the world.

The park contains 119 known limestone caves, and a paved underground trail allows visitors to tour about three miles of them. The interior is full of geologic formations small and huge, such as stalactites, stalagmites, helictites, columns, boulders, pits and domes.

Carlsbad Caverns has an outside, too. Some forestland dots the mountains, which are interspersed with some canyons—but the above-ground part of the park is composed of primarily grassland and desert shrubland. Twenty-six species of cactus grow in the park, including the blossoming prickly pear and claret cup, as well as strawberry hedgehog and Torrey yuccas.

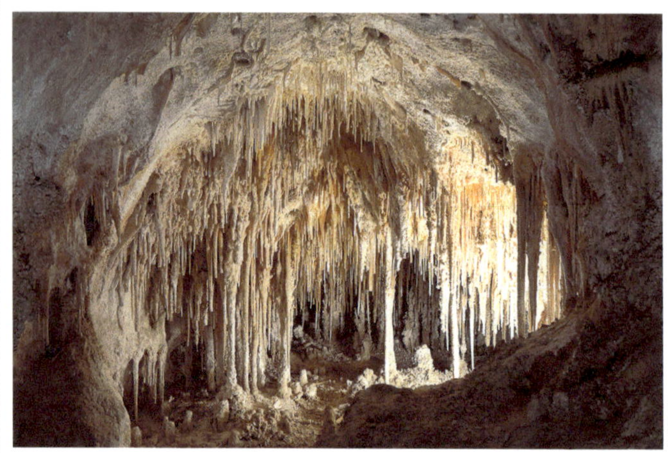

NPS Photo

Carlsbad Caverns National Park

Other wildflowers are found in the park, too, including Lindheimer's morning glory and orange butterflyweed.

Wildlife at Carlsbad Caverns is representative of the standard Chihuahuan Desert population, including javelinas, mule deer, coyotes and great horned owls, and whiptail, spiny and horned lizards. In the forest you might spot an occasional elk, in the grassland a sporadic pronghorn. But the undisputed mammalian stars of the park are the Mexican free-tailed bats. From mid-April through October (but peaking in midsummer), the bats make a mass exodus from the cave entrance every evening at sunset, at a rate of as many as 5,000 per minute. It's a daily extravaganza—a major event in the park's schedule. Photographing them requires a special-use permit, but the logistics are worth the trouble.

LOCATION TIPS > The 8.2-acre Big Room is perhaps the most photography-friendly cave in the entire park system. Not only is it huge, beautiful and creatively lit, but using a tripod is permitted, even on self-guided tours. A 1.25-mile trail circumnavigates the room. Moreover, underground photography is a perfect activity for creatively whiling away the midday's harsh sunlight. For landscape photography, travel the Walnut Canyon Desert Drive at either the beginning or the end of the day. The 9.5-mile gravel road affords views of Rattlesnake Canyon and upper Walnut Canyon, and plenty of general desert scenery. Noncontiguous Rattlesnake Springs is a 24-acre wetland oasis famous for the wide assortment of birds it attracts, and is designated by the National Audubon Society as an Important Bird Area.

CHANNEL ISLANDS NATIONAL PARK
California

SITUATED a dozen miles off the southern California coast, five rugged islands collectively form Channel Islands National Park, home to pristine coastline, beautiful seascapes, and rare and abundant wildlife, all surrounded by horizons of Pacific Ocean. The landscape is more of a seascape, as most of what you'd want to photograph will include water. The shoreline is a mix of sand beaches, dramatic sea cliffs, caves, lagoons and natural bridges. Tide pools dot the shores at low tide, and on overcast days are prime locations (many consider them the best in California) for photographing anemones, starfish, urchins, barnacles, mussels and more.

The flora of the park is most vibrant in winter and early spring, when rain rejuvenates the plants of the islands after months of being beaten brown by unrelenting sunlight. The 10-foot-high sunflower trees are a great photography subject, as are the expanses of goldfields in spring.

Channel Islands is not considered a wildlife park in the same vein as Yellowstone or Denali, but it does offer the photographer some unique fauna opportunities. Due to their isolated location, the islands have nurtured several indigenous species. Most famous is the island fox, a housecat-size subspecies that is not difficult to find and photograph. Other examples include the island spotted skunk, the Baja California treefrog and several types of lizard.

The park is an important breeding ground for California sea lions and northern fur, northern elephant and harbor seals, all of which can be seen and photographed at various times of year. Other mammals frequent to Channel Islands are several species of whale. From a private or commercial boat you can photograph gray whales in winter, and blue and humpback whales in summer—and sometimes minke whales, orcas and others—performing traditional whale activities such as swimming, spouting and breaching.

Channel Islands is a superb location for avian photography, as the park is a nesting ground or stopover for hundreds of species of land birds, shorebirds and seabirds. Bald and golden eagles, barn owls, meadowlarks, brown pelicans, western gulls, cormorants, black oyster-catchers, plovers, sanderlings, and many more can be photographed, as well as several endemic species, including the island scrub jay on Santa Cruz Island.

Underwater photographers, whether snorkel- or scuba-assisted, will find a multitude of clear, life-filled sites to explore. The waters around the island are famous for kelp forests and the wildlife that inhabits them, including such photogenic subjects as sunflower stars, giant sea bass, California spiny lobsters, garibaldi, sea urchins and moray eels. Photographers and divers also enjoy access to submerged shipwrecks, the most renowned of which is the S.S. Winfield Scott, a sidewheel steamer that sank in 1853. That loss led to the eventual construction of the Anacapa Island Lighthouse, a 39-foot white tower on the eastern point of the island.

LOCATION TIPS > Inspiration Point overlooks the narrow Anacapa Island curving its way through the ocean toward the horizon. It's a fantastic photography location at either the beginning or end of day, accessible via an easy 1.5-mile hike from the island's visitor center. Point Bennett on San Miguel Island supports one of the largest populations of seals and sea lions in the world, though to see it you'll have to hike 16 miles round-trip, partly with a ranger. May and June see the highest concentration of pinnipeds, but you can find a healthy number of them anytime. Another intriguing spot along the same hike is the Caliche Forest, a geologic concentration of caliche-covered snags that stand a few feet higher than the surrounding sand. The Sea Lion Rookery at Santa Barbara Island is an excellent spot to photograph sea lions, both on land and under water.

CONGAREE NATIONAL PARK

South Carolina

FLANKED by the Congaree River on the south and the Wateree River on the east, Congaree National Park preserves 41 square miles of near-virgin bottomland hardwood forest towering over vast floodplains. The forest is often swamp-like and the tree canopy is high, so most of the scenery is best photographed (generally speaking) in fog, in light rain, under the diffused light of overcast skies, or when clouds are blocking the midday sun. But as much as this park is about the trees, it's also about the water that floods the forest roughly 10 times per year. The two rivers and countless lakes, ponds, creeks and streams provide ample opportunity for photographing reflections of the vibrant flora above the waterline.

The fact that the forest is old-growth is not trivial. Centuries of overlapping life exist here, meaning that every brook and cranny has something calling it home; every detail of this place has more detail within, so photographing here is very much about making composition out of chaos. Towering over all are trees of record heights—some of the tallest trees in the eastern U.S., some of which stand over 150 feet high. Moreover, all of that life is diverse—within Congaree reside over 300 species of animals (not including bugs) and over 80 species of trees (including loblolly pines, sweet gums, laurel oaks, hickories and sycamores).

Though not known for its wildlife, the park is home to some species of interest to photographers, including white-tailed deer, river otters, turtles, raccoons, marsh rabbits, wild hogs, frogs, red-shouldered hawks, barred owls, herons, wood ducks and woodpeckers. Several species of spiders are scary enough to be dynamic photo subjects, and if you want to photograph snakes, you can rest easy (or not) knowing they won't be scarce. Most of the wildlife is easiest to spot near the lakes and along Cedar Creek.

Congaree is not a park you drive through. The one park road—called National Park Road—is as utilitarian as its name: It gets you to the visitor center and to the primary trailheads. Aside from that, you'll be on foot or in a boat. Over 25 miles of trails thread the park, ranging in length from three-quarters of a mile to 11 miles, all with hardly any elevation gain. You may also canoe or kayak, which is perhaps the ideal way to photograph the heart of Congaree.

LOCATION TIPS > The easiest, most accessible and most popular trail is the Boardwalk Loop, but it should not be disregarded, as either a conduit or a subject. Its two sections measure a little over a mile each. The Low Boardwalk hovers over swampy flats of bald cypress and water tupelo—if you want to photograph cypress knees, this is a good place to be. The Elevated Boardwalk tours a forest of bottomland hardwoods and upland pines, and ends at Weston Lake, a nice spot to find wildlife, captivating reflections and fall color. The Weston Lake Loop Trail meanders through old-growth forest, along a cypress-tupelo slough and then aside Cedar Creek, which bisects the park from east to west. For an even longer tour of this waterway, paddle the Cedar Creek Canoe Trail, which extends from the northwest corner of the park to the waterway's juncture with the Congaree River. At the visitor center, purchase a copy of John Cely's map, which traces the old logging roads that you can use for hiking to spots not marked on the official park map.

CRATER LAKE NATIONAL PARK

Oregon

THE DEEPEST LAKE in the U.S. and one of the clearest in the world, Crater Lake fills the caldera of Mount Mazama, a defunct volcano in the Cascade Range. Twenty-six miles of rim encircles the vivid, blue water with cliffs that rise up to 2,000 feet above the shore.

Wizard Island, on the west side of the lake, is a cinder cone ascending 760 feet above the waterline. It's one of the defining features of the landscape, as it makes images of the lake much more visually interesting than a blank expanse of water would, and also helps to provide a sense of scale. Phantom Ship, the only other island in the lake, is an aesthetically unique stand of volcanic spires that rise almost 200 feet above the water.

Aside from the lake, the surrounding topography holds various additional photographic subject matter. Wildlife is abundant, including bald eagles, Stellar's jays, Roosevelt elk, mule deer, red fox, marten, porcupines, snowshoe hares and the occasional black bear. Summer wildflowers can be found throughout the park, particularly on the aptly named Castle Crest Wildflower Trail.

And as can be expected in the Cascade Mountains, the park is home to a few waterfalls (along with plenty of cascades during the spring melt). Videa Falls is the most notable. A 200-foot cascade through gray volcanic rock, it is rather photogenic from the right angles, is long enough to creatively home in on different segments, and is right next to Rim Road. Conversely, Plaikni Falls is relatively short, is located a mile into the wilderness, and is nestled in jagged bluffs, surrounded by forest, moss and wildflowers.

Crater Lake is an excellent location for winter photography. It receives about 44 feet of snowfall annually, but the lake hardly ever freezes over. A limited amount of snowmobiling is allowed, but you can have nearly full access to the park on snowshoes or cross-country skis (weather-permitting). The winter skies can be remarkably blue; snow on the surrounding mountains, the crater rim and Wizard Island enhances an already beautiful landscape. The backcountry is also fertile ground for the winter photographer, with snow-filled flats, snow-covered trees, snow-laced forests and the leading lines of extensive drifts remaining undisturbed for long periods due to infrequent passerby.

LOCATION TIPS > In warmer months, the 33-mile Rim Road is a (relatively) quick way to scout and access vantages for lakescape photos. Countless spots accessible from the road and from Rim Trail (particularly on the west side) surround the caldera, providing different angles suitable for different weather and light conditions. Mount Scott Trail leads through a pumice field, into and out of a hemlock forest, past wildflowers and up the side of the mountain, all while revealing alpine scenery and views of the lake (particularly in morning light). The Cleetwood Cove Trail provides the only legal access to the lakeshore, and also leads to the dock for the seasonal tour boat; both are the only options for water-level photography. The Pinnacles are 100-foot rock formations formed by ancient volcanic activity. They're easy to reach, and a trail provides various angles for photographing them.

CUYAHOGA VALLEY NATIONAL PARK

Ohio

IN RECENT TIMES, most new national parks were "upgraded" from the status of national monument. Conversely, Cuyahoga Valley National Park was upgraded from being a national recreation area. The difference is apparent: This park is more about things to do than things to see. But that doesn't mean it's a substandard photography location; rather, it means that there are some subjects to photograph here that don't exist in other national parks—golf and skiing, for example, or working farms and farm markets. Still, nature photographers need not fret; the park has plenty of fauna, flora, landscapes and seasonal variety to keep anyone's camera indefinitely busy. Forests, rolling hills, river scenes, gorges, waterfalls and wildflowers all await, as do more than 100 small lakes and ponds and over 1,500 designated wetlands.

The Cuyahoga Valley Scenic Railroad is one of the park's better known cultural attractions. Built in 1880 primarily to transport coal and other freight, it now operates as a conduit for tourist excursions. It also serves the photographer well. You can flag the train at a boarding station and use it for quick access between trailheads or other destinations—for instance, you could park your car, roam on a long one-way hiking or cycling trip, then just ride the railroad back. The train also serves as a photographic subject—it's visible from many locations as it ribbons its way through the heart of the park, ambling through valleys and pine stands, through meadows and marshes, over high trestle bridges and along the banks of the Cuyahoga River.

One of Cuyahoga Valley's trademark natural features is its collection of about 70 waterfalls—an impressive total, considering that the park is one of the system's smallest. Brandywine Falls is the most renowned, is easy to hike to, and is a particularly photogenic spot in the fall when the surrounding red maples turn … well, red. While many waterfalls are best photographed when the flow is high, Brandywine is arguably more attractive when lower flow rates create a bridal-veil effect. But despite Brandywine's popularity, a prettier waterfall experience is found along Spring Creek, home of Blue Hen Falls and Buttermilk Falls. (The latter is not on the park map, but can be found a short distance downstream from Blue Hen.) Neither is as high as Brandywine, but both are in more intimate and aesthetic settings. Bridal Veil Falls and Great Falls are also notable, as is Linda Falls after a rainfall.

LOCATION TIPS > Beaver Marsh is a great spot for photographing aquatic wildlife, otters, waterfowl, songbirds, sweet-scented water lilies and, of course, beavers. The marsh is a beautiful and ethereal spot on a misty morning, when the sun burns through to reveal the still waters and the snags that stand among them. Covered bridges are a rare sight in national parks, but Cuyahoga Valley is home to one originally built in the late 1800s. Everett Covered Bridge—truss-patterned and painted bright red with white trim—crosses Furnace Run in the southwest section of the park. The river has plenty of rocks to use as foreground elements, which create rapids in the right conditions. The multi-arched Brecksville-Northfield High Level Bridge spans the Cuyahoga River and the scenic railroad; the three can be photographed together from the east side of the river or from the downstream Station Road Bridge. For reflections of autumn color on a calm day, try Sylvan Pond. Also explore Indigo Lake, which is known locally as a good birding site.

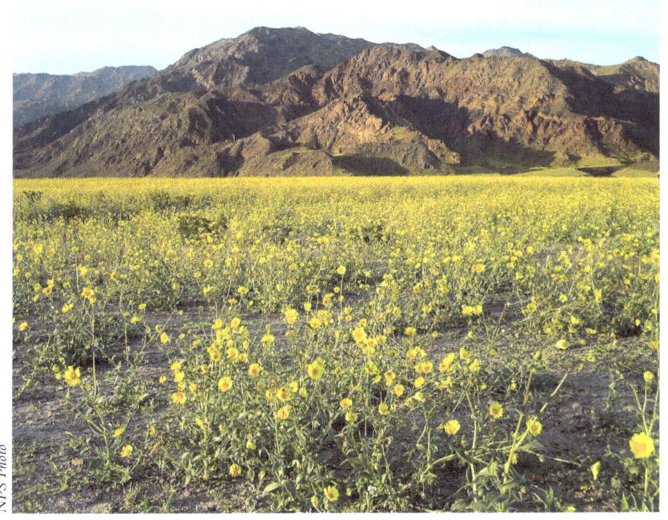

NPS Photo

Death Valley National Park

DEATH VALLEY NATIONAL PARK

California / Nevada

DEATH VALLEY claims a lot of superlatives in the national park system. It's the hottest park, the driest park and the lowest in elevation. It also might be the best for desert landscape photography.

Photographers are drawn here for many reasons, including the rolling sand dunes, the jagged mountains, the geometric patterns of salt flats, rocks that move, and more. Death Valley is also one of the premier parks for night photography. Many of the landscapes are ideal to shoot under moonlight, and the night skies are so pristine that the International Dark-Sky Association has designated it a gold-tier dark-sky park.

The bad news about shooting in Death Valley is that the weather is almost always dry and cloudless, so you won't often see dynamic colors in the sunrise and sunset skies, and you won't often be shooting under diffused light during daytime. The good news is you can feel relatively certain that you'll know what the weather and quality of light will be every morning, every day and every night, so you can scout locations knowing that you'll almost surely be able to work the way you envision.

Another fortunate feature of Death Valley is the variety of opportunities that accompany its size; as the largest national park in the contiguous United States, the topography varies in texture and aesthetic. In February or March, those landscapes might even be decorated with wildflower displays that can range from pedestrian to spectacular depending on the timing of the winter rainfall.

One unique location in Death Valley sees weather combinations so extreme that they produce a phenomenon that appears paranormal. In the depths of The Racetrack, in a remote valley between the Cottonwood Mountains and Last Chance Range, a dry lakebed features windblown rocks and boulders that have left depressed paths in the desert floor. The result is an opportunity for peculiar images of rocks that have clearly traveled long distances with no apparent means of movement.

LOCATION TIPS > If you had to name an iconic scene in Death Valley, it would probably be the sand dunes. But interestingly, they aren't a dominant feature of the park. Where you do find them, though, they're a great photographic subject, serving as foregrounds for wide and distant desert vistas, or for images of patterns and light. The most famous are the Mesquite Flat Dunes near Stovepipe Wells; another prominent, albeit less-visited, spot is Eureka Dunes in the north end of the park. Despite its reputation for being so dry, Death Valley does contain an interesting aquatic feature: Badwater, a shallow spring-fed pool of saltwater that provides morning reflections of the Panamint Range. For multi-layered landscapes, stop at Zabriskie Point and wander around with a camera and tripod, especially in sunrise light. To photograph the sunrise itself, check out Dante's View, a terrace on Coffin Peak that overlooks the valley.

DENALI NATIONAL PARK & PRESERVE

Alaska

HOME TO Mount McKinley, the highest peak in North America, Denali is perhaps Alaska's most famous park. It is one of the state's top tourist destinations, despite its distant location and the ban on private motor vehicles from all but 15 miles of its only thoroughfare.

Denali is a six-million-acre subarctic landscape that is practically impossible to explore comprehensively. Almost the entire park is accessible only to hikers, climbers and fliers. One hundred sixty miles of the Alaska Range divides the northern and southern halves, the latter of which is raw and remote mountain wilderness. Unless your backcountry chops are top-notch, views of the southern park will likely come only from the heights of an aircraft. That said, Denali is an excellent place for aerial photography. Planes and pilots can be found in the outlying towns, and commercial air tours originate from as far away as Anchorage and Fairbanks. Some will even land you on a glacier or mountain lake.

Most visitors, however, base their trips from Denali Park Road. Though you can drive only 15 miles in, you can bike or hike the remaining 77 miles. Alternatively, and most popularly, you can use the well-developed bus system to shuttle you anywhere the road goes. If you see a spot you'd like to explore, just alert the driver and you will be let off in the middle of anywhere.

And that's a good place to start. As with most parks, to see and photograph the best views, you want to get off the pavement and onto the earth. The challenge here is that Denali does not have a developed trail system. (And, for the record, the pavement here is actually gravel.) However, you can hike pretty much anywhere you like. Want to wander across the tundra, traverse that river and disappear into the trees toward that mountain? Go ahead. Awaiting are boreal forests, snow-covered mountains, sheer cliffs, glaciers, rivers, lakes and more. Amongst all that is some of the wildest wildlife in the U.S. Spend a little time wandering Denali and you'll likely find grizzlies, caribou, Dall sheep, moose, coyotes, fox, golden eagles, etc.

LOCATION TIPS > Eielson Visitor Center is known for its incredible views of Mount McKinley—when it's visible. The mountain is locally famous for being so large that it creates its own weather, which 80 percent of the time obscures it from view. So if you want to photograph the park's native-language namesake, you will best your odds by staying at least five days. Reflection Pond is a nice spot to photograph McKinley on the horizon and (as the name suggests) reflecting in the calm morning water. The area of Wonder Lake is good for bird photography, with its expanse of bogs and ponds, and is also a good spot to look for larger wildlife at dawn and dusk (which in midsummer are virtually the same thing). For views of the Alaska Range, try Polychrome Pass, home to multicolored volcanic rock bluffs, wildflowers and myriad small mammals.

DRY TORTUGAS NATIONAL PARK
Florida

LIKE BISCAYNE, Dry Tortugas National Park is made mostly of water. Of its 100 square miles, only about 100 acres are dry land, composed of seven small islands about 70 miles due west of Key West. More than 90 percent of that land mass is made up of the three largest islands: Loggerhead Key, Garden Key and Bush Key. This remote Gulf of Mexico location offers true horizons for sunsets and sunrises, and dark night skies in between.

The central feature is Fort Jefferson, a hexagonal, 19th century island fortress with a minor but important place in U.S. history. The site is a worthy subject for historical photography, and the construction also lends itself nicely to detail compositions of masonry and ironwork, and for the patterns of repeating brick archways inside the perimeter wall. Garden Key Lighthouse, a relatively short, iron tower, oversees the fort.

For the avian photographer, Dry Tortugas is notable for its bird population, consisting of mostly migratory species that rest or nest on the islands during late winter and the first half of spring, and in early- to mid-fall. Relatively predictable subjects include brown noddies, gulls, pelicans, cormorants, belted kingfishers, kingbirds, swallows, nighthawks, boobies, orioles and a slew of warblers. And particularly noteworthy are sooty terns and magnificent frigatebirds (both beautiful to photograph), as their only nesting grounds in the United States are located in the park.

But perhaps the finest photography opportunity is under water. Sandy shoals, sea-grass beds and some of the finest coral reefs in the country surround the keys and dot the seafloor. The clear water is home to a variety of sea life, including nurse sharks, squid, angelfish, parrot fish, triggerfish, damselfish, grouper and smallmouth grunts. Dry Tortugas is also home to its namesake animal: (in English) large sea turtles. While snorkeling or scuba diving, you may have the chance to photograph loggerhead, green, leatherback, hawksbill and Kemp's ridley turtles swimming alongside you.

LOCATION TIPS > The 30-acre Loggerhead Key is three miles west of Fort Jefferson and can be accessed via kayak by prepared, experienced paddlers on a calm day (or, of course, via a larger vessel). The island is home to Dry Tortugas Lighthouse, a 150-foot brick tower surrounded by palm trees, sand dunes and open water. Under that water are the Little Africa Reef and the relatively nearby Windjammer shipwreck, both fine locations for underwater photography. For a good coral reef that's easier to access, try the shallow-water patch reefs 50 yards west of Fort Jefferson. Bush Key—a landscape of mangrove, bay cedar and sea grape—is excellent for bird photography; it's off-limits to foot traffic during nesting season, but you can still photograph with a long lens from a kayak, canoe or boat.

EVERGLADES NATIONAL PARK

Florida

THE EVERGLADES has a mystique about it that extends beyond the community of park aficionados. It's certainly not the only swamp in the country, but for most of the American public, if you mention alligators and snakes and flamingos, it's the Everglades that comes to mind. Those who know the park well will agree that the gators and such are the bona fide face of the local environment, but they'll also tell you that the magic of the Everglades extends far beyond those subjects. (The caveat is that flamingos hardly ever visit. But you're likely to find every other North American wading bird at some time of the year.)

This is one park where you'll need to choose your season carefully. To photograph birds—a lot of birds—plan for late winter. If focusing on flowers, then early spring. If you want to shoot storms and sit in nature's sweat lodge and feed clouds of mosquitos, then summer. Most photographers visit between January and April.

Everglades is a perfect example of a park where sticking to the paved road will shield you from a majority of what's available to see and photograph. Only two major roads service the Everglades, the main park road and the Tamiami Trail (which only skirts the northern boundary before traversing Big Cypress National Preserve—a side-trip location that should not be missed). To be exposed to the rest of the landscape, you'll have to hike, kayak or canoe. (Despite the iconic mental images people have of airboats in the Everglades, they're actually prohibited within park boundaries.)

Once you're out of the car, you'll be exposed to one of the wildest environments in the U.S. You'll be surrounded by water (ponds, estuaries, marshes and seas) and wildlife

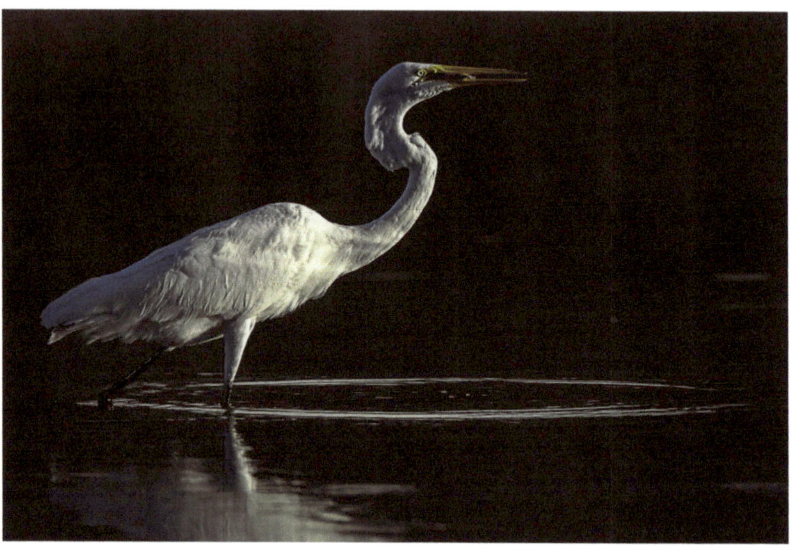

Everglades National Park

(especially birds and reptiles). You can explore shoreline, see miles across the flat sawgrass marshes, or immerse yourself in mini forests on tree islands. And due to the unimpeded views of eastern and western horizons, combined with the year-round warmth and humidity, you'll see fantastic sunrises and sunsets. The one difficult aspect of working the Everglades is the challenge of landscape photography in such a flat environment—you can test your creativity by trying to take on the landscape anyway, or you can fill your days with the multitude of other opportunities in the park.

LOCATION TIPS > The Anhinga Trail is one of the best spots for bird photography in the national park system. The conditions are so perfect for feeding that scores of wading birds frequent the area despite the fact that humans frequent it, too. The trail is also a good spot to photograph alligators up close from the relative safety of the boardwalk. Drive to the end of the main park road and visit Flamingo, where you can circle the trail around Eco Pond for more birding opportunities, and look near the marina for the endangered American crocodile. A 15-mile round-trip tram road circles through Shark Valley, the heart of Everglade's river of grass. But don't take the shuttle—bike or hike. You'll find wildlife, panoramic views and a 65-foot observation tower at the halfway mark. The tower is a good vantage point for photographing sunrises or sunsets, if while getting to or fro you don't mind traveling seven miles past snakes and alligators in the dark. If you're eager for a rugged, weeklong-plus trip through raw nature, consider canoeing or kayaking the Wilderness Waterway, a 99-mile water trail along the unsettled western side of the park.

GATES OF THE ARCTIC NATIONAL PARK & PRESERVE

Alaska

GATES OF THE ARCTIC is the northernmost of the U.S. national parks, and is a preserved section of the Brooks Range, the northernmost chain in the Rocky Mountains. The park is so far north that it lies entirely within the Arctic Circle.

Why is Gates of the Arctic's northerliness so important? Because it correlates to what might be the best light for landscape photography in the entire park system. At these high latitudes, the sun hovers near the horizon for very long periods of time; in other words, golden-hour light here endures significantly longer than in the middle and low latitudes. In midsummer, the warm light after sunrise and before sunset can each last for hours. Even in winter the conditions are amazing for photography; daytime might last only a few hours, but all of it will be with the sun very low in the sky, illuminating the landscape with crisp, clean, beautiful light.

All of that sunshine falls on one of the least tamed landscapes in the country. No roads enter Gates of the Arctic, and no trails traverse it. At over 13,200 square miles, it's the second-largest national park in the U.S. Its mountains, which reach over 8,000 feet, cover almost all of the park. Within them are glacial valleys and alpine wetlands. On them are boreal forest and arctic tundra. Between them flow six National Wild and Scenic Rivers: the Alatna, John, Kobuk, Noatak, North Fork Koyukuk and Tinyaguk. Among them live black and grizzly bears, red fox, moose, wolves, wolverines, beavers, Dall sheep and Arctic ground squirrels. Through them migrate three herds of caribou—over half a million individuals—twice per year. Over them fly bald and golden eagles, rough-legged and red-tailed hawks, great-horned and short-eared owls, snow and Canada geese, peregrine and gyrfalcons, and warblers and kingfishers and loons.

LOCATION TIPS > Water travel is a good way to experience greater distances of the park. A solid photography trip can be planned along the Alatna River. It's one of the easier water routes in the park, with its 83 miles rambling among the heart of the Brooks Range. The drift (and a little rookie-level whitewater) will bring you through both tundra and spruce-hardwood forest, past views of snow-capped mountains, near lakes and along gravel river beds leading to expanses of alpine meadows. The Alatna will also bring you past the Arrigetch Peaks, which many consider to be some of the best scenery of the park. These very pointy, black granite spires rise sharply above the surrounding cirques, with a few mountain lakes and tarns scattered about. A multi-day hiking/camping expedition in the Arrigetch area is an excellent option for photographers. Flanking the Koyukuk River, Frigid Crags and Boreal Mountain are the "Gates of the Arctic," dubbed so by an explorer in 1929. From the heights of a flight in a bush plane, the tableau is spectacular, with the river snaking through the valley and the peaks rising above. It's also another great area for a backpacking photography trip.

GLACIER NATIONAL PARK

Montana

GLACIER NATIONAL PARK is one of the premier destinations for wildlife and landscape photographers. As its name implies, the park contains glaciers, but the most notable features of the terrain are the effects of past glaciers: dramatic mountain peaks, rock walls, valleys, amphitheaters, erratics, etc. What makes this a photographer's paradise is the buffet of scenes embedded in and around its 175 mountains and 760 lakes. For instance, if you're looking for a great place to shoot a mountain reflected in the cool, clear waters of a valley lake, in Glacier you'll have thousands of spots to choose from.

Of course, you can work with the park's namesake features, too. The challenge with photographing glaciers from afar is that they usually just look like snow on a mountain; to capture any sense of their enormity, you often need to get closer than a wide valley away. Fortunately, some of Glacier's 700 miles of hiking trails help you do that. Grinnell Glacier is perhaps the most accessible.

Glacier's main thoroughfare, Going-to-the-Sun Road, is one of the most scenic drives in the United States, and was a model for how to plan automobile routes through national parks. At

50 miles long, the road winds around mountainsides, edges along valleys and waterfalls, and passes lookouts of near and far lakes and glaciers, all while serving as an easy launching point for many of the off-the-beaten-path locations you might want to wander to.

The park is also famous among photographers for its wildlife. Walk around for a week and you might think Noah's Ark grounded there. With varying levels of ease, you'll find black bears, grizzlies, wolves, coyotes, fox, moose, bison, elk, pronghorn, deer, mountain goats, bighorn sheep, marmots, squirrels, pikas, eagles, falcons and more.

LOCATION TIPS > Generally, most photographers agree that the scenery is better on the east side of Glacier. (Just be careful when reading the word "better"—the west is still scenic enough to be its own park.) One notable exception is in autumn, when the maples and aspens color the landscapes on the west side more than on the east. Wild Goose Island in St. Mary Lake is visible from an overlook toward the east end of Going-to-the-Sun Road. It is very easy to access, is beautiful (especially in morning), and thus is one of the most photographed places in Glacier. Commencing at Logan Pass, the Highline Trail heads into backcountry. In just a few miles it passes some great views of Mount Oberlin, Mount Clements, Mount Cannon, Mount Gould and Grinnell Glacier, along with valleys and basins, wildflowers and likely some mountain goats. On an overcast day, head to Trail of the Cedars, a mile-long catwalk that loops through a forest of cedars and black cottonwood. The trail also features Avalanche Creek, a dynamic run of whitewater through a picturesque, moss-lined, red-rock gorge.

GLACIER BAY NATIONAL PARK & PRESERVE

Alaska

GLACIER BAY is relatively new not just as a park, but also as a landscape. Two hundred years ago it wasn't a bay at all—it was just a glacier. In the two centuries since, that glacier has retreated more than 60 miles, leaving behind a series of fjords, inlets, lagoons and islands, all surrounded by towering snow-capped mountain ranges, long rocky shorelines, and dense spruce and cedar rainforests. The sheltered waters can often be glass-smooth, providing excellent opportunities to photograph reflections of all that scenery.

The park highlight for most people is the glaciers, especially the tidewater variety that terminate at water's edge. At up to 250 feet high, just the faces of these frozen monstrosities are a fine photography subject, either as landscapes or for focusing in on the detailed patterns of ice and sediment. But the real show is when they calve: Huge sections fracture off the terminus and thunder into the water below, creating massive splashes, whitewater, waves and brand new icebergs.

The confines of the park are also home to most of the same wildlife you would find inland. But in addition to that is the sea life living in and around the water, which accounts for 20 percent of the park's 3 million acres. The abundant animal population includes brown and black bears (and even some brown black bears), mountain goats, wolves, coyotes, moose, red fox and porcupines. And that's just on land. In the water are whales, seals, sea lions, porpoise, sea otters, etc. The air brings a few animals, too: about 275 species of puffins, cormorants, loons, gulls, ducks, eagles, songbirds and other feathered photography subjects.

The catch is that accessing all of this is not as easy as at most parks. No roads lead to Glacier Bay, so you'll need to travel there via air or water. Few trails have been blazed, and those that have been stretch for only a cumulative 14 miles. But, trail or not, you are permitted to hike just about any land you can access, especially the many rocky shores of the bay. Otherwise you can navigate the park by boat (one that you own, or that you rent or charter in a nearby community), or let the NPS boats ferry you to destinations. The adventurous, self-sufficient and weather-wary photographer may even want to tour the park via kayak.

LOCATION TIPS > As the hub of the park's services, Bartlett Cove is relatively easy to access, and is also a beautiful spot with many options for photography. You can hike (this is the only spot with blazed trails) or kayak to great scenes (including the Beardslee Islands), and on calm days you may be able to photograph reflections of the Fairweather Range in still, protected waters. Bartlett River Trail meanders for a few miles through spruce and hemlock forest, then past moss-coated glacial erratics and along lagoons, and terminates at the river. Further into the park, Margerie Glacier is excellent for photography (as is the entire Johns Hopkins Inlet it melts into). You'll need to

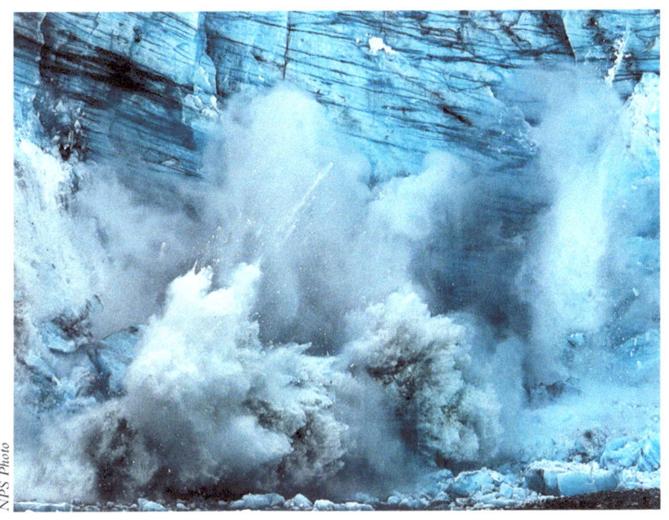

NPS Photo

Glacier Bay National Park & Preserve

be on the water for the best angles, especially for photos of the calving ice. The park offers a daily tour boat that includes a stop at Margerie, as do local tourism outlets. However, to achieve the flexibility that the best photography requires, you'll probably want to be in your own boat (responsibly distant from the glacier). You can use those same options to access Beartrack Cove, site of a famous Ansel Adams photograph. It offers calm, often-navigable waters, hikeable coastline, lush sedgeland meadows and foothills, access to the Beartrack River and enviable mountain views. Wildlife is most often spotted on shore, especially at low tide; also look for large mammals in inlets, where they can frequently be spotted foraging and swimming.

GRAND CANYON NATIONAL PARK

Arizona

It's more than one mile deep, up to 18 miles across, possibly six million years old. And it's one of the jewels of the national parks. Its beauty transcends the park system, as even people untouched by nature or geology are drawn to its rim. The Grand Canyon exceeds all superlatives. It's more than a natural wonder—it's one of the very special places in this world. And for the photographer, Grand Canyon National Park holds so much potential that people have made entire careers from capturing images primarily of this one place.

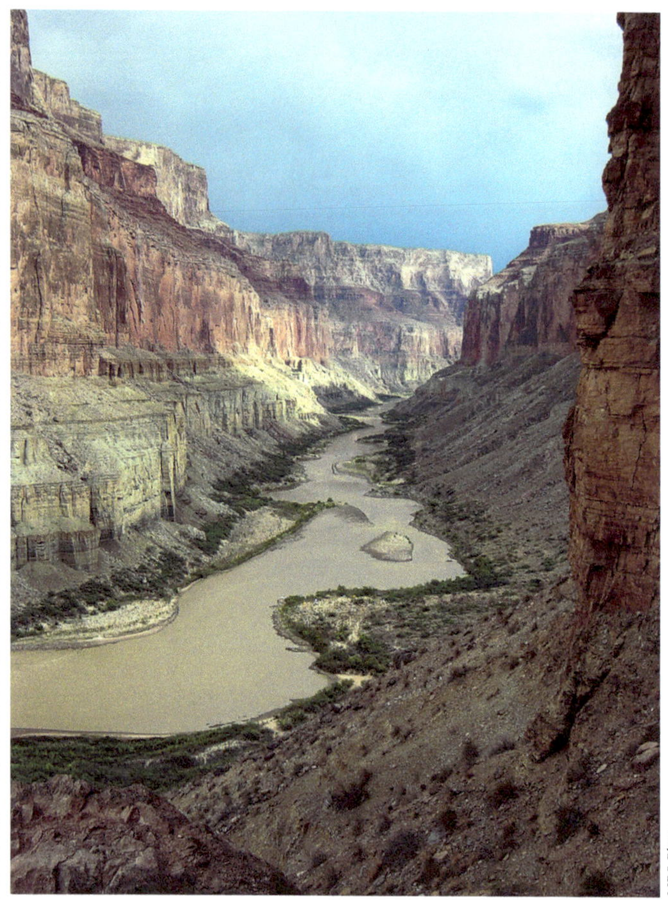

NPS Photo

Grand Canyon National Park

The Grand Canyon is the result of a persistent Colorado River eroding the plateaus of northern Arizona, exposing about 40 identified layers of geologic history. In its wake, the river left mesas, plateaus, buttes, pinnacles, hoodoos, ridges, gorges, promontories, cliffs, caves and rock formations for modern photographers to use for filling memory cards. The canyon floor is mostly scrubland and riparian vegetation. The scenery changes with the elevation—the scrub gives way to pinyon-pine and juniper forest, which gives way to ponderosa pine, spruce and fir at the rims.

The canyon may seem an easy place to photograph, but the reality is that light conditions are usually not ideal, particularly from the rim—flat light reveals little interesting in such a vast and nuanced arena, and strong midday light creates far too many difficult shadows and exposure issues in such a harsh landscape. The best times for photography are at night, either for stars and star trails or for moonlit scenes; during the blue hours, when cool tones fill the canyon and sky; and just after sunrise and before sunset, when the light is warm and streaming horizontally through the canyon, creating patterns and juxtapositions of illumination and shadow. The canyon also shines after rainfall wets the rock face, enhancing the colors of the geologic layers, and during thunderstorms, when massive clouds add depth to the scene and variety to the sky. Lightning is also common during storms, and can often be photographed from safe distances across the expanse of the canyon.

LOCATION TIPS > You can think of your location options in three groups: the South Rim, the North Rim and the canyon interior. The South Rim is the most visited portion of Grand Canyon and houses most of the services. The overlooks are outstanding (for example, Grandview Point and Navajo Point), but can also be crowded with photographers during the best light. To find more seclusion and original angles, try hiking the paths between overlooks. The Rim Trail, in particular, is a great option. The North Rim is, on average, about 1,000 feet higher than the South. (It's also markedly quieter—only about 10 percent of the park's visitors explore it.) The above-rim scenery is a bit different—for instance, you'll find more aspens here, more fall color, prairies and grassland, and also bison (or, more accurately, a local hybrid/subspecies known as "cattalo"). The view down is much like the South Rim's, except for different apparent rock and land formations, and the light hitting the canyon at a different relative angle. At the far western end of the North Rim, challenging and time-consuming to reach, Toroweap Overlook offers perhaps the best perspective of the Colorado River cutting through the canyon. Exploring the interior of the Grand Canyon opens another world to the photographer, giving access to features such as streams, waterfalls, sandy beaches, cactus, gila monsters etc. Rafting the Colorado River is not for the water-weary, nor for the time-limited, and requires very careful considerations when bringing along expensive, aquaphobic photo gear. On the other hand, it provides unique and unparalleled views of the canyon. For sunrise and sunset photography, Grand Canyon has about as many good spots as it does rock formations. Some of the many noteworthy spots are Hopi Point, Lipan Point, Bright Angel Point, Point Imperial and Cape Royal.

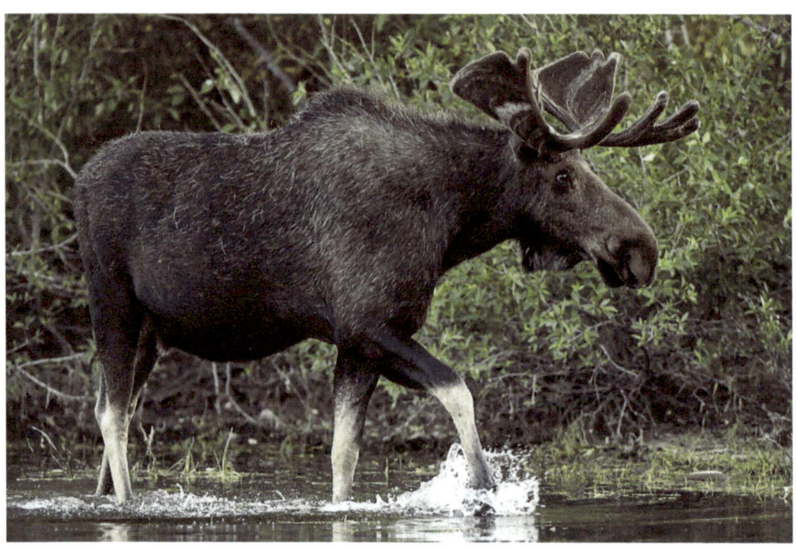

Grand Teton National Park

GRAND TETON NATIONAL PARK
Wyoming

THE WORLD doesn't have many mountain scenes like Teton. The valley of Jackson Hole is about 15 miles at its widest point. Relatively flat, you can view it from east to west, a wide plain of sagebrush punctuated only periodically by aspen groves, the occasional lone tree and stretches of the Snake River. Then, at the western edge, the valley stops abruptly, as the steep Teton Range thrusts nearly 7,000 feet up from the valley floor.

The mountains are craggy, pointy and almost always snowcapped. Eight peaks rise to an elevation of over 12,000 feet, including the 13,776-foot Grand Teton. The park is filled with varied opportunities to frame these mountains in different ways: behind hillside tree lines, along open meadows, reflected in placid lakes, and fronted by wide rivers winding through the valley.

The sun rising across Jackson Hole bathes the scene in amazing light, but it's the quiet few minutes prior that is the real prize: the alpenglow turning the mountains into a glow of red or pink. When the conditions are right, that is when the most successful Grand Teton photographers make their best work.

The park also features all the wildlife you would expect in Wyoming, including black and grizzly bears, elk, moose, wolves, coyotes and more. Historic structures also dot the landscape, including old barns and log houses—and the buck-and-rail fences that line the valley meadows are one of the most defining features of the region. Many miles of hiking trails can bring you around the valley floor or into the mountains, where you'll find glaciers, ponds, waterfalls, caves and canyons.

LOCATION TIPS > The Snake River's Oxbow Bend is one of many great locations in the park for photographing the mountains reflected in water, and is perhaps the most famous. Even photographers who shy away from "tripod holes" will want to spend at least one morning here. It's that beautiful, and the area offers enough latitude to move around and create something original. In fall, the riverbank is laced with the yellow of aspens (and the glint of tripods). Toward the southern end of the park, Mormon Row is home to a few old barns that are popular foregrounds to the mountains rising behind. Like some other parks, Grand Teton has a lot of primitive roads (some unmarked) that are open to people willing to venture off the pavement for views seen less often. A good example is the four-wheel-drive-only River Road, which slithers along the west bank of the Snake River for about 10 miles. Any back-country hike here will be memorable and productive. Hiking through the mountains is strenuous, but the network of loop trails makes it easy to customize a route based on time requirements and desired scenery. The 18-mile Cascade Canyon-Paintbrush Canyon loop is perhaps the most popular, as it's a manageable microcosm of all the park has to offer.

GREAT BASIN NATIONAL PARK

Nevada

THIS REMOTE PARK on the very eastern edge of Nevada rises from the desert floor high enough into the mountains to be home to a permanent ice field. On the way up through the elevations you'll find rock formations, forests of 5,000-year-old trees, groves of aspen and Douglas fir, oak woodland, grassy meadows, alpine lakes and streams, and deep caves. What this little-visited park lacks in popularity, it makes up for in variety.

The scenery is renowned among area photographers as a prime autumn location, as the aspens burst into color backed by rock formations and mountain skylines. Spring brings a mix of wildflowers common to both the southwestern deserts and other parts of the Rocky Mountains, including evening primrose, desert mallow, paintbrush, mountain bluebells, monkey flowers, clover, roses and lilies. The fauna end of the nature scale carries some weight, too. Because of the wide range of climate zones, the park supports a variety of wildlife, from coyotes, mountain lions and bighorn sheep, to pronghorn, jackrabbits and beavers.

The caves are perhaps Great Basin's most famous feature. Over 40 are known to exist in the mountains, though only two are open for touring by the public. Of those two, only one would be considered a photography destination: Lehman Caves, a marble labyrinth of stalactites, stalagmites, helictites and flowstone. (The second accessible cave is intended only for permit-based caving.) Even in Lehman, the photography options are limited, as you cannot enter alone. If you join a tour during the day, rules bar you from using a tripod, and using one is critical to making decent exposures in the dim artificial light. The better option, if you're willing to pay a moderate hourly rate, is to apply for an after-hours photography permit; you still need to be with a guide, but you can bring a tripod and won't have to work in a crowd. The conditions are ideal for creative light-painting.

Due to its remote location, Great Basin has some of the darkest skies in the park system. It's an excellent location for astrophotography and moonlit landscapes.

LOCATION TIPS > The Wheeler Peak Scenic Drive winds into the mountains and along Lehman Creek, affording views of ridges, cliffs and valleys, displays of spring wildflowers, and access to several trails worthy of photographic exploration. The Bristlecone-Glacier Trail brings you to and through two of the park's main attractions, the Wheeler Peak Glacier and a bristlecone pine grove. The five-millennia-old trees are unique photography subjects, with their twisted trunks and branches creating abstract compositional elements. An even larger grove of bristlecone grows on Mount Washington, though it's more difficult to access, via a harrowing primitive road. Aspen groves are found in many locations; some of the best flank Snake Creek and Baker Creek, line the banks of Stella Lake and Johnson Lake, and dot the mountainsides below Wheeler Peak. Lexington Arch is the park's most famous rock formation, a 60-foot-high limestone arch that is believe to be the remnant opening of a long-since collapsed cave; it can be photographed up close and from many spots along the last half-mile or so of trail that leads to it.

GREAT SAND DUNES NATIONAL PARK & PRESERVE

Colorado

ABOUT HALF a million years ago, sand in Colorado's San Luis Valley began blowing toward the Sangre de Cristo Mountains. The mountains halted the progress of the sand, which then began collecting into piles. In the days and millennia that followed, the sand collated into the largest dunes in North America. That one feature—the 30-square-mile dune field—is the marrow of the experience at Great Sand Dunes National Park & Preserve, especially for the photographer.

The dunes are exceptional for photography in two ways: as an element of the landscape, and as a subject for abstract images. One of the classic approaches to photographing the dune field is to use it as a foreground to the mountains; the latter are snow-capped for three-quarters of the year, which creates an environmental contrast between the desert sand and the cold peaks.

Additionally, trapping the dunes against the foothills is a large sand sheet, where you'll find grassland and shrubland that can serve as a foreground to either sand-dune or mountain scenes (or to both, if you find the right angle). Hiking into the dune field, the photographer can use framing techniques and deep depth of field to juxtapose the lit portions of dunes with the shadows they produce, using the winding ridgelines, patterns and contours as compositional elements. This strategy is particularly effective at the end of the day, in warm, waning daylight. (Morning light is blocked by the mountains until about an hour after sunrise.)

Though the dunes are spectacular and are the reason most photographers travel here, they're certainly not the only natural beauty within the park's boundaries. The Sangre de Cristo Mountains border the dunes on the north and east, with peaks rising a mile above the valley floor. The highest layer of the ecosystems in the park is alpine tundra, which accommodates only a little more life than the dunes at the bottom, but is also rugged terrain with a dramatically different aesthetic. The ecosystems between those two extremes are vibrant, including subalpine meadows, spruce-fir forests and foothill stands of pinyon pine, aspen and cottonwood. The mountains also contain five lakes and some unnamed tarns that are worth exploring for alpine reflections, fall foliage and wildflowers. Various wetlands are also scattered in the valley, where they attract cranes and assorted shorebirds.

LOCATION TIPS > Some of the best easy-to-reach spots for photographing the dunes backed by the Sangre de Cristo Mountains are just off the park road near the visitor center. One trick to photographing the dunes is avoiding footprints in the scene; most tourists don't venture past the first ridges, so photographers probably should. The park has an open-hiking policy for the dune field—no trails necessary, so roam where you will. Medano Creek, born of seasonal snowmelt, flows around the eastern and southern edges of the dune field. It's a nice foreground for landscapes, and is a good spot to look for animal tracks in the morning. If you have a reliable four-wheel-drive vehicle, healthy fitness level and good backcountry shoes, consider the trek to Medano Lake. The backcountry-worthy vehicle is needed to drive the Medano Pass Primitive Road nearly 12 miles—through meadows, forest and plenty of views of (and crossings over) Medano Creek—to the head of Medano Lake Trail. Once on foot, you'll hike four miles to Medano Lake, through spruce-fir forest and aspen groves, following the creek to its source. The lake lies in a depression in the mountaintop, and if you amble up the flanking ridge, you can photograph an aerial view of the dune field a mile below.

GREAT SMOKY MOUNTAINS NATIONAL PARK

North Carolina / Tennessee

STRADDLING the line between eastern Tennessee and western North Carolina, Great Smoky Mountains is the most visited of the national parks. What brings people here is one of the oldest landscapes in the United States, right in the heart of the Appalachian Mountain chain.

The Smoky Mountains get their name from the blue haze that lifts above the valleys and around the peaks, caused by the massive amounts of condensation wafting from the trees. Many overlooks in the park (whether at the side of the road or a trail) offer quintessential views of mountain ridge after mountain ridge receding toward the horizon, cast in blue tones, or in warm pastels at sunset, each a little lighter than the former.

The park teems with 2,900 miles of rivers and streams, along with scores of waterfalls and cascades—some that you

Great Smoky Mountains National Park

can drive to, some that you can take short walks to, and some that you can make hours-long hikes to. Along those drives and hikes you are almost certain to observe large wildlife. Deer are everywhere, herds of elk reside in the forests and meadows at Cataloochee, and the park is home to more black bears per square mile than any other place in the country. In spring, mountain laurel and dogwood bloom among the forest's young pale-green foliage; and in fall, birch, beech, maple and cherry turn in one of the park system's best displays of seasonal color.

Great Smoky Mountains also preserves historic areas, one of which (Cades Cove) is so conducive to photography that you could spend an entire trip around its 11-mile loop road and never exhaust yourself of inspiring scenes.

LOCATION TIPS > In Cades Cove, spend time at the two gravel roads that trisect the loop road: Hyatt Lane and Sparks Lane. Both are often quiet even when the rest of the area is not, and offer views of meadows, forests, hills and the surrounding mountains. Cades Cove light is best in morning. On two days per week, no automobiles are allowed in the area until almost noon—creating the opportunity for a nice, quiet photographic journey on foot or on bicycle. From the top of Clingmans Dome, the highest point in the park, you can photograph sunrise or sunset, and, if you're lucky, valley fog from above. The Roaring Fork area sees fewer visitors than many other parts of the park, but offers some beautiful hikes to forest streams and waterfalls. Grotto Falls is one of the more picturesque. The 25-foot waterfall can be photographed from both sides of the stream, and also from behind, as the trail curves under the overhang.

GUADALUPE MOUNTAINS NATIONAL PARK

Texas

THE GUADALUPE MOUNTAIN range stretches south from New Mexico into the far east of Texas, away from the areas that most non-Texans know about. For 65 miles it rises above the flats, like an elevated island, finally culminating at El Capitan, a bluff of sheer, thousand-foot limestone cliffs that ascends suddenly and dramatically from the floor of the Chihuahuan Desert. The southernmost 10 miles of the range forms the core of Guadalupe Mountains National Park. Other topographical features include woodland canyons, conifer forests, semiarid grassland, desert shrubland, sand dunes and spring-fed oases.

The park's canyons are of particular interest to landscape and nature photographers. The walls protect microenvironments that offer, quite literally, a change in scenery from the other low-lying areas. McKittrick Canyon is named by some as the most beautiful place in Texas, especially in fall when the red and yellow foliage lends a vibrancy that contrasts with the surrounding neutral-toned canyon. In the north section of the park, Dog Canyon offers secluded forests, open meadows and trails along ridges and atop peaks.

The park's wildlife roster includes coyotes, mule deer, gray fox, javelinas, black-tailed rabbits, collared lizards and rattlesnakes, along with other species that are either nocturnal or otherwise evasive (either way, they're rarely seen). Elk inhabit the park, but are generally observed only in the mountains. Tarantulas also inhabit the park, but are generally observed only in autumn. Common birds are red-tailed hawks, western scrub jays, peregrine falcons, golden eagles, turkey vultures and sandhill cranes.

LOCATION TIPS > The hikes to the tops of Guadalupe Peak and El Capitan reward with their aerial views of the desert floor—not just from the top, but also from myriad spots on their switchback trails. Moreover, the summit of the former includes a great view of the latter, with the perspective of the

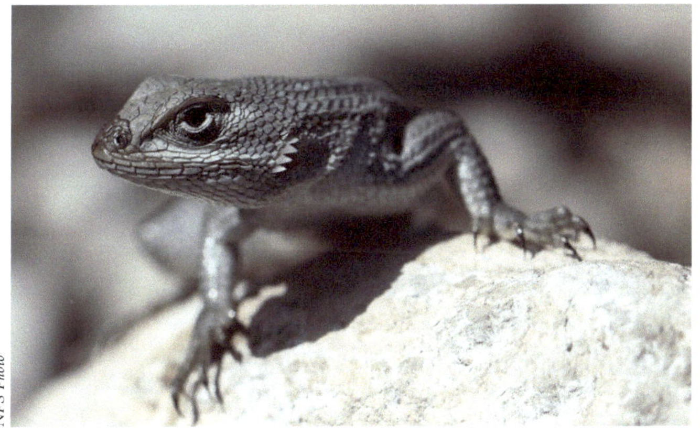

NPS Photo

Guadalupe Mountains National Park

desert floor as a distant background. For ground views of El Capitan, hike the El Capitan Trail or drive the primitive road to Williams Ranch. In summer, afternoon storm clouds can mottle the light on the bluff, making for great photography conditions; just be adequately wary of lightning in the open desert, where you'll be the tallest thing around. The springs in the park (such as Mazanita Spring or Smith Spring) are good places to wait for wildlife, particularly mule deer, particularly at the beginning and end of daylight hours. Toward the western end of the park you'll find the Gypsum Sand Dunes—2,000 acres of bright-white gypsum grains that drift as high as 60 feet. Nearby are even more expansive red sand dunes composed of quartz grains.

HALEAKALA NATIONAL PARK

Hawaii

On the island of Maui, Mount Haleakala rises more than 10,000 feet above the Pacific Ocean. This dormant shield volcano is at once a photography subject and a platform for photographing the surrounding landscape, from the mountainside carpeted with lush tropical vegetation to the surreal cinder-cone desert interior of the 2,700-foot-deep summit basin. Thirty-five miles of trails traverse the basin (dubbed the "Wilderness Area"), allowing for an intimate photographic exploration of the volcano.

The park contains five distinct ecosystems, so from the summit to the coast, you'll find different types of landscapes.

Shrubland, rainforest, riparian habitats and more give the photographer near-infinite options for how to frame this paradise. Even within the Wilderness Area, the aesthetics are different from east to west.

Haleakala has a bountiful supply of interesting plants and wildflowers. The most iconic is the Haleakala silversword, which is endemic to the park (it's not even found elsewhere in Hawaii). It's a stout rosette of hundreds of narrow silver leaves that stretch upward from the ground. A silversword flowers only once in its lifetime (as much as 90 years), but is equally photogenic with or without blossoms. Also endemic to the park are four species of geranium. These and other plants and flowers can be seen and photographed in a garden at the Headquarters Visitor Center, as well as in numerous spots in the wilderness.

As can be expected on a Hawaiian island, the park is home or stopping-ground for a wide selection of bird species. Examples include the native Hawaiian goose and the Hawaiian petrel, along with some species not named after the islands, such as pheasants, java sparrows, egrets, frigates, cranes, plovers, various cardinals and endemic honeycreepers. If you like to photograph endangered species, Haleakala is a good place to explore—it's home to more of them than any other unit of the park system.

LOCATION TIPS > Photographing sunrise from atop Mount Haleakala is practically a rite of passage for visiting the park. Locals will tell you that it never looks the same twice. You definitely will not be the only photographer (or onlooker) there, so arriving early is prudent—meaning it's best to arrive in predawn hours when you can stake out both a parking space and a tripod spot. A less populated surround can be found by hiking the short Pa Ka'oao Trail to the top of a small hill. While you're waiting for daylight, you can photograph stars in one of the darkest skies in the civilized world. After sunrise, you can photograph the backlit cinder cones in the basin, either from the rim or by hiking in. One of the routes in the Wilderness Area, the Sliding Sands Trail, is good for spotting silverswords in the wild. Near the coast, the Pipiwai Trail leads through a photogenic bamboo forest and to several waterfalls, including the Falls at Makahiku and the 400-foot-high Waimoku Falls—all of which are fine subjects under overcast skies. For the limited but impressive coastal vistas in the park, hike the half-mile Kahakai Trail.

HAWAI'I VOLCANOES NATIONAL PARK

Hawaii

NATURE HAS BEEN building Hawai'i Volcanoes National Park for 70 million years. Also, some of it was made yesterday. With two of the world's most active volcanoes (Kilauea and Mauna Loa) continuously contributing new terrain, you could truly photograph a somewhat different landscape from one day to the next without even moving your tripod.

From time to time the lava flows in different places, at different volumes, but the overall effect is relatively consistent: This place grows. In fact, the island is 500 acres larger than when Kilauea commenced its current eruption in 1983.

As the name of the park implies, the primary attraction is the volcanoes. But these aren't tall stratovolcanoes that dominate the aesthetics of their surroundings (such as Mount Rainier); rather, they're shield volcanoes, which spread out for miles in all directions and increase in elevation gradually. They look more like really big hills. Because of that, the photography opportunities are found primarily in the details of the volcanoes—the craters, the steam vents, the lava flows.

At the active Halema'uma'u Crater you might have a chance to photograph lava, but will almost always be able to shoot at least the gas plumes (which can be otherworldly, especially if backlit). Also, you can likely capture the glow of an unseen lava lake illuminating the crater under blue-hour conditions or at night. For actual flowing lava, you may be able to hike out into some of the lava fields—in some spots you can get quite close (just be sure to follow the park's safety guidelines). While journeying out on the crust, another possible subject is the dark, smooth contours of hardened pahoehoe lava, the surface of which can contain beautiful patterns that make good macro subjects.

Because some of the more interesting features of the volcano can be so vast, the opportunities for aerial photography are fantastic. Many local plane and helicopter pilots provide the service of chauffeuring people over the smoking volcanoes and steaming shore rifts. It can be pricey, but is probably not an excursion to miss.

LOCATION TIPS > Crater Rim Drive provides easy access to some interesting spots. Examples include overlooks where you can photograph wide-angle views of the caldera and the

Halema'uma'u Crater (particularly at sunset or dusk, when the intensity of its glow complements the luminosity of the sky), or use a telephoto lens to frame select features, such as volcanic gasses rising from the crater pit. Along the same drive you can access the Thurston Lava Tube, which provides the unique opportunity to photograph the interior of a lava cave, along with the lush fern forest outside. From the end of Chain of Craters Road you can hike across pahoehoe fields to the sea, and may even be able to view and photograph lava flowing on land or steaming while pouring into the ocean. However, if that is your goal, the prudent and most productive practice is to go with a safety-first tour or guide—or at least discuss your plans with, and ask for feedback from, a ranger at the visitor's center.

HOT SPRINGS NATIONAL PARK

Arkansas

THIS PARK differs from others in that its focus is primarily on man-made bathhouses rather than on unique or breathtaking natural features.

The hot springs that the park is named after do exist, but not in their original state. They were altered in the 1800s to flume the water into Bathhouse Row in downtown Hot Springs, Arkansas. They were re-altered over a century ago and now are completely covered, routed into reservoirs for storage and distribution. You can still bathe in the houses, which is why just about everyone who goes to this park goes to this park.

Despite that, a photographer can find some things to do here. You can, of course, photograph the bathhouses—they are alluring historic structures (some of Gilded Age architecture), and are somewhat unique for the U.S.

But if you want to shoot the types of things that most people venture into parks to shoot, you'll probably want to drive on the roads through Hot Springs' hills and valleys, and then hike along the 26 miles of trails. There you'll find some wildlife opportunities in the form of small mammals (the largest being coyotes), amphibians and birds (herons, swans, vultures, eagles, owls and such). The forests of the park provide good opportunities for photographing wildflowers (beebalm and dogwood, in particular), but are arguably at their best in fall.

LOCATION TIPS > Bathhouse Row is on Central Avenue, in the heart of the city of Hot Springs—so you won't have trouble spotting it. Hot Water Cascade is the spring that appears the closest to its natural state, but you'll have to work to find a good angle. On a cool morning, you should be able to photograph steam lifting off the water. If you're willing to take a two-mile walk, hike the Hot Springs Mountain Trail; on a sunny day you can photograph some nice scenes from the overlooks, and on a cloudy day you can shoot the mixed hardwood and pine forests. For a longer saunter through remote areas of the park, try Sunset Trail. This 10-mile route passes through various types of terrain, to the highest point in the park, and by Ricks Pond. Because it's punctuated with occasional parking lots, the trail is easy to hike in sections, so you don't have to commit yourself to long treks in order to venture into remote corners. One particular area of interest is Balanced Rock, where you can photograph the eponymous boulder and other outcroppings, and get a decent view at sunset.

ISLE ROYALE NATIONAL PARK

Michigan

SURROUNDED by the waters of Lake Superior, Isle Royale isn't quick to get to. The closest mainland harbor is 18 miles away, so you need a boat or a seaplane to ferry you out. Once there, getting around the park is easy if you're willing to travel by kayak, canoe or other watercraft. But Isle Royale—the largest island in North America's largest lake—also has 165 miles of trails, so much is accessible by foot, as well.

All that paddling and walking will bring you through some of the most pristine water wilderness in the United States. The coastline is rugged and rocky, and the shore weaves in and out of inlets and bays, around points and barrier islands. For more delicate scenes, the south side of the island tends to slope at a more gentle pace into the lake; the northern side tends to be more dramatic, with higher promontories that drop into the water. Because the 45-by-9-mile Isle Royale and the accompanying archipelago orient from southwest to northeast, they feature a nearly endless supply of tripod spots for sunrises and sunsets. Being far from cities, the park also has exceptionally dark night skies, a clear view of the Milky Way, and frequent sightings of the Northern Lights.

The trails weave through Northwoods forests, along ridge tops, around bays, and past marshes and streams and inland lakes. But you'll be able to access even more of the park if traveling by water. Though some of the lakeshore can be treacherous for novice kayakers and canoeists (ask a ranger for advice and guidelines), most is easy to paddle and to navigate with some basic knowledge and a good map. You can also move from inland lake to inland lake using portages, which is a great way to visit some of the more remote spots.

On the wildlife front, Isle Royale is most famous for its wolf and moose populations, though a visitor is much more likely to see the latter. Other local critters include beavers, red squirrels, trumpeter swans, geese, loons and amphibians of all varieties.

This is also one of the few national parks that offers something to the lighthouse photographer, as there are four lights within Isle Royale's boundaries. Three of them, however, are on barrier islands accessible solely by boat—only Rock Harbor Lighthouse is on the main island, but still takes work to get to.

LOCATION TIPS > Hiking Greenstone Ridge can be a trip by itself, and many park visitors use it as such. It mostly beelines the center of the island while leading through forest—but that forest occasionally opens up into elevated views of waterfront channels and barrier islands. Most notable, perhaps, are the overlooks on Mount Franklin and Mount Desor. Tobin Harbor is a nice spot to photograph, especially in fog (not uncommon), either from shore trails or from a canoe or kayak. There you'll find docks and moored boats, along with myriad islands, points and wooded shores that you can juxtapose in compositions. Unlike most parks, there aren't many go-to spots for viewing and photographing wildlife; but if you want to improve your chances for finding moose, try situating yourself at the marshes or ponds at the beginning or end of daylight, or near the natural salt lick at Hidden Lake. To photograph fox, look around your campsite.

JOSHUA TREE NATIONAL PARK

California

MANY ASSUME that Joshua Tree National Park is mostly about the plants that it's named for. But while the aesthetic of so much of the park is defined by the Joshua trees, there's so much more to love about this place.

The trees *are* a great photography subject. With their tall bare trunks topped by a burst of upstretched branches, further

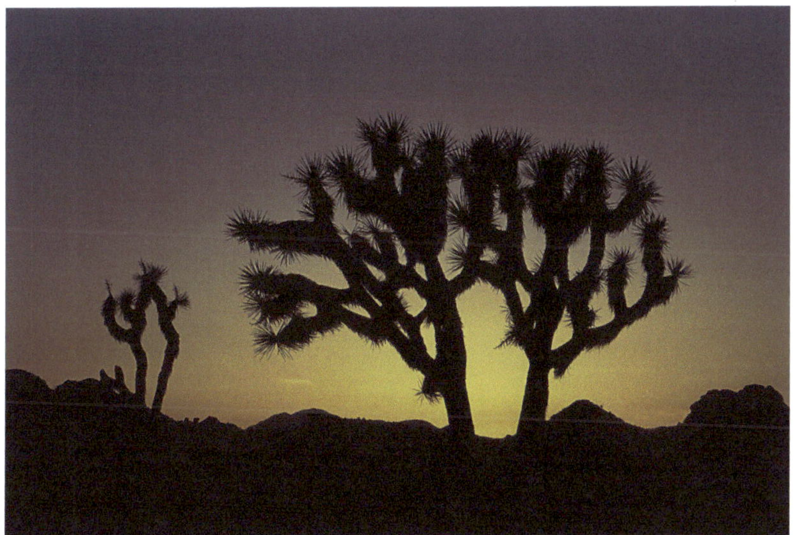

Joshua Tree National Park

topped by a veritable explosion of long evergreen leaves, they present a unique and dynamic component to an otherwise challenging desert landscape. Photographically, they look great isolated as singular subjects, in bunches as part of the environment, and as sharp and distinctive shapes when silhouetted in front of sunrise, sunset, dawn or dusk skies. And if you're lucky you might be able to catch some trees in spring bloom, a somewhat unpredictable occurrence.

Joshua Tree offers a wide range of other subjects, as well, due to the three distinct ecosystems that fall within its boundaries. You'll find oases and desert planes, mountains and valleys, dry lakes and sand dunes, monoliths and canyons. With the varying terrain comes varying wildlife, as well. The park is home to bighorn sheep, mule deer, coyotes, snakes, bobcats, rabbits and fox. The region is also a popular stopover for migratory birds, and home to golden eagles and roadrunners.

Being well away from big cities, Joshua Tree is also an optimal locale for night photography. Whether shooting star trails, Milky Way skies or moonlit landscapes, you can find just about as much to photograph after dark as during the day.

LOCATION TIPS > At the south end of Wilson Canyon, the Cholla Cactus Garden is a perfect place to spend a long time on a short trail. Though relatively small in acreage, this forest of short cacti is good to photograph either at sunrise or in late afternoon. Barker Dam is one of the few areas to find water, which grants chances to shoot reflections of the flora and surrounding rock formations. Hidden Valley is an oasis in the northwest corner of the park. Though the loop trail through the area is only one mile long, you could circuit it over and over and never run out of things to photograph. It's essentially a garden in the desert, and one of the best places to find wildflowers and cacti that you can easily frame against backdrops of granite rock formations.

KATMAI NATIONAL PARK & PRESERVE

Alaska

THE KATMAI REGION literally exploded into a national park. In 1912 the Novarupta Volcano erupted in what was the world's largest volcanic event of the 20th century. Exploration ensued, and six years later, for preservation and study, the area was established as a national monument.

Katmai National Park still features the site of the eruption, known as the Valley of 10,000 Smokes, named after the array of remnant fumaroles in the landscape following the blast. These days the land smokes no more, but this 40-square-mile ash flow—rife with canyons, gorges, rock formations and surreal landscapes—is a terrestrial highlight for photographers. Beyond the ash field, Katmai is home to 15 still-active volcanoes and other mountains and valleys, as well as hundreds of freshwater lakes, ponds, rivers and streams, unspoiled Pacific coastline, lowland tundra, and lush sedge flats.

Alas, the topography is not why most people visit Katmai. Overwhelmingly, the primary allurement is brown bears. A lot of them live here (over 2,000), and they reliably frequent the Brooks Camp area, a few dozen at a time, to feed on spawning and dying sockeye salmon in July and September. Bears wander the whole park during the warmer half of the year, and are spotted regularly by anyone venturing through. If you need help when the bears are scarce at Brooks Camp, you can find it from local guides, particularly ones who own planes.

Incidentally, Katmai supports populations of other wildlife, too, such as moose, caribou, seals and otters. Birds are also abundant, including great-horned owls, black oystercatchers, greater yellowlegs, harlequin ducks, bald eagles, gulls, ravens, magpies and puffins.

LOCATION TIPS > The easiest place to photograph brown bears is from the viewing platforms at Brooks Camp. The platforms (crowd-controlled by park rangers) overlook three spots on the Brooks River where bears congregate with some unfortunate salmon. The most dynamic photographs are generally made at Brooks Falls, a short waterfall that bears sit either under or atop to catch salmon with their paws and jaws, sometimes in midair. Katmai is the opposite of most parks in that the wildlife is easy to find while the great landscapes take some work to reach. For the latter, one of the more easily attainable options is hiking to the top of Dumpling Mountain. The trail affords access to alpine tundra, subalpine meadows sprouting with wildflowers such as lupine and wild geranium, as well as views of Lake Brooks and Naknek Lake with Brooks River ribboning between. A more ambitious option is to paddle the Savonoski Loop, an 80-mile trek on rivers and lakes flanked by mountains and open plains. The route includes the Bay of Islands, an excellent spot to photograph islands (obviously) and skerries among calm, reflecting waters. Scenic flights will help you reach and photograph the remote backcountry, and can be chartered in pretty much all the surrounding towns.

KENAI FJORDS NATIONAL PARK
Alaska

THE RELATIONSHIP between mountains and ice is central to the scenery in Alaska's smallest national park (which is still larger than 42 parks in the rest of the country). The dominant feature is the Harding Icefield, a 700-square-mile slab of frozen water up to one mile deep. The peaks of some buried mountains point upward from the field, forming islands in the ice known as "nunataks." Nothing in this landscape is uninfluenced by ice.

Branching off Harding are at least 38 glaciers, including some ending in the Gulf of Alaska and some in alpine lakes. Those that terminate at the coast do so into the fjords—long, narrow, and incredibly grand inlets formed by past glacial activity. The fjords are a natural habitat for the area's marine wildlife, such as sea otters, Stellar sea lions and harbor seals, along with resident orcas and other whales that sometimes venture in.

Other mammals in the park include black and brown bears, and moose, all of which are frequently observed and photographed. Kenai Fjords is also a fine spot for avian photography. Bald eagles are common, as are golden eagles, magpies, black oystercatchers, peregrine falcons, and shorebirds and seabirds. Additionally, horned and tufted puffins nest on the cliffs of the park's islands.

LOCATION TIPS > The easiest notable spot to reach in Kenai Fjords is the area around the Exit Glacier. A short road enters the northeast of the park, ending at a nature center. Paths branch off to various views of the glacier and to its outwash plain, where you can photograph the terminus and the streams running through the dark glacial sediment. Also here is the head of the Harding Icefield Trail, an eight-mile round-trip strenuous hike that traces the clifftops east of the glacier, traverses meadows, passes through cottonwood and alder stands, then terminates at an expansive view of the ice field. The trail is one of the most likely places in Kenai Fjords to see black bears and mountain goats, and the road to the area is good for spotting moose. Bear Glacier is the largest in the park, and empties into Bear Lake, which is sheltered from Resurrection Bay and the Gulf of Alaska by a narrow moraine. This confluence of geology creates relatively calm waters that trap a high concentration of icebergs (some of which have black bands from the glacier's flow stripes), making for a rather extraordinary seascape. Excellent photography is possible from kayaks and the shoreline—of everything from the icebergs to seals seeking the security of isolated waters to the flow-striped glacier creeping toward the lake's edge.

KINGS CANYON NATIONAL PARK

California

PERHAPS no other fact evidences the photographic potential of Kings Canyon quite like this: One of the noted proponents and Congressional lobbyists who helped get it founded as a national park was Ansel Adams.

The canyon is one of the deepest in the U.S., at 8,200 feet from top to bottom. However, as visually impressive as it is—looking much like Yosemite Valley without the waterfall—the canyon is but one of many attractions for the photographer. The natural features in and around the canyon (including other canyons within the park's boundaries) provide a wide spectrum of subjects to aim a lens at.

Some would argue that Kings Canyon's sequoia groves are more photogenic than Sequoia National Park's (which borders Kings Canyon directly to the south). Grant Grove is so spectacular that it used to be its own national park. It contains the General Grant Tree, the largest sequoia in the grove and one of the largest trees in the world. Redwood Canyon is home to the biggest grove of sequoias (and also some meadows and shrubland), navigable via 16 miles of trails.

The backcountry is pristine alpine wilderness. It comprises some of the most beautiful mountain scenery in the Sierra Nevada; forests of incense cedar, cottonwood, aspen, pine, oak and fir; meadows of grasses, shrubs and wildflowers; and the riparian ecology of the Kings River and its many cousins. The river is an admirable photographic subject, as it roars or calmly flows through the valley (depending on location and time of year), through various landscapes and ecosystems. Placid lakes, ponds, tarns and other wetlands provide ample opportunities for finding reflections of rock formations and alpine scenery. Kings Canyon is also home to numerous waterfalls and countless cascades, such as Roaring River Falls (iconic and accessible), Mist Falls (a popular stop on the hike to Paradise Valley) and Grizzly Falls (which ends an 80-foot drop by crashing into boulders).

LOCATION TIPS > Zumwalt Meadow is easy to hike to and around, and is pleasant to photograph, as well. The meadow sits on the valley floor, with lush greenery providing a softer aesthetic than found in most other areas of the park. The Kings River flows through the grasses, framed by the distinctive granite walls of Grand Sentinel and North Dome. The Woods Creek Trail to Paradise Valley includes some waterfalls, inspiring valley views, peaceful riverside forest scenery and rugged rock formations. The John Muir Trail is one of the most remote hikes in the contiguous Unites States, and highlights what is perhaps the most scenic parts of King Canyon's backcountry. The trail requires a serious commitment, but brings you through several treasures of the eastern half of the park, such as McClure Meadow, Evolution Valley, Le Conte Canyon and the distinct 3,000-foot peak of The Citadel. The trail also passes through the Rae Lakes, a pristine and remote area well-suited for a several-day photography expedition. The area is also reachable via other, easier routes, one being the 41-mile Rae Lakes Loop, which is among the most popular backcountry hikes in the park.

KOBUK VALLEY NATIONAL PARK

Alaska

LOCATED entirely within the Arctic Circle, Kobuk Valley National Park is one of the most unspoiled wildernesses in the United States. The park has no internal infrastructure—no roads, no trails, no facilities. As a visitor, you're on your own and must carry anything you need for as long as you plan to wander, including the knowledge to stay safe in those conditions. For locomotion, many people who spend time in the park do so by boating the tranquil Kobuk River, and then beaching and hiking when the need or fancy strikes. (Aerial touring is also popular, as is having a bush plane shuttle you in and out.)

The river crosses through the southern third of the park, so calmly that the current is often not apparent. The waterway winds for 61 miles through varying topography, including 150-foot high bluffs, treeless tundra, and boreal forests of alder, spruce and birch. The river is not only conduit, but subject as well: It has enough straights, bends and oxbows to allow for a variety of compositional approaches. The Kobuk River Valley is sheltered by the Baird Mountains to the north and the Waring Mountains to the south—both are difficult to tour, but are also photogenic. They comprise myriad ecosystems, including layers of alpine tundra peaks that recede into the skyline.

The stars of Kobuk Valley's wildlife are the caribou. The largest herd of caribou in Alaska, numbering about half a million, crosses Kobuk Valley during the spring and fall migrations. In late August and early September, with a little scouting and luck you can photograph them swimming across the Kobuk River with their nearly-full rack of midseason antlers. Other wildlife in the park includes black and grizzly bears, gray wolf, moose, fox, mink, waterfowl, mosquitos and black flies. (For the latter two, a macro lens is useful—or bug spray.)

In fall, the aspens and the tundra scrub change color, adding yellow and red splashes to the landscape. The park is open in winter and can be traveled via snowmobile and dogsled, in addition to human power (i.e., via snowshoe or cross-country ski). Kobuk Valley is a harsh place in winter, but in addition to providing raw, frozen scenery, it's a good spot for viewing the aurora borealis. All year, night skies are immaculate.

LOCATION TIPS > The Great Kobuk Sand Dunes are an iconic sight. Rising as high as 200 feet and stretching for about

25 square miles, it is the largest active dune field in North America. Two other sets of dunes are in the park, as well: Little Kobuk Sand Dunes and Hunt River Dunes. The latter, while not the grandest of the three, is the easiest to reach from the water. Onion Portage is a good spot to watch for the fall caribou migration to cross the Kobuk River. It's such a good bet, in fact, that you may also see local Inupiat hunting there. In the southern half of the park, that great northern-Alaska light is even more useful than at Gates of the Arctic, because fewer mountains block the horizon-hugging sun.

LAKE CLARK NATIONAL PARK & PRESERVE

Alaska

THOUGH named after the 50-mile-long lake in its southwest reaches, the character of Lake Clark National Park is at least equally the result of the dominance of its Chigmit Mountains. The mountains range from the shores of Cook Inlet to the middle of the park, where they taper into foothills and a tundra plateau.

Scattered between and about is everything you would expect from Alaska. An untold number of alpine lakes, ponds and tarns reflect the mountains and attract the region's extensive spectrum of wildlife. Nine hundred square miles of glaciers are still reshaping the terrain, still slowly creeping through the mountains, carving valleys and repositioning geologic features. Two volcanoes, Mount Iliamna and Mount Redoubt, still send steam skyward, and the latter erupted as recently as just a few years ago.

Lake Clark is the largest of the park's lakes, and, while beautiful, is far from being the most eye-catching of the set. Turquoise Lake, nestled in a glacial valley, is colored by glacial silt. The Twin Lakes, near a backcountry ranger station, are surrounded by mountains that offer not only a scenic backdrop, but also unlimited vantage points. Crescent Lake is a great spot for photographing bears, and its head is fed by photogenic streams that pour in from nearby valleys.

The park also contains three designated National Wild and Scenic Rivers (the Mulchatna, Chilikadrotna and Tlikakila), along with 123 miles of coastal shoreline on the Cook Inlet. The seaside salt marshes are perhaps the most dynamic eco-

Lake Clark National Park & Preserve

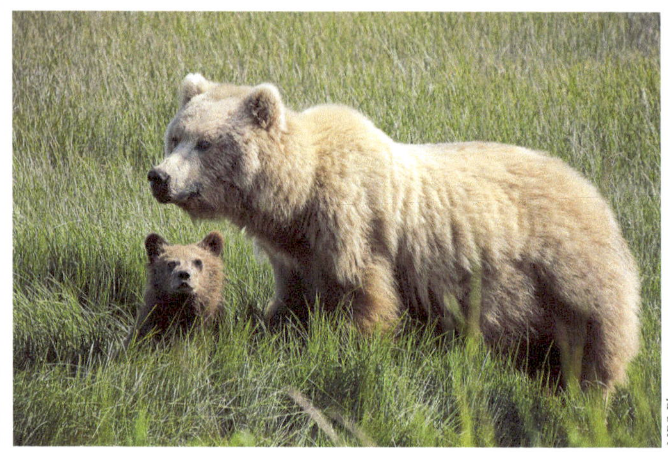

NPS Photo

systems in the region, supporting a variety of wildlife such as bears, moose, otters, waterfowl and shorebirds.

The bears are one of the most evident mammal species. Brown and black bears inhabit the entire region, though the brown outnumber the black and tend to scare them off—so you don't see the latter much. Bears are easiest to spot in the coastal areas, where they feed on sedge and dig for clams in the tidal flats. During salmon runs, they can often be spotted along the streams, rivers and lakes. Lake Clark also has resident gray wolves, moose and Dall sheep. Caribou are common in the foothills and tundra plains, though they number far fewer than a couple of decades ago.

LOCATION TIPS > The only maintained trail system in the park begins close to Hardenberg Bay, near the National Park Field Headquarters at Port Alsworth, on the south-central shore of Lake Clark. The trails lead past bogs and a beaver pond, through birch groves and tundra meadows, to Tanalian Falls and Kontrashibuna Lake, and to the top of 3,900-foot Tanalian Mountain, where you'll find inspiring views of the aforementioned lakes and the surrounding peaks. During salmon runs, look for brown bears at the Kijik River, Chinitna Bay and Silver Salmon Creek. For a backcountry experience, consider basing yourself at a lake or glacier for few days and embarking on day hikes to different spots for photography. If you want to stay mobile, a great trek is moving south to north, or vice versa, between Twin Lakes and Telaquana Lake. Many route options are available, bringing you past views of glaciers, mountains, tundra, streams, waterfalls and... well, lakes. One popular backcountry spot to visit is the Proenneke Cabin at Upper Twin Lake. It was the residence of Dick Proenneke—a naturalist, writer and filmmaker who lived there for 30 years—and is now recognized as a National Historic Site.

LASSEN VOLCANIC NATIONAL PARK
California

About a century ago, Lassen Peak would not have been a fun place to be. From 1914 through 1917, a long series of eruptions reorganized the landscape into what we now preserve as Lassen Volcanic National Park. Though it hasn't erupted again in about a century, Lassen is still an active volcano, and its surface has the geothermic features to prove it.

Most of those geothermic spectacles are concentrated in several regions of the park, a few of which can be visited. (Others are isolated from touring, but can be seen from a distance.) The most popular accessible geothermals are those at Sulphur Works, Warner Valley and Bumpass Hell. In these and a few other spots, photographers can tour steaming fumaroles, mud pots and boiling springs.

Lassen Peak is still a dominant scenic component of the park. It stands about 2,000 feet above the surrounding wilderness, is the southernmost active volcano in the Cascade Range and one of the largest by volume in the world. Other volcanoes are dispersed around the park, too. In fact, Lassen Volcanic is one of the few places in the world with volcanoes representing all four of the categories that geologists sort them into: shield, composite, cinder cone and plug dome.

The park also contains a fair number of alpine lakes fit for photographing reflections of the surrounding forests, volcanic topography and snow-capped peaks. Manzanita Lake is iconic as a foreground for vistas of Lassen Peak, and nearby Reflection Lake serves much the same purpose. The 1.5-mile trail around Manzanita is one of the most popular scenic hikes, and one of the best spots for photographing birds. Streams can be found throughout the park, but especially in the more mountainous western half.

Lassen Volcanic is also known for the fall-color displays in the aspens, for winter landscapes and for the lightning that Lassen Peak attracts during storms. In spring, wildflowers such as iris, violets and lupines burst from the meadows.

LOCATION TIPS > In the northeast corner of Lassen Volcanic, the area around Cinder Cone is a must-photograph location. The dark-gray cone rises over 700 feet from the surrounding landscape, which is a field of pumice and loose cinder dotted with sparse pines. You can climb Cinder Cone and photograph the crater and its concentric double rims, which offer fascinating juxtapositions of light and shadow when side-lit or back-lit. From the rim, you can also photograph outward toward colorful Painted Dunes and the black Fantastic Lava Beds, both topnotch land features, and both worth photographing from ground-level, too. Kings Creek Falls is a split cascade that flows down 50 feet of volcanic rock face surrounded by ferns and other lush vegetation. It can be accessed via a rocky 2.5-mile round-trip hike that follows Kings Creek through a forest of hemlock and lodgepole pine, and through Lower Meadow, a good place to spot mule deer. Upper Meadow is also good for observing wildlife, and for photographing Kings Creek flowing through the grasses with Lassen Peak in the background. The Cluster Lakes are an assemblage of more than a dozen small alpine lakes and ponds within about a one-mile radius, all in similar settings but with slightly different aesthetics. The 11-mile hike in, around and back from the Cluster Lakes is easy enough to complete in a day, but also makes for a potentially productive overnight backcountry trip.

MAMMOTH CAVE NATIONAL PARK

Kentucky

BENEATH almost 53,000 acres of Kentucky's woodland hills and valleys lies the world's longest known cave system. Though only 390 miles of caves have been mapped, experts believe the system extends more than 1,000 miles. About 10 miles of the caves are available for visitors to explore, including the banks of subterranean rivers and lakes. The underground contains various geologic formations, including stalactites descending from the cave ceiling and stalagmites ascending from the floor, along with domes, chambers, pits and dripstones.

Mammoth Cave features some terrestrial subjects, as well, navigable by boat or by hiking some of the 84 miles of trails. Photographers interested in plant life will find an impressive breadth of it at the park (including 1,300 species of flowering plants), as it's located in a transitional zone between ecosystems and climates, which creates varied habitats. The hills are covered with several types of dense forest, including oak-hickory in the uplands, oak-cedar on dry south- and west-facing slopes, and oak-pine along ridgetops. The park finds itself awash in color in autumn, as oak, beech, dogwood, sassafras, red maple, black gum and tulip poplar fringe the forests in golds, oranges, reds and purples.

Starting as early as late February and lasting through spring, many wildflowers bloom among the trees, along the riverbanks and in the small meadows. Species commonly found include prairie dock, bluebells, wild geraniums, purple and prairie coneflower, culvers root, tall coreopsis, and numerous samples of blazing star, sunflower, goldenrod, aster and black-eyed Susans.

LOCATION TIPS > Photographing in the caves presents some logistical challenges, including that they're sparsely lit, and tripods are not allowed. However, the park does sometimes offer a ranger-led opportunity that caters to photographers: the Focus on Frozen Niagara tour. This easy walk traverses only a quarter mile, but allows for 90 minutes of photographing (with a tripod, if you want) Rainbow Dome, Crystal Lake, Moonlight Dome and the Frozen Niagara flowstone. Above ground, the Green River is a peaceful waterway winding through the forests of the park, and is particularly attractive for photography on misty mornings and in autumn. Wander around the river's Turnhole Bend, which offers vantages of the water and the sandy banks curving through the trees. During rainfall, search out caves that may have water falling from atop the entrances, which can be beautiful to photograph from inside.

MESA VERDE NATIONAL PARK

Colorado

THE PRIMARY PURPOSE for Mesa Verde National Park, and therefore the primary attraction within, is the preservation of 600 cliff dwellings constructed by ancestral Puebloans who inhabited the area as long ago as the sixth century. Nestled in canyons and alcoves above the Montezuma Valley, the dwellings are part of an extensive archeological treasure of more than 4,800 sites in the park's 52,000 acres.

For the photographer, the dwellings are of interest as part of the overall landscape, as well as for the details. Overlooks and trails provide the former. For the latter you'll need closer access to the structures, which often—but not always—requires hitching yourself to a tour. The more intimate opportunities abound, from photographing shafts of light streaming through ceiling doorways to hand-hewn ladders descending into stone-walled living rooms, and various structures such as kivas and towers.

Aside from the cliff dwellings, photographers will also find other archeology. Of particular interest are the mesa-top sites. Far View was the most populated area, with about 50 known villages in only half a square-mile. The dwellings at the Far View sites, rather than being crafted of smooth sandstone blocks and sheltered by overhanging cliffs, are built of thousands of rectangular stones and sit aside unimpeded views of the surrounding landscape.

Despite all the great historic structures, Mesa Verde comprises more than ruins. The park is rife with beautiful vistas, including canyons and tablelands, wildflowers, stunning sunrises and sunsets, and unpolluted night skies. Plenty of wildlife resides here as well, including a population of wild horses that range between Mesa Verde and the bordering Ute reservation.

LOCATION TIPS > Photographing the cliff dwellings can be challenging due to the harsh light. When working the exteriors, overcast skies and shade are your friend; to help you find the latter, the park's website offers some per-site advice regarding the ideal times of day to shoot. Spruce Tree House is the best-preserved cliff dwelling, and is one of the finest for photographing interiors because you don't need to be with a tour for access (for much of the year, anyway), so you may walk and work at your own pace. The quarter-mile trail to the site passes through dense stands of Gambel oak on the canyon floor. It also brings you to the head of Petroglyph Point Trail, which leads past a 12-foot panel of rock art, as well as views of Spruce Canyon and Navajo Canyon. Cliff Palace is the largest cliff dwelling in North America. It provides excellent photography opportunities, but access to the interiors requires being on a guided tour; however, the park does offer a 90-minute, reasonably priced tour tailored for photographers. Almost five miles of the Mancos River flanks the eastern edge of Mesa Verde, and its moist banks provide a home for plant life not readily found in other parts of the park, such as cottonwood, willow, buffaloberry, mosses, orchids and ferns. If photographing here in the fall, the river is a good place to scout for color.

MOUNT RAINIER NATIONAL PARK

Washington

On a clear day, Mount Rainier defines the skyline for dozens of miles around. It's dramatic and massive (more than twice the height of surrounding mountains), thrusting from the landscape in the classic conical shape of a stratovolcano, and always topped with snow and ice. Despite its prominence, it's not the only photogenic feature the park has to offer.

If the volcano is the most famous icon of the park, the second most famous is the annual wildflower bloom. The peak display is in July and August, when the subalpine meadows are carpeted with lupines, daisies, lilies, paintbrush, cinquefoils, marigolds, bear grass and hundreds of other species. Flowers also bloom in the forests, aside stream beds and along lakesides. (In the latter two spots you can find one of my favorite floral subjects: monkey flowers.)

The park also contains a good number of lakes—many of which serve as perfect mirrors for photographing reflections of Mount Rainier—along with countless rivers, streams and creeks that wind down the mountainsides and through forests and meadows. Numerous waterfalls also make fine photography subjects, particularly Spray Falls, Paradise Falls, Comet Falls and Christine Falls. All the waterfalls tend to be at their best during spring thaws and autumn rains.

The weather around Mount Rainier complements the photography opportunities found within. In fact, for any weather you may encounter, there is a subject nearby that is well suited for it. Early- and late-day light sweeps across the open meadows and illuminates the namesake mountain unimpeded by the lower peaks in the Cascade Range. Fog and mist frequent the terrain, bringing a different mood to many scenes and obscuring otherwise busy backgrounds. Overcast skies are common and serve to diffuse the sunlight for close-up flower photography. And almost-daily rainfall recharges the waterfalls and brings the forests to life, particularly the rainforests of the northwest corner of the park.

Mount Rainier is also an excellent destination for winter photography—most roads are closed, but snowshoeing and cross-country skiing are permitted. The network of trails around Longmire, in particular, offers relatively easy winter access to nice scenery. Moreover, this is one of the few parks that permit some snowmobile access.

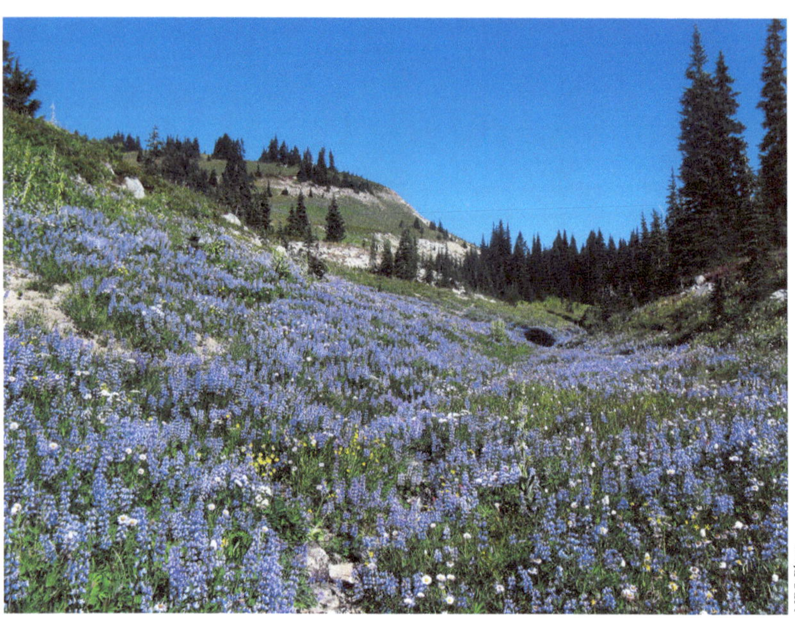

NPS Photo

Mount Rainier National Park

LOCATION TIPS > Mount Rainier has enough miles of roads for a good drive, and many of those miles are flanked by lens-worthy scenery. But those roads really are utilitarian: Their primary purpose is to get you and your camera to trailheads so that you can hike to some of the best mountain landscapes in the park system. For photographing reflections, definitely visit Reflection Lakes, which are not only beautiful but also easy to access. Also try Tipsoo Lake. And remember for both locations that reflections are usually best just before and at sun-up, before morning breezes bring ripples to the lake surface. For wildflowers, many spots are amazing, and perhaps the most famous of them (and most crowded, at times) is the Paradise area. Hike the 5.5-mile Skyline Trail for views of mountain skylines, wildflowers and waterfalls, including Myrtle Falls and Sluiskin Falls. For forest photography on an overcast day, try the Grove of the Patriarchs, a stand of western red-cedar, Douglas-fir and western hemlock situated on an island in the Ohanapecosh River. The one-mile trail crosses a suspension bridge, which is also a good photography subject. For a two-week backcountry photography adventure, consider the rugged 93-mile Wonderland Trail that circumnavigates Mount Rainier, passing and traversing alpine lakes and meadows, suspension bridges, glaciers, rivers, forests and waterfalls.

NATIONAL PARK OF AMERICAN SAMOA

American Samoa

THE NATIONAL PARK of American Samoa is one of the newest, most remote and least visited national parks. Those attributes are likely interrelated. It is also the only U.S. national park south of the equator.

The park is set upon three volcanic islands—Tutuila, Ta'u and Ofu—and within its boundaries are peaks of cloud forests, slopes of rainforest and expanses of Pacific Ocean. But it's the shoreline between those that will interest many photographers. From there you'll find opportunities for photographing seascapes and landscapes with cliffs and mountains rising above the water.

Wildlife photographers will find no large land animals—three species of bat (one with a three-foot wingspan, the flying fox) are the biggest wild mammals on the islands. Birds, however, are abundant. In particular, the Pacific imperial pigeon, or lupe, is beautiful and relatively common in the rainforests and around the bays. Also flitting about are collared kingfishers, bristle-thighed curlews, terns, boobies, frigatebirds, honeyeaters and tropical doves.

Culture photographers, however, will find one large mammal of interest: humans. The park is home to several villages, some secluded, where the locals are known for their friendliness and hospitality. (There's even a program that allows you to stay at local homes, perhaps the most preferred form of lodging for park visitors.) Just note that regional etiquette dictates asking permission before photographing people.

LOCATION TIPS > Ofu is home to a beautiful palm-lined, coral-sand beach interrupted by scattered boulders and edged by steep mountains that rise dramatically from the shore. At the north tip of the Ofu section of the park is Pola Island, an S-curve of sheer, tree-topped cliffs that are particularly picturesque as seen from the air or water. However, you can also find views of Pola from Vatia, a village on Tutuila, and from the Tuafanua and Pola Island trails. Underwater photographers will want to investigate the sea turtles and 900 species of fish in the crystal-clear waters of the park's coral reefs. The reefs at Olosega and Ofu are the most notable, the latter particularly for its size: 350 subsurface acres.

NORTH CASCADES NATIONAL PARK
Washington

FAR NORTH on the Washington-Canada border, in the heart of the Cascade Range, is one of the best spots in the park system for alpine photography: North Cascades National Park. The mountain scenery is so stunning and extensive that some call North Cascades "the American Alps."

But North Cascades offers more than just the mountains—you'll also find one of the forces that shaped the park's topography: glaciers. Over 300 of them are scattered among the peaks, along with numerous snowfields. All that frozen water melts a bit during the warm season, creating or feeding the parks' 500-plus lakes and ponds, its myriad swamps, marshes and beaver-dammed wetlands, and its countless rivers and streams. In many places the water is a unique shade of turquoise, due to the fine sediment created by the glaciers grinding the landscape. The glaciers also fuel another feature of the park that's popular for photographers: So many waterfalls and cascades dot the region that one would be foolish to try to guess the number, let alone count them.

As with many mountainous areas on the U.S. west coast, the two flanks of the Cascade Range are ecosystematically different. The west side traps much of the moisture moving landward from the Pacific, creating very green old-growth rainforests—dense woodlands of hemlock, red cedar and Douglas fir—much of it carpeted in moss, ferns and mushrooms. Alongside clearings you can also find groves of red alder, which along with bigleaf maples provide a colorful show in autumn. The east side is a more sparse and dry hilly landscape of sagebrush, pine, spruce and cottonwood.

LOCATION TIPS > Artist Point, beautiful and easy to access, offers a 360-degree view of mountain terrain, with nearby wildflower meadows and reflective lakes, all surrounded by Mount Baker on the west, Mount Shuksan on the east, and other various peaks of the Cascade Range. Several trails allow for easy wandering. In particular, try the Chain Lakes Loop, a six-mile jaunt past awe-inspiring views and several alpine lakes. You can use a wide-angle lens to capture grand panoramas, or a telephoto to isolate features of the landscape. The Horseshoe Basin Trail is ideal for the backcountry photographer. It passes more than a dozen waterfalls while leading to a large, hilly tundra meadow laced with wildflowers and tarns. The North

Cascades Highway bisects the park for about 80 miles. Along the way you'll find a plethora of photographic opportunities, including mountain skylines, waterfalls and the Skagit River, in addition to dramatic views of Ross Lake, Gorge Lake and Diablo Lake.

OLYMPIC NATIONAL PARK

Washington

OLYMPIC NATIONAL PARK is a jewel of wilderness situated on the Olympic Peninsula in northwest Washington. The confluence of weather patterns and ecosystems creates a diversity of landscapes and subjects for the photographer that is scarce in all but a few parks.

Olympic has three distinct regions for photography: the mountains, the rainforest and the coast. All offer drastically different and dynamic scenery and, best of all, they each often come packaged with the ideal light for the photographic possibilities they contain.

With 7,300-foot Mount Olympus as the centerpiece, the mountains rise and fall in jagged and random succession, a cascade of peaks and valleys that drift over the landscape toward the Pacific Ocean on one side and the Strait of Juan de Fuca on another. The few mountain roads and the many mountain trails lead visitors above the clouds that frequent the peninsula and offer direct views to both sunrises and sunsets, along with inexhaustible supplies of alpine scenery. Within this landscape live black bears, black-tailed deer, northern spotted owls, raccoons, snowshoe hares and endemic Olympic marmots. The many subalpine meadows support thriving communities of wildflowers, including lovely avalanche, glacier lily and an extensive population of lupine.

Moisture moving inland from the ocean gets trapped on the western slopes, fueling expanses of rainforest. This vibrant environment—large tracts of it old-growth—is about as green as a scene can be. The leaves are green, the undergrowth is green, and the moss and tiny plants that cover every surface are green. Everything that's growing appears to be on something else that's growing. And because the rainforest is almost always under cloud cover, you can usually get even exposures that allow for saturating the green to its full potential. Living among this beautiful, always-dripping chaos are an unseemly number

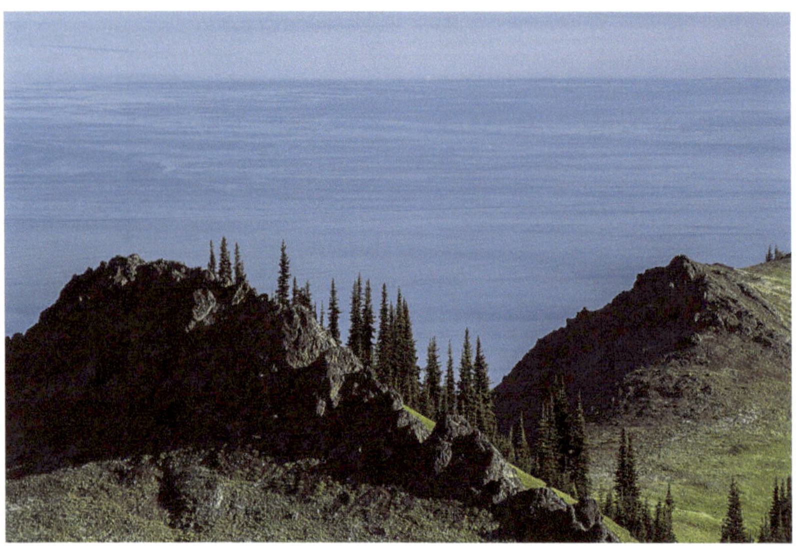

Olympic National Park

of bugs, bright-yellow banana slugs, and portions of the largest unmanaged herd of Roosevelt elk in the northwest.

To the west of the primary section of Olympic is 73 miles of wilderness coastline, much of it accessible only by boat, trail or beach-hiking. Tall sea stacks stand offshore, large enough to support their own ecosystems on top. Mixed in are dramatic rock formations and high cliffs, and sandy beaches lined with enormous piles of scattered and weathered beach logs. The frequent fog that rolls in makes for moody conditions for photography, especially when infused with late-day sun.

LOCATION TIPS > Hurricane Ridge is a good starting point for finding and photographing mountain scenery. Trails of varying lengths branch in multiple directions, through meadows and along ridges. The black-tailed deer in this area are renowned for their indifference toward humans, including photographers. A hike to nearby Hurricane Hill affords access to great mountain views and hillsides of wildflowers and marmot burrows. The Hoh Rain Forest features a couple of loop trails that you can circle over and over again and see something new every time. Tripods and polarizing filters are required equipment here, as are rain gear and waterproof shoes. Any of the beaches are great for photography, but on a cloudy day make a note to explore Ruby Beach, a topnotch spot for photographing tide pools. Starfish, anemones, barnacles and sea urchins are common.

PETRIFIED FOREST NATIONAL PARK

Arizona

PETRIFIED FOREST is unique in that it's one of the few parks created not for its beautiful vistas, but rather for its geologic riches. Nearly a quarter-billion years ago the area was quite different, rife with life and rivers. Felled trees fossilized into one of the densest collections of petrified wood in the world, leaving behind a treasure of compositional elements for the modern photographer. The colors of the remnant logs vary throughout the park—from red to gold to black—providing a nice variety worth moving around for.

Unfortunately for the landscape photographer, all of that petrified wood lies around terrain that, while sensational to look at, mostly lacks dynamic features to base an image around. You can find some rock formations in the park, and some grassland, and some mesas and buttes; but in many areas, a fair amount of creativity is needed to add interest, depth and dimension to compositions. Another challenge at Petrified Forest is that it enforces daylight-only visiting hours (to curtail fossil theft), so being on-site for sunrise and sunset light is not as easy as at most other parks—here it requires either a special-use permit or registered backcountry camping.

As sparse a landscape as Petrified Forest is, the northern section comprises some of the best sites of Painted Desert, one of the more beautiful badlands in the park system. The eroding landscape reveals bands of geologic color in the hills, particularly reds and oranges that glow warmly during golden hour.

The park also offers opportunities for archeological photography. Puerco Pueblo is the 800-year-old remains of a sandstone-block village that was home to an estimated 200 people. The area also contains petroglyphs, as does Newspaper Rock, which is relatively nearby. At the south end of the park, Agate House is a millennium-old pueblo built of petrified wood that was reconstructed in the 1930s by the Civilian Conservation Corps. And a more recent archeological site is the segment of old Route 66 that runs through Petrified Forest—the only such stretch of the old highway in any of the national parks.

LOCATION TIPS > The road in the northern section of Petrified Forest features several lookouts with excellent views of Painted Desert, along with easy access for commencing hikes into the landscape. Kachina Point in particular is an area worth exploring for colorful desert topography, especially in morning light. Kachina is one of the termini for the mile-long Painted Desert Rim Trail, which provides a nice overview of the area and wanders through some of the only woodland in the park. Blue Mesa offers more variety in hue, in the hills of highly textured, blue-toned bentonite clay. Overlooks provide impressive panoramic views of the badlands, and the Blue Mesa loop trail brings you to the valley floor, where you'll find warm-colored petrified wood to juxtapose against the cool-colored backgrounds. Giant Logs Trail, though short at just under a half-mile, passes among some of the most impressive logs in the park, in terms of size and color.

PINNACLES NATIONAL PARK

California

WHAT DO you get when an ancient earthquake splits a 23-million-year-old volcano in half? A broken terrain of rock formations, mountain views and caves that in 2012 became the United States' newest national park.

Over 30 miles of hiking trails roam among Pinnacles' rocky spires, lush grassland, oak-pine woodland and jagged scree. In the spring (widely considered the park's most picturesque season), flora brings color to parts of the landscape in the form of green grasses and multicolored wildflowers, such as lupine, California poppy and manzanita. Fall brings a bit of color as well, primarily in the cottonwood and sycamore trees. All of those elements function to add softness and visual life to an otherwise rugged environment. You can portray that dynamic in photographs by juxtaposing the botanic with the geologic, the life with the earth it springs from.

Wildlife opportunities are better at other parks, but this does happen to be one of the few places to photograph California condors in the wild. Prairie falcons soar among the spires, and the greater roadrunner, California thrasher, turkey vulture, Stellar's jay, yellow-billed magpie, lesser goldfinch and canyon wren also call the park home.

Moreover, Pinnacles is a good park for cave photography. Though not as long as those at Mammoth Cave or Carlsbad Caverns, Pinnacles' talus caves are in some ways easier to photograph. The reason is in the geology: Because these caves are formed by boulders fallen into sheer canyons, light leaks in at points, granting creative opportunities not found in deep underground chasms.

LOCATION TIPS > The High Peaks Loop trail is just under 10 miles long, and is not always an easy hike. But it brings you through a fair representation of the park's scenery. You could easily spend a day hiking and photographing in one direction, then doing it backward the next day to reverse your view of the light on the rolling hills, wildflowers, canyons and pinnacles. And then you can hike it again and again for a few days afterward, at different times of day, without exhausting the creative options. High Peaks is a particularly stunning area that is becoming one of the iconic scenes of the park. You can photograph it in early- or late-day light, and can silhouette it against the setting sun. The Bear Gulch Reservoir offers opportunities for photographing rock formations and their reflections, and one of the trails leading there brings you through one of the two primary cave systems in the park.

REDWOOD NATIONAL AND STATE PARKS

California

AUTHOR JOHN STEINBECK wrote, "No one has ever successfully painted or photographed a redwood tree." Regardless, you should try. Redwood National Park is one of the more breathtaking environments in the United States. Standing among the redwoods is at once daunting and peaceful. You feel small, but invigorated at being part of something so big. Yes, as a photography subject it's challenging. That's just a better reason to approach it, especially when it's so beautiful.

Fortunately, Redwood does provide a little help. A trick to depicting size in a two-dimensional photograph is juxtaposition—including a smaller, recognizable element in the frame that will help the viewer appreciate the scale, and therefore the magnitude of your primary subject. To help you do that, the floor of the redwood forests have smaller trees, bushes and carpets of ferns.

The park also features one of the country's more renowned rhododendron blooms—usually occurring sometime between mid-May and mid-June—which adds soft color to the scene. The region's weather helps the photographer, too, as coastal fog often rolls into the forest in morning and late afternoon, especially in summer. The fog will help you isolate trees from the background, or you can depict them disappearing into the heights of the mist. When the morning fog begins to dissipate, you can turn toward the sunrise and photograph the crepuscular rays streaming through the forest.

Should you tire of trees, you can also visit the water. Redwood is home to 40 miles of pristine Pacific coastline, where you can photograph seascapes, sea stacks, boulders, seals, tide pools and driftwood, along with some of the best sunsets in the park system. If you'd like to aim your lens at wildlife, you can find elk, bears, fox and bald eagles. And though this isn't the best park for waterfalls, Trillium Falls is worth the relatively short hike.

LOCATION TIPS > Most photographers prefer working in the groves at the northern end of the park, particularly Stout Grove—and Lady Bird Johnson Redwood Grove is a good spot to photograph the rhododendron in spring. Southern areas of the park can also be great to shoot, such as the scenes found on the Damnation Creek Trail, which includes stands of coastal redwoods, forest floors of giant ferns, and a terminus at rocky coastline. Enderts Beach has perhaps the best tide pools, where you can photograph starfish and sea anemone, among other shallow-dwelling ocean life. The beach is accessible via a half-mile trail through forest. Elk can be found in many areas, but be sure to look in the appropriately named Elk Meadow off Davidson Road. Keep in mind that Redwood National Park is part of a larger system that includes fantastic state parks which also protect the redwood forests. In particular, Del Norte Coast Redwoods State Park and Jedediah Smith Redwood State Park offer great photography opportunities.

ROCKY MOUNTAIN NATIONAL PARK

Colorado

One of the foremost U.S. locations for alpine photography is, by no coincidence, named after the country's most prominent mountain range. With many miles of strategically laid road, Rocky Mountain National Park offers plenty of spectacular landscape photography opportunities that are easy to access via car. That's why this park attracts as many visitors as Yellowstone despite its significantly smaller size. Subsequently, in high season (midsummer) the roads and trailheads can be crowded. But the park also boasts 355 miles of hiking trails, some with lengths and elevation gains that scare off casual tourists, so there's always someplace quiet to photograph in Rocky Mountain.

The primary attraction is, of course, the mountains. The park's 415 square miles are home to countless peaks, including 78 with altitudes over 12,000 feet. What also reaches that height is Trail Ridge Road, a picturesque 48-mile drive that connects the east and west sides of the park. Eleven miles of the drive are above the tree line, winding through alpine tundra and bushland, while the other miles meander through groves of aspen and forests of spruce and fir, and past views of valleys, meadows and mountain skylines.

The forests of Rocky Mountain light up in the fall when the aspens turn yellow and gold. In many spots this color weaves among the dark evergreens; juxtaposing the two, you can create abstract compositions of the intermingled colors. Moreover, the first snow usually falls in early autumn, dusting the colored trees with white, providing another great opportunity for photographers who serendipitously time their trip perfectly at the uncertain edge of the seasons. Weather brings other opportunities as well, as fog and violent lightning storms are common to the area.

Wildlife photographers, too, find plenty of subjects at Rocky Mountain, particularly with the elk that frequent the meadows in early morning and at the end of the day. Other mammals commonly sighted include moose, bighorn sheep (particularly in late spring), mule deer, coyotes, beavers, snowshoe hares and yellow-bellied marmots. Black bears and mountain lions also inhabit Rocky Mountain, but are seldom seen.

LOCATION TIPS > The area around Bear Lake is what an entire national park might look like if it was designed by landscape photographers. The many trails in this region lead to Fern Lake, Odessa Lake, Lake Helene, Spruce Lake, Cub Lake, Emerald Lake, Dream Lake, Haiyaha Lake, The Loch, Sky Pond, Mills Lake, Jewel Lake and, of course, Bear Lake—all within just a few forested miles of one another. All are fine locations to find wildlife and wildflowers, reflections of mountain and forest scenery, and more. Moreover, that same compact trail system will bring you to Timberline Falls, Alberta Falls and Fern Falls, past numerous cascades and streams, and through groves of aspen and conifers. The Bear Lake area is a great winter destination, too, as you can snowshoe or cross-country ski to all the aforementioned spots. Old Fall River Road is an 11-mile gravel road that a photographer might need an entire day to drive when accounting for the many photo opportunities along the way. The trip will lead you past waterfalls, streams, ponds, an alluvial fan, ridges and meadows, and through tundra and groves of pine and aspen. The road itself is also a nice subject, as its curves and switchbacks create leading lines and visual elements for both simple and complex compositions. The eastern side of the park is popularly regarded as the better half for scenic photography; but that only means you're likely to find more solitude and tourist-free landscapes on the also-beautiful western side, where you'll see a healthy selection of beaver ponds and meadows.

SAGUARO NATIONAL PARK

Arizona

SAGUARO is a park based mostly around one thing: cacti. They are, to be fair, very large cacti—up to 60 feet tall. The park features a rather large forest of them in the southern Arizona desert, split into eastern and western halves by the city of Tucson.

The primary cactus of the park is its namesake, the giant saguaro that is a visual icon of the American southwest. But you'll also find other cacti, including barrel, prickly pear and the photogenic teddybear cholla. Lest you think a cactus is boring to photograph, try it backlit by warm light, when the rays of the sun highlight each of its thousands of needles; or silhouetted affront a sunrise or sunset, showcasing its unique form against the colored sky; or in spring, when it blooms with white, yellow, green and pink flowers.

Saguaro National Park provides photographers with the usual selection of desert wildlife, including coyotes, roadrunners and jackrabbits. You may also observe fox, javelinas, spotted owls, white-nosed coatis and horned lizards in the desert, and black bears, white-tailed deer and raccoons in the mountains. Bobcats and mountain lions live throughout the park, but are elusive. And though rare to see, you may also be able to photograph a desert tortoise.

The landscape photographer will love this Sonoran Desert environment as well, with its canyons and rock formations that bring interest to a terrain that appears to be barren only at first glance. While Saguaro is not an ideal place for photographing the night sky (due to the nearby lights of Tucson tainting the darkness), it does provide a fitting setting for moonlit scenes.

LOCATION TIPS > Many photographers believe the west side of the park offers the best photo opportunities. The Bajada Loop Drive will bring you through foothills filled with saguaro and through flatter terrain with enough contour to make it interesting for photography. The 11-mile Hugh Norris Trail is a great place to seek out landscapes, from both the desert floor and from overlooks. On the east side, Rincon Mountain rises high enough to support different tree species at different elevations, providing habitats that range from desert to oak woodland to pine forests. On Cactus Forest Loop Drive, at about the five-mile point is a nice spot for shooting the sun setting over the desert. Keep your eye out for southwestern winters that are unusually wet, as they can prompt breathtaking spring wildflower blooms in the park.

SEQUOIA NATIONAL PARK
California

ONE OF THE United States' oldest national parks protects some of the world's largest and oldest trees—the magnificent sequoias of the southern Sierra Nevada. The trees aren't as tall as the coastal redwoods, but that doesn't make them easier to photograph—the sequoias still reach over 300 feet high. They are also incredibly wide—up to 45 feet in diameter. The largest of the park's sequoias is also the largest tree by volume in the world: Known as General Sherman, it stands 275 feet high, is 36.5 feet wide at the trunk, and has a calculated volume of over 52,500 cubic feet. The inherent photographic challenge is accurately revealing such enormity in a small and two-dimensional format.

Giant Forest's 40 miles of hiking trails lead through the park's most notable sequoia grove. This is where General Sherman has its roots, and the area also contains several photogenic sequoia-encircled meadows. The Congress Trail and the Trail of the Sequoias are particularly famous for their views of hundreds of impressive specimens. The trees often grow in stands, and the closer together they are, the easier they are to photograph well (generally speaking). Fallen logs are scattered on the forest floor, providing opportunities for a different perspective and creative element. If you want to photograph sequoias in winter, Giant Forest is where to be, as the park permits snowshoeing throughout the area.

The trees are the face of the park, but Sequoia also offers beautiful backcountry scenery. The Sierra Nevada topography was created by glaciers, rivers and seismic activity, leaving behind jagged mountaintops, deep valleys, boulder-strewn meadows, dramatic canyons and countless caverns. The park is known for its wildlife, too, particularly its conspicuous population of black bears. Also common are yellow-bellied marmots, coyotes, mule deer and squirrels.

Sequoia is not regarded as a waterfall park, but it does include one such feature that is relatively well-known: Tokopah Falls. Unfortunately, the breadth of it is not great for photography. But it does offer the opportunity to isolate its components in creative ways, and to photograph the many cascades you'll see while hiking there. Additionally, the park contains over 3,000 alpine lakes and ponds, and 2,600 miles of rivers and streams, most notably the Kings, Kaweah and Kern rivers.

LOCATION TIPS > In Giant Forest, Crescent Meadow is big enough to be beautiful and small enough to photograph as a whole among the surrounding sequoias. As with any forest meadow, one of its rewarding features is that you can photograph tree stands from the outside, giving the appearance of being immersed in a grove while being more free with composition and angles of light. The meadow sprouts with wildflowers in summer, and is a good place to spot bears feeding among the open grasses. Much of the same can also be said of Round Meadow. Moro Rock is a nice location for photographing the sun setting over the forested hills and peaks of the Western Divide. Alternatively, the rock is a nice subject as a 245-foot granite dome rising from the trees. It can be photographed in sunset light from parts of the nearby trail. Mineral King is a subalpine glacial valley in the southern region of Sequoia, loved by backcountry hikers and campers, but visited by few others. Photographers will find quiet views of mountain peaks, riparian habitats, meadows, lakes and tarns. If interested in cave photography, certainly explore Crystal Cave, a marvel of polished marble stalagmites and stalactites. Be aware that tripods are not allowed, but portions of the interior are artificially lit.

SHENANDOAH NATIONAL PARK

Virginia

IN SOME OF the oldest settled land in the U.S. sits one of its oldest national parks. It's a beautiful park, though wily: It makes a photographer work to find most of its worthy subjects.

Shenandoah is almost entirely covered in deciduous forest, and consists of 300 square miles of the Blue Ridge Mountains, which in the park range in elevation from 530 to 4,051 feet. From many vantage points, the mountains layer into the horizon, creating one of the more famous peaceful landscape tableaus in the nation. Water runs down the sides of those slopes just about everywhere. Seventy mountain watershed basins produce about 90 streams that flow into rapids, cascades and waterfalls in every corner of the park, and through wetlands, marshes and swamps.

The main hardtop tributary of Shenandoah is Skyline Drive, the 105-mile two-lane road that bisects the east and west halves, terminating at the south into the Blue Ridge Parkway (another fine photography destination). Skyline Drive is the sole destination for many visitors, as it's famous for spectacular views of the Appalachian Mountains and surrounding countryside. It's particularly popular in fall as one of the east coast's most renowned leaf-peeping hotspots—meaning that it's also great for autumn photography. Due to the varying elevation, you can find peak color somewhere in the park at any time of the fall-foliage season. Along Skyline Drive are the heads or intersections of almost all of the park's 500 miles of trails, so the road serves as your starting point to just about anything you'll want to photograph.

Shenandoah has less of a wildlife selection than many of the other parks, but is known for its prominent populations of white-tailed deer and black bears. The former are the easier to find, especially around Big Meadows, but you can't spend much time in the park without spotting the latter, as well. Coyotes, eastern cottontail rabbits and gray squirrels also reside in Shenandoah.

LOCATION TIPS > If you want to photograph cascades of mountains, you need not venture far from Skyline Drive. Nearly 70 pull-offs and overlooks will provide you with plenty of opportunities. However, note that because Shenandoah is such a slim park, most of the overlooks look over developed farmland and small towns. If you prefer your mountain photos

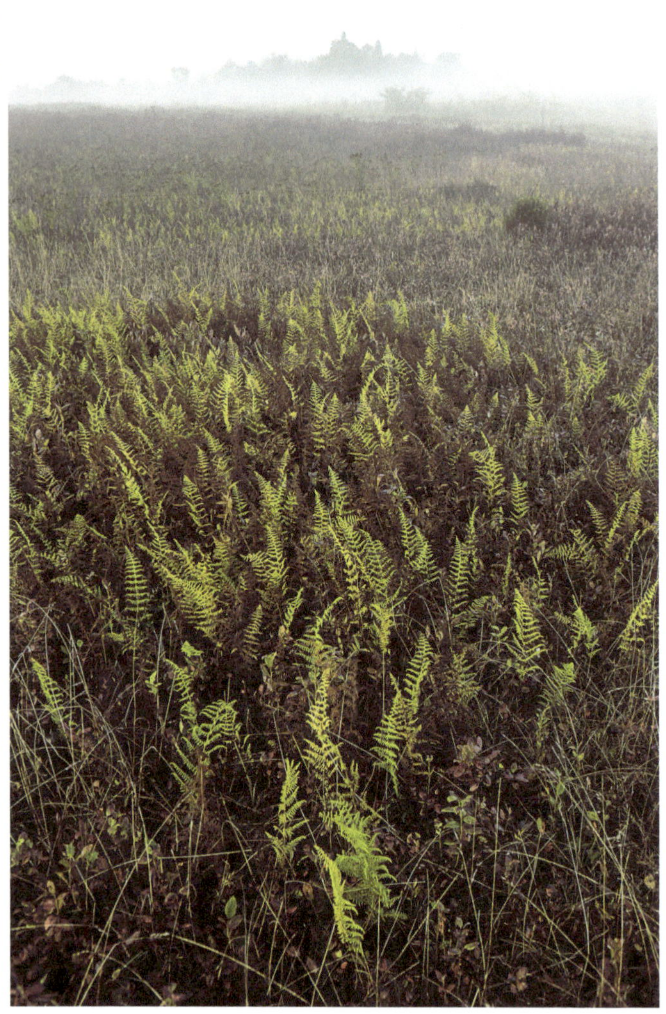

Shenandoah National Park

to be nature-only, try the pull-offs that face north or south (and just the latter for winter sunrises and sunsets). For overlooks away from the road, short-hike just about any stretch of the Appalachian Trail, 101 miles of which wind through the park's mountains. Waterfalls are one of Shenandoah's primary photographic attractions, but every one of them requires a hike with an elevation gain on the return trip. For an efficient waterfall expedition, try hiking the Cedar Run/Whiteoak Circuit. With photography, it can easily be an all-day expedition, and the trek back to Skyline Drive is strenuous—look forward to a 3,000-foot elevation gain in three miles. But the effort will bring you past eight waterfalls, several forest pools and many more cascades than you could keep track of. The star of the photo spots in Shenandoah is Big Meadows, a five-acre clearing in the middle of the park. It's easy to access, a marvel to just stand and look at, and offers a wealth of lens subjects. A walk on the flanking fire road can swiftly bring you to the less-visited southern end, where you can saunter along the tree line searching for early- and late-day wildlife. Game trails slither through the meadow, allowing you access to lone trees, boulders, wildflowers, ferns, wild blueberry, seasonal wetlands and more. Big Meadows is an especially great location in fog, which, fortunately for photographers, blows in frequently.

THEODORE ROOSEVELT NATIONAL PARK

North Dakota

Located in the North Dakota badlands, Theodore Roosevelt National Park is a celebration of a scenic and quiet landscape, and of the man who for a good portion of his life was inspired by the wildness of that land. Theodore Roosevelt spent parts of 15 years as a resident and cattle rancher along the region's Little Missouri River. The experience shaped his philosophy of conservation, which eventually led to him signing five national parks into existence when he served as the 26th president of the United States; he also created 15 national monuments (five of which later became national parks) under the Antiquities Act, which he signed into law.

Roosevelt's Elkhorn Ranch is one of the three separate units of the national park. On his old ranchland, only some of the foundation of the structures remains. But the surrounding wilderness is much the same as Roosevelt experienced. Cottonwoods stand among the river meadows, alongside cliffs, buttes and plateaus. Still, the most dramatic scenery of the park belongs to its north and south units.

The North Dakota badlands are similar to those in South Dakota's Badlands National Park, but with a little more vegetation and a lot more wildlife. Depending on where you are, the rounded badland hills take on warm and/or cool tones, from beiges and reds to blues and grays. Mixed in are interesting rock formations, such as caprocks and spherical sandstone concretions. Relics of the region's glacial past remain, too, in the form of granite glacial erratics in the North Unit.

The grassland prairies at Theodore Roosevelt are also part of its unique aesthetic. In the wet season, these green expanses add color to the otherwise dry landscape, as do the wildflowers after a rainy spring. Park wildlife such as bison, elk, pronghorn, and white-tailed and mule deer can often be found grazing among the grasses.

Black-tailed prairie dogs are common, and many of their towns are well marked on the official map; some you can drive to, and remote towns can be reached via hiking. These areas are also good spots to watch for carnivorous wildlife, such as coyotes, hawks and golden eagles, which hunt the prairie dogs. The most noteworthy mammal found in Theodore Roosevelt is the small population of wild horses. Several bands of five to 15 roam the park, particularly in the upland plateaus and in Painted Canyon.

LOCATION TIPS > Oxbow Overlook is one of the iconic vistas of Theodore Roosevelt. Located at the end of the North Unit's 14-mile Scenic Drive, the overlook offers an elevated view of the Little Missouri River snaking through the badlands. The view is most colorful in fall, when the leaves of the cottonwoods along the riverbank turn gold. From the overlook, hiking either direction on the Achenbach Trail affords more vantage points and river-level access. For another S-curve view of the river, but in the South Unit, hike the half-mile (round-trip) Wind Canyon Trail. Distinctive mushroom-cap hoodoos can be found along the Caprock Coulee Nature Trail and the Petrified Forest Loop.

VIRGIN ISLANDS NATIONAL PARK

Virgin Islands

PRIMARILY located on the Caribbean island of St. John, Virgin Islands National Park is a 19-acre paradise of pristine shores, coral reefs and tropical forests, and countless historic and prehistoric archeological sites.

The primary attractions for most visitors are underwater, in the form of numerous coral reefs, sea-grass meadows, sandy bottoms and forests of mangrove prop roots. Each environment houses the wildlife that you would expect to be living there: 500 species of tropical fish (including starfish and puffers), sea turtles, rays, crustaceans, sponges and more. Moreover, the crystal-clear water makes this an ideal park for snorkeling and aquatic photography.

Back on land, you can remove your underwater housing and mount a telephoto lens to photograph the myriad birds found on the shore, in the forests and everywhere in between. They include pelicans, red-tailed hawks, mangrove cuckoos, hummingbirds, egrets, herons and 50 species of indigenous tropical birds. Other wildlife photography opportunities involve bats, crabs, iguanas and a selection of invasive species, such as (yes, seriously) wild donkeys.

Moving in from the coast, you can explore swamps, scrubland and upland tropical forest, and survey the view from St. John's highest point, Bordeaux Mountain. Hiking trails or water transportation (including kayaks) can bring you to the many bays and beaches around the park, which all harbor seascape scenery. The beaches, depending on their location on the island, come in a few varieties (sand, coral and pebble), which lend a different aesthetic to different spots.

Surrounding the park in a three-mile band is Virgin Islands Coral Reef National Monument, established to protect the coral reefs, mangroves and sea-grass beds around St. John Island. Most of it is accessible only by boat, aside from Hurricane Hole, which you can hike to, and which happens to be the part you'd most likely want to visit.

LOCATION TIPS > Trunk Bay is the most popular spot on the island, especially among tourists—but that's not necessarily a reason to stay away from it. It's a beautiful spot, one frequently named among the most scenic beaches in the world. Beneath the waves you'll find a snorkeling trail, but due to the heavy swim traffic the coral is not pristine. Cinnamon Bay also has good snorkeling, and both of these spots rent the required gear in case you haven't traveled with your own. The Reef Bay Trail will bring you through different kinds of forest and a variety of tropical flowers, past historic structures and millennium-old petroglyphs, to a seasonal waterfall, and finally to Genti Bay, a great spot for a swim or a snorkel or some seascape photography. Hurricane Hole is known for its remote atmosphere and peaceful waters, which provide excellent snorkeling conditions for photographing sea life and the colorful coral growing among the roots of coastal mangroves. The area is also rife with seabirds and wading birds that are relatively easy to photograph from land or kayak.

VOYAGEURS NATIONAL PARK

Minnesota

Set at the very top of the contiguous United States, Voyageurs National Park is a land of Northwoods lakes and islands—a lot of them. Forty percent of the park is water; sixty percent comprises the Kabetogama Peninsula and the 900 islands that surround it.

Thirty lakes are within the boundaries of Voyageurs. The four main lakes (Rainy, Kabetogama, Namakan and Sand Point) are the aquatic hub of the park, and are the primary conduits for traveling within. Each of the other 26 lakes are either on the peninsula or one of the islands. Many are connected by navigable narrows or portage trails, which is what makes water travel here not only nearly necessary, but also pleasant and efficient. The earthy parts are also punctuated with other wetland features, including streams, swamps, marshes, bogs and ponds (natural and beaver-induced).

Along the edges of the land, 600 miles of lakeshore squiggle into bays and inlets, providing sheltered pockets of wilderness lined with rocks and cliffs, and flanked with hardwood or boreal forest. White, red and jack pines mix with spruce and fir. Among them are stands of both birch and aspen, with some maples and oaks interspersed, which tinge the landscape with golds, oranges and reds in fall. On the ground—lining streams and bays, covering island meadows and rocky points—over 400 species of wildflowers bloom at various times of the warm seasons.

Moose are perhaps the park's most picturesque mammalian resident, and can sometimes be spotted around water at the fringes of daylight. White-tailed deer are common, and otters, fox, weasels and snowshoe hares make occasional appearances. Gray wolves aren't often seen, but there's a good chance you'll hear them at night. And because of all the water, birds are a common sight at Voyageurs, particularly those that enjoy lake food. Bald eagles are prevalent, as are ring-billed and herring gulls, great blue herons and common loons.

For locals, winter is a popular season for exploring Voyageurs, and traveling photographers can do the same with relative ease. Ice roads are plowed on the lake surface, allowing for car travel to a few places normally accessible only by boat. Snowmobiles are also allowed on the ice, as well as on 110 miles of marked snowmobile trails on the peninsula and islands.

Snowshoes and cross-country skis allow you to branch out even further to photograph one of the country's most unique landscapes in its harshest state.

LOCATION TIPS > Some good, accessible scenery can be found around the Ash River Visitor Center, which you can drive to. The lake views from the nearby shores are nice at both sunrise and sunset. From the visitor center, hike the 2.5-mile loop to Blind Ash Bay, a quiet spot that is beautiful with a morning mist floating over the water, especially in autumn. Some of the best photography spots on the water tend to be the countless coves that are carved into the islands and the shores of the Kabetogama Peninsula. Those are, generally, the most predictable places to find wildlife, and tend to be placid in the morning. The peninsula is where to look for moose, as almost all of the park's population lives there. Anderson Bay features bluffs that rise 80 feet from the waterline. They're a nice photography subject, but moreover, hiking to the top affords terrific views of Rainy Lake and the nearby points and offshore skerries. At 9.5 miles, the north-south Cruiser Lake Trail traverses the peninsula, connecting several lakes and ponds while roaming through forest and along ridges.

WIND CAVE NATIONAL PARK

South Dakota

POSITIONED at the merging point of the Great Plains and the Black Hills, Wind Cave National Park offers the photographer far more than its name suggests.

The park's 143 miles of limestone caves are known primarily for their air movements—not for dazzling interiors, like some of the other caves in the park system. However, the geology of these caves does include some interesting formations, such as boxwork, frostwork and flowstone. Photographing the interior requires either some compromises or some cash. Access is permitted only with tours, and some don't allow photography. A few tours do allow photography, but none allow tripods. If you want to use support, you'll need to apply for (and pay for) a special-use permit, which may or may not be granted.

If the idea or logistics of a cave shoot aren't appealing, then perhaps the other half of Wind Cave will be: the upper, outdoor half. The sunlit part of the park comprises over 44 square miles of prairie grassland and ponderosa pine forests.

Wind Cave National Park

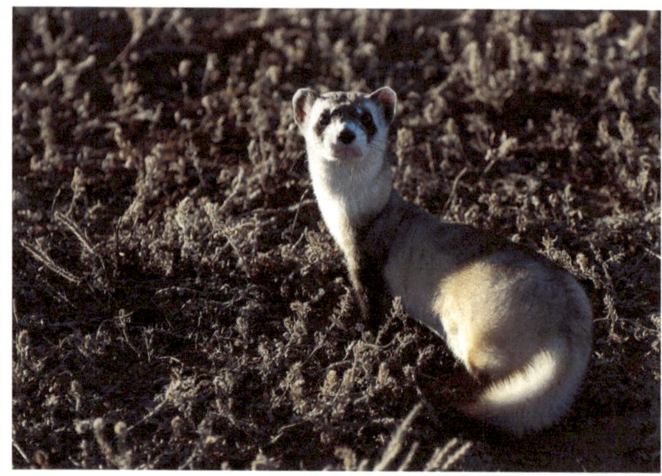

NPS Photo

Because of the transition of ecosystems across the park, a wider variety of wildlife can be found here than might normally be expected in such a relatively small area. Prevalent birds include prairie falcons, red-tailed hawks, golden eagles, western meadowlarks, woodpeckers and wild turkeys. Resident mammals include elk, pronghorn, coyotes, black-tailed prairie dogs, and white-tailed and mule deer. Bison were reintroduced to the park in 1913, and excel here—they number about 400, many of which are rather conspicuous. In 2007, another species was reintroduced: the rare and highly endangered black-footed ferret. They're nocturnal and spend almost all of their time underground, so you're unlikely to see one—but they have been seen, and they have been photographed.

LOCATION TIPS > From the main scenic roads, generally speaking, the landscape photography opportunities are in the south of the park, and the forest photography in the north. For more remote landscape opportunities, try the East Bison Flats Trail, which rolls along the hills of the prairie and affords views of the Black Hills. Wind Cave supports multiple prairie dog towns. One of the most accessible is near the junction of Routes 87 and 385, and a backcountry town can be found along the Sanctuary Trail. Incidentally, the towns are also good places to look for coyotes and black-footed ferrets, because both eat prairie dogs. On the east side of the park, two primitive roads ramble through more remote grassland, and are an excellent spot for photographing herds of bison and pronghorn.

WRANGELL-ST. ELIAS NATIONAL PARK & PRESERVE

Alaska

PERHAPS THERE IS NO SURPRISE in the fact that the largest U.S. national park is in the largest state. Wrangell-St. Elias National Park & Preserve in southeast Alaska is huge—21,000 square miles, six times the size of Yellowstone. It contains a massive array of mountain peaks, expanses of tundra, boreal spruce forest, ocean shoreline, alder and willow thickets, alpine meadows and lakes, and rivers and waterfalls.

Those mountains also contain the largest glacial system in the U.S. Over 25 percent of the park is covered with glaciers, including one—Malaspina Glacier—that is larger than Rhode Island. Kennicott Glacier is one of the more popular for photography, as it can be accessed relatively easily and has pronounced flow stripes that can be used to lead the eye in compositions (as seen from Mount Donoho, in particular). Hubbard Glacier also is notable in that it begins in the second-highest mountain in North America and is the largest tidewater glacier on the continent, with its six-mile-wide, 600-foot-tall face calving into Disenchantment Bay. Some of the glaciers can be hiked across, providing unique angles for photography. And some contain ice caves that can be explored and photographed (though this is certainly a risk best taken with the assistance of an experienced guide).

Due to its size, location and variety of habitats, Wrangell-St. Elias has a large and diverse wildlife population. The park contains one of the continent's heaviest concentrations of Dall's sheep, which you can find in the mountains—along with, of course, mountain goats. Black, brown and grizzly bears (the latter two are subspecies, but justify being differentiated) are common, as are several other large mammals, such as bison, wolves, moose and caribou. Local birds include trumpeter swans, bald eagles, spruce grouse, woodpeckers and great horned, boreal and northern hawk owls. On the coast you may find sea lions, harbor seals, sea otters, porpoises and whales.

Due not only to its size, but also to the beauty of the topography, Wrangell-St. Elias is tremendous for aerial photography. Scenic flights may be chartered from many nearby towns. Bush pilots can also leave you in the backcountry (landing on, for example, a glacier) and return to pick you up at a predetermined date and location.

LOCATION TIPS > The easiest self-reliant way to get into Wrangell-St. Elias is by driving or biking one of the two unpaved roads that enter the park: McCarthy Road and Nabesna Road, which are 60 and 42 miles long, respectively. Both pass extensive views of mountains, rivers, lakes and wilderness; both provide access to scores of trailheads of varying lengths; and both dead-end at the sites of retired mines. Along McCarthy Road, two railroad bridges over a century old make interesting photography subjects. The Kuskulana River Bridge spans a 283-foot gorge at 200 feet above the water. The all-wood Gilahina Trestle curves unkept and unsteady through the forest, 90 feet over the river. From the small town of McCarthy (within the park, at the end of the appropriately named McCarthy Road), you can drive, bike or hike to Kennecott, a preserved mountainside mining community. Nabesna Road, in the park's northern section, is more primitive and less traveled. For coastal scenery, consider exploring Icy Bay on a multi-day kayak trip. The bay borders the St. Elias Mountains, which rise to 18,000 feet within 10 miles of shore—it's the highest coastal mountain range in the world. The bay is home to fjords, calving glaciers, icebergs, shoreline wildflowers, marine mammals and sea birds.

YELLOWSTONE NATIONAL PARK

Idaho / Montana / Wyoming

YELLOWSTONE is perhaps the ultimate playground for photographers. As long as your camera is working, you can never be bored here. And, frankly, you likely wouldn't be bored without the camera, either.

A large expanse of wilderness—much of which is contained in an active caldera—makes for a wide spectrum of photo opportunities that range from wildlife to landscape to geology. The most notable of those is probably the countless number of geysers. Old Faithful is the most famous, but while it is amazing to watch, it's not even close to being the best to photograph. And the geothermic features don't end there. You also see a steady supply of fumaroles, hot springs and mud pots of all sizes, shapes and colors. You can photograph these features as simple subjects, or get creative and use them to complement the aesthetics of the surrounding landscape. For example, dense steam from hot springs can be used to silhouette tree skeletons,

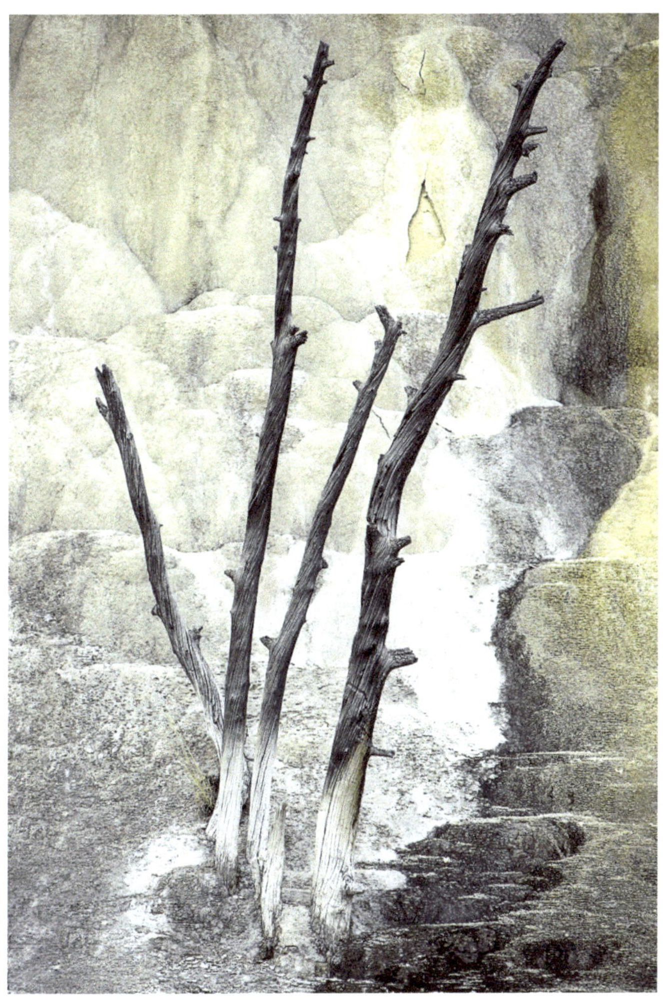

Yellowstone National Park

or the steam from hundreds of fumaroles can be backlit to create an otherworldly tableau.

Yellowstone is also renowned for its wildlife. Bears, bison, elk, deer, moose, pronghorn, bighorn sheep and coyotes are prevalent. Wolves also populate the park in several places, and while not easy to get close to (you're not supposed to try—you have to hope for luck that they'll get relatively close to you), it's not impossible to come away with a photo of one. And all those opportunities shadow the many more smaller animals you'll encounter, from raccoons and badgers to eagles and other birds of prey.

Just as spectacular as the geothermals and wildlife are the landscapes. Yellowstone has meadows and mountains, rivers and lakes, and so many waterfalls that new ones are still being discovered. Each region of the park is aesthetically distinct, so you can alternate between different areas, and therefore different subjects, throughout your trip in order to maintain a day-to-day variety of photographic experiences.

LOCATION TIPS > Try shooting at Mammoth Hot Springs in the morning, when the warm sunlight streams through steam, and makes the oranges and reds of the pools almost glow in front of your camera. For iconic scenes of the majestic Yellowstone River, explore the Hayden Valley on the eastern side of the park loop road between Fishing Bridge and Canyon Village. The latter is home to Yellowstone Falls. To say they're photographed "often" is an understatement, but there's a reason why: They are stunning. The view of Lower Falls from Artist Point is one of the most photographed scenes in the park system. If you want to photograph geysers, research which are the most photogenic, which are the most predictable, and which are the most frequent. When all those traits intertwine, those are the perfect spots for photography. White Dome Geyser is perhaps the best at combining those three factors, and is adjacent to Great Fountain Geyser, one of the most beautiful whether it's erupting or not. The Lamar Valley is prime wolf habitat, and the landscape is wide open and stunning—particularly in morning light. It is also one of the few areas of Yellowstone open to automobiles in winter.

YOSEMITE NATIONAL PARK

California

THE YOSEMITE VALLEY is perhaps the most beautiful place in the United States. The valley is flanked by El Capitan and Cathedral Rocks, is backed by Half Dome, is carpeted by dense pine forest, and is adorned with Bridalveil Fall placed so perfectly in the scene that you might think it was painted in. It is not hyperbole to suggest that this one view inspired the entire national park system.

Though it wasn't the first national park, Yosemite was the first expanse of land set aside by the federal government for preservation, and it has since become one of the top choices for landscape photographers. The valley is a large part of why.

Though it represents only a tiny percentage of the park, the Yosemite Valley attracts the most tourists and the most artists. It's filled with rivers, creeks, ponds, rock formations, boulders, meadows, groves, wildflowers and wildlife. The latter includes black bears, coyotes, mule deer, hawks, marmots and squirrels, none of which are hard to find.

The valley is also home to a sizeable share of waterfalls. The aforementioned Bridalveil, which tumbles 620 feet, isn't even the tallest. That achievement is claimed by the 2,425-foot Yosemite Falls. Sentinel Falls, Ribbon Fall, Nevada Fall and Vernal Fall are also great for photography, as are countless others. ("Countless" is how the park literature officially describes the total.)

The caveat to all this great waterfall photography is that you would be wise to partake in it before late summer, when most of the falls dry up for the season. Most start flowing midwinter, as the mountain snows begin to melt. Their flow volume is highest in spring, when they generate so much spray that you can photograph rainbows (and moonbows) in many locations. That same spray, however, makes the falls challenging to work near, so early summer might be a more attractive choice for photographers wary of getting their gear wet. Another popular waterfall is Horsetail, which in late February (weather permitting) is backlit by the setting sun, turning the water bright orange against the dark face of El Capitan.

LOCATION TIPS > If you're photographing Yosemite, you probably want to photograph the valley. The most famous spot is Tunnel View—that's where Ansel Adams made one of his signature images, "Clearing Winter Storm." Common wisdom suggests that the most usable light is from late afternoon through sunset, and is at its best angle in spring and fall. Cooks Meadow is a good place to easily access some great valley scenery: spring wildflowers and wildlife, and views of Yosemite Falls and Half Dome. Also worth trying is the trail to Mirror Lake, where, in spring, you can photograph reflections of Half Dome. (The lake dries as summer sets in.) Drive up to Glacier Point for vast views of the valley, especially at the end of the trail to Sentinel Dome. This area is perfect for sunrises, sunsets, night skies and moonlit landscapes, and for using a long telephoto lens to isolate distant features. If you encounter overcast conditions, consider heading to Mariposa Grove, where you can photograph about 500 sequoias (though probably not all in the same image).

ZION NATIONAL PARK
Utah

COVERING AN AREA of only 229 square miles, Zion is certainly not the biggest park, but it packs a lot into its relatively small size. In fact, many photographers would put it at the top of their list of most photogenic national parks.

What is so stunning about Zion? In one word: everything.

The park's prime feature was carved by the Virgin River: a red and white sandstone canyon so deep and narrow that the rays of the sun reach the bottom only minimally. That might sound like a bad thing for a photographer, but it results in juxtapositions of light and shadow that present infinite creative opportunities. Moreover, it enables all-day photography—the shade and shadows and warm bounced light create varying conditions during all daylight hours; the light changes so drastically that you can return to the same spots at different times of the same day and photograph them differently. The possibilities in Zion are so diverse and contiguous that you may need to force yourself away from photography to allow for time to eat and to move from place to place.

Besides the light, even the scenery varies. At the bottom of the canyon you'll find roaring river rapids and tranquil streams, free-falling waterfalls and dripping cascades. The terrain can be shrubby or rocky, bare or home to groves of cottonwood, willow, cactus or juniper. You can photograph in wide expanses flanked by hanging gardens of ferns and mosses, or in narrow slot canyons of smooth rock face colored in a spectrum of creams to reds.

Over the canyon rim, the topography inspires a different sort of creativity. Mountains and rock formations, deserts and river views all provide ample fodder, especially for photographers willing to hike into the wilderness.

And Zion offers all of this all year long. The greenery is at its peak in summer, as are the waterfalls that tumble down the canyon walls after thunderstorms. In fall the canyon's cottonwoods will turn yellow and the maples orange and red. Winter brings snow to the landscape—always to the mountains and sometimes to the desert. And in spring the canyon walls and desert floor become adorned with the color of cliffrose, slickrock paintbrush, marigolds and more.

LOCATION TIPS > The Watchman is a distinctive mountain peak in south-central Zion. You can photograph it well from

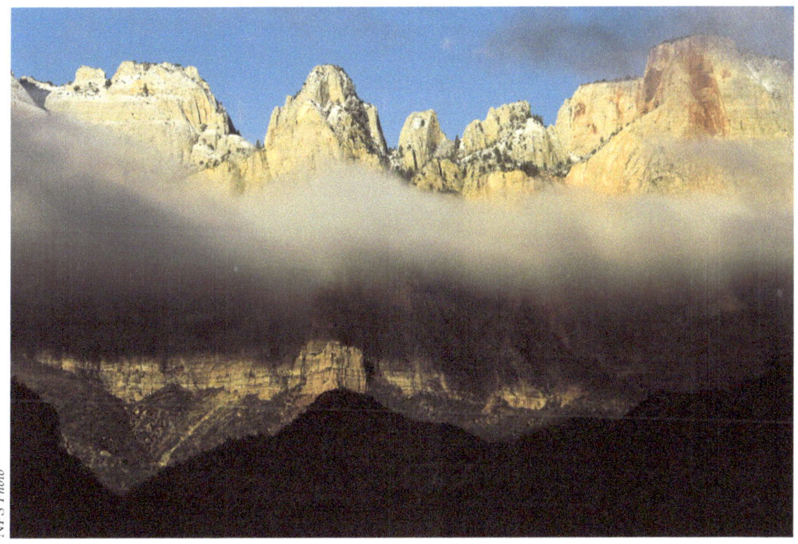
NPS Photo

many locations, but the popular spot to do so (for good reason) is from the bridge over the Virgin River at Canyon Junction. From there you can frame the sky reflected in the river as it meanders through the landscape toward the peak. Emerald Pools is a desert oasis where you can photograph waterfalls and streams, cliff face and boulders, wildflowers and rich-green ferns. The Checkerboard Mesa at the far eastern side of the park offers patterned sandstone, rich with swirls and leading lines that make for great compositional building blocks. It's a reliable option for shooting on overcast days. In Zion Canyon, everywhere is a place to plant a tripod, but consider hiking The Narrows. You'll get wet (you should definitely inquire about the water levels, especially in summer), but you can spend the entire day trekking toward better and better photo opportunities of pools, the river, flora and colorful canyon walls.

FURTHER INFORMATION

THROUGHOUT this book I mentioned assorted resources, services, publications, apps and products that help me when planning and executing a photography project in a national park. Though I included brand names in the text when appropriate, I didn't do so always, lest the book sound like a vehicle for moving merchandise.

However, I do think it's useful to know how to obtain information about some of these things in case you're interested in seeing how they might help you, too. Also included here are some additional resources that may be of interest to like-minded photographers.

WWW.PHOTOGRAPHINGNATIONALPARKS.COM

The website for this book. It features other associated items, including more information about the national parks, e-guides for photographing specific parks, ebooks and a free question-and-answer e-newsletter.

WWW.NPS.GOV

The official website of the National Park Service, it's the gateway to just about any information you need to start learning about the parks or to plan a trip to photograph one. You can also find information about national monuments, battlefields, historic sites, etc.

NATIONAL PARK MAPS

The official portal for downloading maps of any national park is www.nps.gov/carto. The maps are free and in the public domain, so you can print copies to use for planning a trip.

WWW.NATIONALPARKS.ORG

The website of the National Park Foundation, the official charity of America's national parks. The website has a good amount of useful information about the park units, news, an e-newsletter and more.

WWW.NPCA.ORG

The website for the National Parks Conservation Association—the only independent membership-based organization that supports the entire park system, and publisher of the quarterly *National Parks* magazine.

WWW.NATIONALPARKSTRAVELER.COM

National Parks Traveler is a membership-based website that offers general information and in-depth features about the parks, guides to various activities, and a "Parkipedia" wiki for members' favorite trails, lodging, wildflower blooms, etc.

PHOTOGRAPH AMERICA

Since 1989, California-based Robert Hitchman has published a quarterly travel newsletter for photographers. Many issues have covered national parks and the surrounding areas. Back issues are available for purchase individually or in regional packages. www.photographamerica.com

THE NATIONAL PARKS: AMERICA'S BEST IDEA

This 2009 Ken Burns documentary chronicles how the U.S. national park system was conceived and created. It's a must-watch for anyone interested in these places.

QT LUONG

Known as the first person to photograph all 59 national parks with a large-format camera, QT Luong obviously has much he can share with other photographers. See his blog for great stories about his park trips. www.terragalleria.com/blog

WWW.LNT.ORG

Leave No Trace is a membership-driven group dedicated to teaching the ethics of environmentalism when using public lands for recreational purposes.

U.S. ARMY SURVIVAL MANUAL

One of the best wilderness survival guides available. You hopefully won't need some parts of it (such as information about evading an enemy), but the sections about living through an emergency situation in the outdoors are valuable. Copies are available for purchase by the general public.

BEST PRACTICES FOR BUSINESS

If you have any desire to make money with your photos, protect yourself and the industry by ensuring you do it the right way. Editorial Photographers (www.editorialphoto.com) and American Society of Media Photographers (www.asmp.org) are excellent resources.

AMOD GEOTRACKER

I've tried many geotracking devices, and this is my favorite: the AMOD AGL3080. It doesn't fit every trait of what I would consider to be the ideal device, but it comes closer than any other product I've seen.

YES WATCH

My solunar wristwatch of choice. (See page 63.) It's made to meet the timekeeping and celestial-tracking needs of nature photographers and others with specialized outdoor jobs (such as astronomers and pilots). www.yeswatch.com

WWW.KENROCKWELL.COM

A valuable, unbiased resource for information on many, many cameras and lenses, along with their technical specifications.

WWW.LIGHTNINGSAFETY.NOAA.GOV

If you want to photograph lightning, you want to know how to do it safely. The National Weather Service offers good information about being around thunderstorms.

ICETREKKERS

A few products on the market improve traction when you're walking on ice. Icetrekkers are my favorite. They stretch over the sole of your shoe (somewhat like tire chains), and have metal corners that dig into the ice while you walk. I'm sure someone could slip while wearing them, but I have *tried* to slip and have failed. They open up otherwise inaccessible winter locations to the hiking photographer. www.icetrekkers.com

APPS

Below are some apps I use on my phone or iPad to help with scouting locations and working in the national parks:

THE PHOTOGRAPHER'S EPHEMERIS

Displays a map of your current location (or any other spot you pick) along with a graphical representation of where the sun and moon will rise and set, and the times for all those celestial events. Very easy to use. www.photoephemeris.com

PHOTO PILLS

Comes with the ability to predict the location, times of day and days of the year for celestial events such as sunrise, sunset,

Milky Way visibility and more. Comes with other tools as well, including calculators for depth of field and time lapse photography. Also comes with a significant learning curve—but its power can be worth the effort. www.photopills.com

SKYVIEW

Point your phone or tablet at the sky and this space exploration app will chart everything it sees: stars, planets, constellations and even the space station. www.terminaleleven.com

TIDE GRAPH PRO

Know when the tides are high and low, and how high and low they'll be. Can save predetermined locations, so no on-site internet connection is required to access the data. www.tidegraph.com

BIRDSNAP

Developed by researchers at Columbia University and the University of Maryland, Birdsnap uses your bird photo to help you visually identify the species. www.birdsnap.com

AUDUBON GUIDES

The National Audubon Society publishes a collection of field guide apps to help users identify birds, butterflies, wildflowers, and so on. www.audubonguides.com

NATIONAL GEOGRAPHIC

Two of their apps are of interest to photographers: National Parks by National Geographic (which offers photography and photo-location tips from the magazine's photographers) and National Park Maps HD. www.nationalgeographic.com/apps

CHIMANI

This Maine-based company offers a series of free travel-guide apps for many of the national parks, which include maps, shuttle schedules, information on scenic views, and safety tips for the area. www.chimani.com

GOOGLE EARTH

The tablet version of Google's renowned electronic atlas. earth.google.com

SOURCES

Much of the national-park information in this book came from first-hand experience and a lot of reading over my 20-plus years of traveling and photographing. In some cases, I had to write about parks I have not visited, and that's when my journalism skills were useful. Every fact has been independently verified from multiple sources, including media-relations personnel at the parks. However, in fact-checking this information, a few particular sources were invaluable:

National Park Services websites and online publications. www.nps.gov

Guide to the National Parks of the United States. National Geographic. 2007. www.nationalgeographic.com

"Photograph America Newsletter." Robert Hitchman. 1989-2015. www.photographamerica.com

INDEX

L

M

www.ingramcontent.com/pod-product-compliance
Lightning Source LLC
LaVergne TN
LVHW052250100826
845147LV00001B/4

* 9 7 8 0 9 8 3 5 0 3 8 2 8 *